PICTURING
CULTURAL
VALUES IN
POSTMODERN
AMERICA

PICTURING CULTURAL VALUES IN POSTMODERN AMERICA

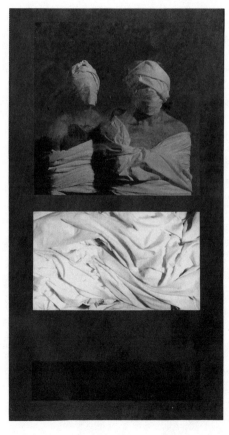

EDITED BY
WILLIAM G. DOTY

THE UNIVERSITY OF ALABAMA PRESS
TUSCALOOSA AND LONDON

Picturing cultural values in
postmodern America

Copyright © 1995
The University of Alabama Press
Tuscaloosa, Alabama 35487-0380
All rights reserved
Manufactured in the United States of America

∞

The paper on which this book is printed meets the minimum
requirements of American National Standard for Information
Science-Permanence of Paper for Printed Library Materials,
ANSI Z39.48-1984.

Library of Congress Cataloging-in-Publication Data

Picturing cultural values in postmodern America / edited by William G.
   Doty.
       p.   cm.
   Includes bibliographical references and index.
   Contents: Within and beyond the picture frame / William G. Doty—
The vertiginous frame / Gray Kochhar-Lindgren—Humanism and the
birth of perspective in Renaissance painting / Stephen Karatheodoris and
William G. Doty—Jung's anti-modern art of the mandala / Daniel C.
Noel—A poetics of the sacred / Jerome Rothenberg—Thinking made in
the mouth / Hank Lazer—Family pictures / Irena S. M. Makarushka—An
apocalypse of race and gender / Mark Ledbetter—The functions of images
and the imagination in moral and ethical reflection / David H. Fisher—
Silent myths singing in the blood / William G. Doty—Renewing rituals /
Matthew Fox—Living a reservation culture / Lynda Sexson.
   ISBN 0-8173-0733-8 (alk. paper)
   1. Postmodernism—United States.   2. Aesthetics, Modern—20th
century.   3. Religion and culture—United States.   I. Doty, William G.,
1939–
B831.2P53   1995
149—dc20   94-13361

British Library Cataloguing-in-Publication Data available

CONTENTS

PREFACE AND ACKNOWLEDGMENTS

Contributors to this collection of essays were often aware of each other's topics but wrote independently. It was fascinating to receive each proposal, and then each contribution, because of the many perspectives we shared, although we were treating independently a wide range of materials. Five of us are teachers in religious studies, all in the broadly defined "religion and culture" area of that interdiscipline: Makarushka at Bowdoin College, Ledbetter at Millsaps College, Noel at Vermont College, Sexson at the Montana State University, and Doty at the University of Alabama at Tuscaloosa. We know the work of one another generally (well enough to argue profitably!) but hardly form a "school."

Karatheodoris taught sociological theory at the University of Alabama, where Lazer teaches English and serves as assistant dean for humanities and the fine arts in the College of Arts and Sciences. Kochhar-Lindgren has taught American Studies at the Universität Regensburg and English at several colleges in Georgia. Rothenberg holds the position of professor of literature as well as that of chair of visual arts at the University of California–San Diego. David Fisher is associate professor of philosophy at North Central College. Matthew Fox is the outspoken editor of *Creation Spirituality*, whose visions of contemporary Christianity have led him to conflicts with the Roman Catholic church and simultaneously to an extensive following among religious persons of all persuasions.

As editor for such disparate essays that yet have so many shared concerns, I thank the contributors for their patience through the several rewrites I suggested, as well as the production staff of the University of Alabama Press for their skills in publishing this collection. Eight of the contributors are linked in some fashion to the Society for Values in Higher Education, and I think they all join me in expressing appreciation for the interdisciplinary richness and intellectual stimulation of our participation in that society.

Two of these essays were subvented by the College of Arts and Sciences of the University of Alabama: the original versions of Irena Makarushka's and Mark Ledbetter's essays were given as Department of Religious Studies Lectures. Likewise, Jerome Rothenberg visited the campus under the auspices of the college, whose ongoing indirect research support I would like to acknowledge. Both my secretary, Betty Dickey, and my computer technician, Kirt Warren, helped manage the electronic versions of the texts. The designer at the University of Alabama Press, Paula Dennis, again provided an attractive cover, based in this instance upon the work of an MFA graduate of the University, Jeffery Byrd, whose involvement with postmodernist modes of representation as well as the baroquely gessoed frames he finds in secondhand shops made him a natural choice. The original is "Walk on Broken Glass," a 1991 forty-eight-by-twenty-four-inch toned photo collage. Byrd teaches photography at the University of Northern Iowa; his works have been exhibited widely, and he was featured in a cover review in *Christopher Street* in 1992.

The editor, Press, and contributors acknowledge with gratitude the following permissions granted by authors and publishers:

- Excerpts from David Antin, *Tuning*. Copyright © 1984 by David Antin. Reprinted by permission of New Directions Publishing Corporation.

OPENING UP A PICTURE FRAME

HANK LAZER

COMPOSITIONS 1

oh currant   do you listen to music other
than what they listen to now   what connection
do we have to the glass and light images on the screen
for years he sat in the self   stinken pajamas
language is the conduit out   au courant
don't push her   she said she doesn't like children
i'm tired of the beige walls in the livingroom
awe current   first they have to find the gene marker
bob   please tell our contestants about the prizes
they can win   first circle all the rhyming words

that scarf looks ridiculous   and orange pants
rastaman caravan   invasion   laserprints
lasersurgery   go light on the eyes doc   cremation evasion
translation of a well known serbo croatian   equation

who taught you that dance step   where'd you get
that jacket   why don't you have any life insurance
why won't you sponsor an underprivileged child
did you file an income tax return for 1984

when does your driver's license expire   how
did you get that scar   when did your eyes
start going bad   why did she keep the peacocks
in the house   do you own a convection oven

the key lies in the hasidic nigun   and
that's the truth   a late night walk   it's
all in the pacing   from bad to verse
and the reverse   i can't make rehearsal tonight but i'll be there tomorrow morning

fishnet stockings   interstices   electron hole
the orbital where the electron should be found
he told me i had the gift of speech but not thought

where can i find something about modern love in
all this   an imagined chinese mode of specificity
all you can do is push the buttons and hope the
damned thing records   jackson hole wyoming

two points determine   a line   why
do you have to justify your margins   and
to whom   align   and the nonaligned
powerful when they vote in a block

that was a great block party they had last
homecoming   heidegger says something about
mystery and proximity   i don't think
the grand jury will dismiss the case   it's
hard to tell ahead of time what the judge
will and will not allow   does it ever
work to sequester them   the rule of law
pity the poor astronaut barfing in weightless space
the media put the famine on the back burner
said it had played itself out   yes
the ribs come with roll and slaw

the return vents help to recirculate the air
blue air clear water   what's my line

you've had enough lines for one night
i'll say

elsie is a name you don't hear that much anymore
god you're not   going to hog   that whole line   are you
get the plaid   i'm sick of seeing you   in solid colors
no wholes barred   stop at the sign of the shell
this is walter cronkite signing off   no holds barred
in order to get the line   you'll have to get your wife to
cosign   net fishing isn't allowed here
shut the fuck up

the best you can do   is create an ellipsis
don't you mean   oasis

From *DOUBLESPACE: Poems 1971–1989*
(New York: Segue, 1992), 131–33.

From "INTER(IR)RUPTIONS 9"

intervalic thought stochastic i am after measuring taking the measure of
monsieur et madame miss your destination manifest this your detonation
and so assailed in this era willing constructions each poet enters the line's den
one two three forwards

From *INTER(IR)RUPTIONS: Poems*
(Mentor, Ohio: Generator, 1992), 3.

PICTURING CULTURAL VALUES IN POSTMODERN AMERICA

WITHIN AND BEYOND THE PICTURE FRAME

The Postmodernist Context and Contents of These Essays

WILLIAM G. DOTY

This introductory essay puzzles the notion of values today, especially in light of the claim that supernumerary narratives are kaput: repeatedly we hear about the ultimate secularization of Western culture, in which "nothing is sacred any longer" except of course when sacred equals commercial or political. A wide range of issues in contemporary society is related to various attempts at finding coherence in the midst of the resulting postmodernist chaos of conflicting meanings (and the often extraordinarily counterintuitive technical or clique language of many postmodernist studies, which we have sought to avoid here). The essay also provides an overview of the issues of the various chapters in the book.

Heidegger's concept of Enframing *has to be brought alongside contemporary statements of hermeneutics (interpretation theories/principles) even as* religion *is redefined not so much as the abstract discourses of metaphysics as in the figurings and imaginings and ritualizations by which contemporary persons project meanings upon an apparently uninvolved universe. Moral and ethical imagery (as we will see in David*

Fisher's chapter) is never nonembodied, and essays here focus repeatedly upon specific social contexts—of images in disputes concerning abortion, the engendered ways males and females "see" differently, the shape of the contemporary marriage in movies, and so forth. The wide focus remains characteristic of the contemporary pluralities that surround us—and of the bombardment of images that enmesh us in their competing claims to represent the most desirable products or virtues.

Not to put too fine a point on it, we live, breathe, and excrete values. No aspect of human life is unrelated to values, valuations, and validations. Value orientations and value relations saturate our experiences and life practices from the smallest established microstructures of feeling, thought, and behavior to the largest established macrostructures of organizations and institutions. The history of cultures and social formations is unintelligible except in relation to a history of value orientations, value ideals, goods values, value responses, and value judgments, and their objectivations, interplay, and transformations. Yet it is no exaggeration to say that the oceans and continents of value, though much travelled, remain almost entirely uncharted in any way suitable to the navigational contingencies of postmodern itineraries.

—John Fekete, *Life After Modernism*

Why must art always be defined as an *alternative* to reality? Sometimes art is a *recognition* of reality, a mode of apprehending and of representing it. And why do we tend to neglect the fact that works of art always exist as *part of* the material world?

—Craig Owens, *Beyond Recognition*

Inaugurating a flashy new intellectual journal, published by Oxford University Press and edited at the University of Texas at Dallas, the highly respected critic Frank Kermode proposed that future *Common Knowledge* contributors might address some of the questions about *values* raised by feminist and minority questionings of the canon and the displacement of literary criticism with cultural criticism. Kermode saw the problem largely as one of standards ("the canon") and the status of the art work—asking, for instance, whether television Westerns and soap operas are worth the careful attention that has been given to works of art—as well as a question of ethical conduct: one cannot preach "Just say no!" if all values are contingent and transcendental ideals or deities are no longer thought to exist somewhere to give them birth.

Part of the usual definition of the postmodern, the acknowledgment of the death of the master narratives or metanarratives of the West—the "big stories" and ruling metaphors, even worldviews—comes from both the right, ready to trash the liberal democratic gains of recent America, and the left, so uncomfortable with the sheer mass of contingent values that its representatives retreat into a specialized and technical jargon almost impenetrable to the uninitiated.[1] Consequently "the new history" looks less at the sorts of idealistic visions or historiographic frames in which events are chronicled than at the specific events of a particular day. A good example is provided by an essay in the *Common Knowledge* symposium responding to Kermode's call that strikes me as more appropriate to discussion of values than most of the others. Tobin Siebers (1992, 67) examines the specific cultural and political context in which the literary-critical school of New Criticism was founded; not only is the general context of the Cold War helpfully adduced, but a particular Sunday edition of the *New York Times* is examined in order to give the atmosphere of the country at the time when New Criticism began its long reign within Modernism.[2]

The decline of the master narrative is evident in schools: advocating the traditional etiquettes taught in the lower grades, not to mention the often quite explicit reference to racial or religious standards, is no longer acceptable. To be sure, a teacher can still cause a child to feel inferior because the child's family does not share the teacher's views on abortion or resistance to a foreign war, but mostly the "foundations" for such views are admitted on all sides as having vanished along with the hickory stick. Hence "anti-foundationalism" or "contingency," the condition in which the much-vaunted pluralism of American tradition comes home with a vengeance: no longer a melting pot (in which the values of the white upper Protestant class actually have dominated), but a coexistence of ethnic-racial habits, a multicultural collaboration, "secularism" as a de facto toleration of many religions and political platforms, rather than an atheistic nonreligiosity.

Culture is conveyed in inflections—what one eats, what sorts of heroines or heroes are admired, where and with whom sex is permitted, et cetera—and postmodernist America is the site wherein various social habits are now clashing explicitly as seldom before. Modernist ideals—such as the primary assumption of the technological age, that of constant growth, or indeed, that of evolution upward—lie shattered now upon the political and ecological realities of an endangered planet. Even as this volume is brought to press in the midst of political upheavals in eastern Europe, belief in long-term twentieth-century assumptions such as the sacred inviolability of the people's revolution has eroded ("the idea of revolution [is] a failure that indeed characterizes the last decades of our century," Vattimo 1992, 40); during the Reagan-Bush decade "relations of inequality, domination, and oppression, many of which were beginning to be dismantled, have become the taken-for-granted structure of social organization" (Grossberg 1992, 313). The verdict is still out on whether the new politics swept into office along with Clinton and Gore will find their fresh agendas stymied by the entrenched congressional projections of class and race, but clearly compromise rather than revolution will remain the leitmotif.

While the essays in this volume are not restricted to ethnic-racial habits, their authors are clearly aware of the underlying ways our culture has shaped itself fundamentally in political, racial, and other terms: they look at the very framing of the ways in which we approach the world, the direction of our "gaze" no less than how we define (variously) the sacred and the secular. They note how judgments of literary merit determine who is "in" and who is "out of" any school of poetry. They point to images of gender domination that still orient motion pictures, of class-based or racial exclusions of others; and they call attention to the ways cultural images produce patterns of ethics that affect us all. I will comment on each of the essays here, or in introductions to each essay, or in the concluding chapter; but the very title of the book compacts its contents: "picturing" in terms of how images are shaped, but also how images are regarded, how they are valued—as unreal or as ideals that determine other nonimaged expressions, how they shape loyalties and party memberships.

The term *cultural* is intended in the way the discipline of cultural studies has operated, not narrowly in an anthropological sense, but rather in terms of focus on the world-at-hand and how it is treated. And *values* is used in terms of some of the issues just raised, as emphasized in a recent study, *Theory and Cultural Value* by Steven Connor (1992, 8): "Value is inescapable. This is not to be taken as a claim for the objective existence or categorical force of any values or imperatives in particular; but rather as a claim that the processes of estimating, ascribing, modifying, affirming, and even denying value, in short, the processes of *evaluation*, can never be avoided. We are claimed always and everywhere by the necessity of value in this active, transactional sense." And surely we are so claimed by values across Postmodernist America, the land that exemplified postmodernism in the arts and architecture well before European analysts began identifying the positive aspects of the design of the casinos in Reno and Las Vegas or the reshuffling of elements of the past in the outlines of new hotels and corporate buildings.[3]

Value has become a slogan word of the New Right—to the point that a group of which many contributors to this volume are fellows, the Society of Values in Higher Education, which originated years ago in the liberal field of academic religious studies and which has been responsible for ongoing dialogue across the disciplines no less than for open inquiry into conflicting values, has had recently to repulse the assumption that it represents the political right rather than (as has mostly been the case) leftist or centrist positions. The problem of determining value drives the novelistic reflections of the author of the famous *Zen and the Art of Motorcycle Maintenance*, Robert Pirsig, in his recent *Lila: An Inquiry into Morals* (1991). Strongly rejecting the objectivism of some forms of modern anthropology (although Pirsig reflects almost nothing of the revolution in contemporary ethnography sketched in Doty 1990), Pirsig's character Phaedrus struggles with pragmatism's dilemma of finding ways of operating not on the basis of a foundationalist "good" or merely "the best choice in a dilemma," but on the basis of "the best resolution of ethical issues for the greatest number of people."

Grounding "quality" as a "universal source of things" that is still not identical with the Platonic Ideas that he is in dialogue with (there are many tipoffs that Plato's *Phaidros* is the intertext to this novel), Phaedrus has to reach out to a capitalized Dynamic Quality, or Metaphysics of Quality, namely, to anything that opposes purely static moralism, in order to ground his ethical system. That he does so by overturning the usual distancing of the subject-*vs.*-object approach to reality is important for our purposes here, since Pirsig supports a discussion of values that is not simply located in claims to absolute, "objective" knowledge, but in *patterns of values*, in orientations to the world as experienced.[4] Hence one might associate his work to some extent with recent "communitarian" thought, or at least with those who point today toward the necessity of recovering communal dialogue about issues long treated as simply irrelevant in a technological climate that favored the individual entrepreneur.[5]

Steven Connor's *Theory and Cultural Value* studies values issues in contemporary academic contexts, noting the "ethical turn" in the various provinces of critical theory, feminism, Marxism, deconstruction, discourse theory, and psychoanalysis (1992, 102). Repeatedly such a turn is criticized by neoconservatives because it involves evaluative thinking, moral choices, and ethical reflection—all of which are more volatile and strikingly less controllable than the process of laboratory experimentation and demonstration, or the positivist and instrumentalist views of education usually associated with the various revanchist calls to "return to the classics." Precisely what a turn to values or ethics will highlight is the distance from the mind's logical thinking to feeling and affect, to the role of "conscience" (literally: a co-knowing in one's community), and to the power of representative images (the "pictures" of our title) in regulating initial responses to behavioral problems.

Lawrence Grossberg develops a telling analysis of the tactics that representative figures of the New Right have utilized to commandeer public discourse: they have managed to divert the terms of the debate about abortion into a one-sided moralism of individual privilege (the "right" to life) and their cleverly chosen affective images ("Abortion stops a beating heart") mask the wider medical and social issues. "More importantly, such appeals displace their commitment and enable them to refuse any real concern for the actual condition of life of the millions of children, in this country, and around the world, who are starving to death or dying from curable diseases, wars, etc." (1992, 271). Not unsurprisingly, antiabortion voices are usually against sex education in the schools also, against prenatal-care clinics for poor families, against rural health-care centers, and against other crucial support facilities for the children *already* being born, so that the rate of childbirth-associated fatalities is higher in the United States than in most Third World nations, and 40–50 percent of America's children now live in poverty, a statistic apparently so frequently repeated that it has lost all power to provoke change (How might one picture *that* cultural value in such a manner as to motivate altering it?).

One can imagine other aspects of ethical matters, such as the deadly visitation of AIDS, or the shape of the family, which will recur in this volume. "For example, a friend who recently became a father described feeling as though every time he speaks of his concerns as a parent, he 'sounds' like a conservative. It is not merely that the Right seems to 'own' the discourse of the family, but that the discourse itself, which belongs to no one, pulls one affectively over to the right" (Grossberg 1992, 283). Or we might cite the tendency to annex the languages of patriotism, so that "real Americans" may not, by implication, argue or demonstrate against what only a tiny portion of the national government may have set into motion; to capture the languages and images means to determine how one may speak even about common experiences and values, and when history can be retold in ways supportive of only one or another political position, the community's conscience becomes merely a party line.[6]

The multiplex questions about the shapes of national discourse cannot be engaged further here. But such a discourse, or the academic discourse to which we just made reference, will be complex in any postmodernist situation, and it is important to recognize the importance of discussions like those instigated in this book, discussions that do not shirk complexity and refuse to waffle before cheap image-setters who want to dominate the use of *family, America, true religion,* or *sexuality.* As Connor notes, "Questions of value and evaluation are inherently complex, since they invariably involve us in acts of self-reflection, as we inspect and evaluate our own acts of evaluation" (1992, 17–18). Just such self-reflection has been central across academic discussions for the last several decades, thanks to the deconstructionist movement, which is an approach to the ways discourses can be analyzed in terms of the very propositions they put forth. The feminist denunciation is subject to feminist denunciation; the political platform is subject to questions about how consistent its claims are with what it professes to represent; and of course the ethical recommendation is subject to queries about the ethics of making recommendations or regulations at all. The situation is complicated in the sphere of ethics and values, since to represent value is always to misrepresent it to the extent that the very structures that dominate our thought may hinder us from apprehending the Enframing nature of values in itself.[7]

Representation and Framing

Deconstructive frameworks are self-analyzing and -questioning frameworks and attitudes; they frequently undermine the contextual authority in which they appear. Connor notes that "to discuss the ethics of deconstruction is to be concerned not with specific values . . . promised by deconstruction, or the principles of right conduct held to be implicit within it, but rather with the ethical force or responsibility which is already in being whenever one begins to perform the work of a deconstructive analysis" (1992, 190). In such a sense the German philosopher Martin Heidegger (1889–1976) was already doing deconstructive analysis when he sought first to dismantle (he used a term that translates "destrual") and then to reassemble Western philosophical metaphysics. Deconstruction in this sense does not mean doing away with something but revisioning it, revoicing it by noting omissions in what is spoken or implied, revising a position in terms of its own revisions of another position—and on and on in a seemingly infinite regress, so that one never reaches a foundation but another arbitrary and transitory formulation, one never attains any single meaning of a symbol or signifier but opens the doors of all symbols and signifiers to others that appear as historical chains or sequences of signification-meanings. Hence we all watched in amazement when in Bulgaria anticommunist protesters sang both an old Beatles' song, "All You Need Is Love," and a pop song written to generate funds for the famine relief in Ethiopia, "We Are the World"—these were not political slogans, but revised significations/applications of music written for entirely different occasions.[8]

So much seems to happen *on the frontiers, the borders* upon which change takes place:[9] and the end of this century seems to be as full of change as were its initial decades! I like Craig Owens's prescient recognition of that postmodernist border-ing; it's not the forward-oriented frontier of modernism, but the confused, multiurban, multiethnic scene so well represented in the television series that began in 1987, featuring Max Headroom, fearless borderline character (he existed in hyperspace among the TV broadcast waves). "It is precisely at the legislative frontier between what can be represented and what cannot that the postmodernist operation is being staged—not in order to transcend representation, but in order to expose that system of power that authorizes certain representations while blocking, prohibiting, or invalidating others" (Owens 1992, 168).

Owens points to the legislative frontiers, but one might as readily point to scientific frontiers where particular framings of information become perspectival blinders toward other possibilities; new paradigms may be excluded from use until finally they become inescapably powerful in their own right and displace earlier models. But such models always parade as "god's truth" views, a.k.a. "scientific knowledge." Hence Emily Martin refers to "scientific knowledge as [being merely] one purveyor of a view of the world from a particular vantage point. This knowledge is often able to masquerade as 'natural fact,' a powerful means by which its vision of hierarchical human relationships is learned and internalized" ("Body Narratives, Body Boundaries," in Grossberg 1992, 409–23; at 411), yet in the process of "naturalizing" a limited and arbitrary perspective, "god's truth" assertions easily become "the only way," the most universal truth, the "purely scientific" means of comprehending an issue, and so forth.

Martin's observation makes evident the relationship between scientific and poetic diction: either represents an attempt to express, shape, or transform meaning, and neither may advance too quickly into uncharted realms lest it face incomprehension on the part of readers. Hence there are linguistic frontiers as well, and a prefatory poem like Hank Lazer's "Compositions 1" or the extract from his "INTER(IR)RUPTIONS 9" at the outset of this book, or a concluding story like Lynda Sexson's, with which this book ends, will seldom be found in works like this today. Pity! Because there are border invasions in both instances: Lazer's language-tumbles (very, very carefully breathed, for all their apparent randomness) break Heideggerian metaphysics into the realm of the beer bash; French and English intermix as the *sounds* mingle. And Sexson's angels in the Garden of Eden aren't really angels, are they? Nor is her Gardener-God any traditional deity of Western religious thought. But in both instances (Lazer's "fishnet stockings   interstices   electron hole" and Sexson's plaintive hint that "in some sense we are all captives of a reservation culture, our heirlooms lost, our only claim consumerism") the role of coherence and tradition, that of experimentation and innovation, and the capitalist individualism of the right or the sociocommunal emphasis of the left, cross boundaries that our everyday ways of thinking try to keep rigidly in place.

Essays here explore several modes of representation of values and the values of representation, and they treat repeatedly how the postmodern pastiche or collage of thought and image operates, how apparently clashing values coexist side by side, how we are all boundary crossers every day. And how we come to the *perspectives* that rule experiences or images out of bounds or include them as "normal," "natural." How we resist the blinkers of the too-simple explanation, the total closure toward others of the bigot. Repeatedly, attention to the framing, the social construction of reality, the consensus by which a worldview is enforced, provokes opening and creativity. We seem more readily able to relinquish our monovisions when we recognize them, when they are pointed out to us, but often that does not happen. It is often necessary to inspect the analytic of another system or thinker first.

Martin found that even a group of highly disadvantaged high school students at the Community Survival Center in Baltimore could learn to demystify the metaphors used to convey facts about human biology in an educational videotape. Her analysis of such metaphors portrays a curious instance of a supposedly so-scientific culture: again and again the imagery utilized to convey biological facts about sexuality replicates a cultural model of masculine priority and dominance, rather than the actual physiology of the reproductive process. Oriented toward the "production of valuable things," the sexual production of male sperm is described typically as being remarkable, creative, amazing, while women's bodies merely "shed" a single gamete each month, and the eggs lie about passively waiting for a thrusting sperm to save them. In actuality, Martin notes, such views have been refuted repeatedly as scientists have demonstrated "that the forward propulsive force of the sperm's tail is extremely weak, so that rather than strongly swimming forward with purpose, the sperms actually flail about side by side, swim in circles, mill around. The current picture is that adhesive molecules on the surface of the egg capture the sperm and hold it fast" (1992, 413).

A culture's root metaphors derive from its worldview; language systems represent conventions by which cultures agree to name realities this way or that, rank this or that social position as privileged, or—as we have just seen—treat one or the other gender as superior. Reality is "socially constructed" insofar as perception is framed by what a society regards as real or unreal, important or trivial, and so forth. Ultimately there is a "tone" to a culture whose megaperspective upon all of reality holds sway across all the spheres of experience and expression.

Several essays in this collection explore the programmatic orientations of the contemporary or postmodernist world, especially following or dependent on the transition into the posttechnological, postatomic world—*post* here standing not necessarily for temporal sequence but for difference (it is important in naming cultural periods to recognize that change is gradual, and that there will always be many persons firmly ensconced within the paradigm that is fading away). Increasingly today *post-* in naming cultural movements indicates self-consciousness rather than time. Hence, as Scott Lash notes (1989, 193), the movie *Fatal Attraction*, analyzed in Makarushka's chapter below, has been seen by several British critics as a post-AIDS film—*not*, that is, as a film reflecting a vanquishing of the disease (hence "after AIDS"), but as a film touched centrally by awareness of the dilemmas of contemporary sexuality.

In art criticism one hears today of post-postmodernism, with reference to the schools of architecture and art that developed in contrast to the mid-century subdivisions of postmodernism charted already by Christopher Jencks (1977, 1987). Robert Detweiler (1989, xi) proposes that the contemporary interpretive scene must be regarded "not only as post New-Critical but also as the era of post-formalism, post-structuralism, deconstruction, post-representation, post-modern, and even post-hermeneutic," and Mark Taylor (1992) argues that much of what has been called postmodernism is more appropriately labeled "modernist postmodernism" that is little but the obverse of classical modernism, an initial stage—from Taylor's perspective, we have yet to engage fully the entry into a *post*modernism that moves beyond modernist obsessions.

The Megaconcept of Enframing

Heidegger's concept of the attitudinal, perspectival worldview (in Heidegger's German, *Ge-Stell* instead of the usual *der Gestell*) will feature in Gray Kochhar-Lindgren's essay here, especially as it is developed in *The Question Concerning Technology* (Heidegger 1977, 19–20, 24–26) and "The Origin of the Work of Art" (Heidegger 1971). The broad issues treated in those monographs, often called up merely by using the term *Ge-Stell* (for which I'll henceforth use the awkward but conventional English translation "Enframing," capitalized to show that it is a technical term), reach across the interpretive questions of representation and framing. The Enframing concerns the orientation of technology in its very essence. It is not just a mechanical frame or a constraint such as Max Weber identified as the "iron cage" that seemed about to strangulate early-twentieth-century culture. Heidegger says that we must "put out of mind the modern meaning of placing or framing" (1971, 85),[10] and yet he focuses precisely on what is represented by that modern *meaning*, on the *ways* our particular era incarnates Being as such in its Enframing—what Heidegger's translator Albert Hofstadter summarizes as "the gathering of all forms of ordering things as resources . . . , the collective unity of all the putting, placing, setting, standing, arraying, arranging that goes into modern technology and the life oriented to it" (Heidegger 1971, 85n). The Enframing is the essence of the technological worldview that so thoroughly objectifies everything that everything *is* only "object," object whose Being is silenced before it has a chance to evidence itself because our attitude is that objects (or nature) can only be manipulated, not heeded, heard, or allowed to question the very Cartesian subject-object attitude of Enframing itself.

Usually technically oriented toward "making sense," making meanings, manipulating what is at hand, we find it difficult to talk about *poetics* as the means by which Being emerges in a particular cultural moment, but that is Heidegger's ultimately optimistic agenda. The crucial passage comes at the end of "The Origin of the Work of Art," but it has been prepared for earlier by discussion of the similarity of Enframing/*Ge-Stell* to figure/shape/*Gestalt* (64), and in a peculiar definition of art as "the setting-into-work of truth. . . . *Art lets truth originate*"; "wherever art happens—that is, whenever there is a beginning—a thrust enters history, history either begins or starts over again" (77, my emphasis). Technology need not mean a constraining, but it ought to mean a freeing of culture; hence Heidegger refuses to blame technology but scorns the modern attitude that argues that "things are in the saddle and ride humankind" and hence believes that humankind has no recourse except to roll over and play dead.

Rather, à la Heidegger, the Enframing is a challenging aspect of Being that disframes and disenchants our boring and entrapping propensity toward Repetition/The Same, in order to enable existence, one's existing outside any predetermining framework such as racial, gender, or ethnic boundaries (cf. Heidegger 1977, 26–27). The danger facing the culture is less that we are entrapped by some monstrous technological mindset than that we *think* we are, and so relinquish the poetic creativity that is the most characteristic human trait. The essence of technology is that it comes to seem powerful in and of itself—that its effects seem unavoidable in that they become the *only* way in which we can live if we are to be part of ordinary life. "The rule of Enframing threatens man with the possibility that it could be denied to him to enter into a more original revealing and hence to experience the call of a more primal truth" (1971, 28). It is easy to forget that previously "the bringing-forth of the true into the beautiful was called *technē*. And the *poiēsis* of the fine arts also was called *technē*" (34). Hence once more a crucial Heidegger essay ends with the issue of the arts, and in subsequent essays collected along with "The Question Concerning Technology," Heidegger cautions about merely orienting ourselves toward the future as if there were mechanical formulas through which the attitudes of the present technological era could "save us."[11] Finally, Heidegger cautions us not to take too seriously our ability to objectify the world into a world-picture or worldview (134) and not to allow "value and the valuable [to] become the positivistic substitute for the metaphysical." In that case values are represented merely as points of view or orientations, and hence, as Nietzsche already realized, values are reproduced mechanically and thoughtlessly, so that a transvaluation of all values is always necessary— what we may name mythopoetics, demythologizing, demystifying, or deconstruction.

Postmodernist Constants

In the rest of this introductory essay I track some of the ways the volume's components overlap and amplify one another; I want to highlight some of the issues frequent in postmodernist discussions that are represented here. Obviously these materials do not all speak with a single voice, since the postmodernist syntheses are temporary collocations of perspectives, not reproductions of a *gran récit* (master narrative) cloned from some central dissemination point. It would hardly be possible today to assemble a set of essays that would speak with one voice, a situation still possible only a generation ago. Today the isolated essay is the predominant mode of publication, and within small circles of like-minded individuals, there are at most panels and symposiums wherein a single technical discourse prevails, no single model having attained a hearing across the postmodernist disciplinary fields. It has been the style for some time now to write in a mode that is cluttered with Lacanian psychological terms, with neo-Marxian, deconstructive, cultural-studies, neo-Freudian, and narratological phrases. Indeed, being "politically correct" in essays seldom means writing simply, but I find that individuals thoroughly imbued with the diction of one or another of the schools rarely comprehend the specialist discourse of another, and the more accessible prose in this book represents an attempt not to ignore the complex layers of contemporary critical language, but to grant it voice through a noncomplex diction.

I am in sympathy with John Fekete, introducing his edited volume *Life After Postmodernism*, when he summarizes: "I have been arguing that with the shift toward what looks like an emerging postmodern cultural framework, the prospects for the renewal of value discourse are compelling and stimulating. I am not talking of a unified axiology, of a single discipline, of an abstraction from specialized studies. What is at issue is an emerging intertextual discursive field in which the point of view of value orientation may disseminate, in which value commentary may take the form of an intervention, and in which a value-theoretical approach may hold greater attractions than the representations of the onto-epistemological tradition" (1987, xiv). The concluding pages of Lynda Sexson's *Ordinarily Sacred* are reprinted as a conclusion to this volume, but this introductory remark by Fekete might have formed a remarkable parallel *introduction* (although this is a less technical volume than the one he edits).

It ought to be obvious (but often is not) that not every individual experiences postmodernist values within the same contexts, either historical or emotional, as every other. Hence any such highlighting reflects as much on the ways I have been engaged in discussions with the other contributors as any normative set of "postmodernist issues" (the same self-limitation I set above in a note listing characteristic features of postmodernism). As Lata Mani cautions, since not all groups are caught in the webs of postmodernity in analogous ways, the very *differences* between modern subjects may be insufficiently engaged because they are inadequately specified; we must be fully aware of the methodological dangers of "a cut-and-paste model of juxtaposition, as if the cumulative pressure of these developments is in itself sufficient to explain the postmodern condition" (1992, 393). If we are to consider religion "posttheologically," in the gap left behind as the master narratives have vanished for many people, we will need to consider religions, and especially the ways different religions differ. Regardless of whether or not they are religions as traditionally identified (although nothing is more striking about the so-called New Age religions than that they recycle long-familiar religious paths!), the contemporary student may no longer presume that some ultimately congruent theological or political unity underlies various religions or ethical values. Instead one must attend to the various socio-politico-historical framings expressed by specific religious formulations, as we face questions of long-term coexistence rather than assimilation and accommodation to some hypothetical religious substrate.[12]

But I suspect that the wise charting of the domain of religion by Lynda Sexson would be agreed to by many of the contributors to *Picturing Cultural Values*. The wisdom of Sexson's *Ordinarily Sacred* (1992) is that she challenges the binary opposition, sacred *vs.* profane, that haunts traditional religious metanarratives. Sexson comprehends the dangers of the labeling of the holy that reaches back into antiquity—the term *kadosh* (Hebrew), or *sacer* (Latin, the basis for *sacred*) meant not only succor but threat; the holy was circumscribed partly because of its propensity to flame out and destroy those who came before it undefended, inappropriately. But Sexson understands as well that the ultimate extreme of the sacred or the profane ought to be the concern of religious attention less than the lack in between, the mixing ground, the boundaries that we use to demark arbitrary spheres of being and influence.[13]

Religion is "a quality of perceiving and knowing," a recognition of the extent to which ordinary reality, for all its profaneness, is simultaneously saturated with the sacred (Sexson 1992, 8–10). Religion is "the consecration of experience, or person, so that the person, or experience, is made whole (holy)" (9); it is "the desire for depth. . . . the experience or expression of the world imagined" (16). Religions provide the adhesive, centripetal impulsion toward an identified center—not necessarily a transcendental center imported from afar, but a pattern giving meaning and framing that contributes to a holistic quilting-together of meanings, "picking up the pieces, improvising, making up and making do" (90). Likewise Sexson treats myth as "the narrative of depth that traces its vertical story on horizontal events" and that serves as "the means of binding together fragmented experience and of giving reality or form to culture" (56). Such a concatenation or bricolage will represent the ways we sustain ourselves, even if only temporarily, with the knowledge of the changing historical moments that make their own claims on what is considered sufficient for those moments.[14]

"Whatever we perceive religiously we 'read'; that is, we interpret—we find meaning in relation to ourselves" (Sexson 1992, 32), hence the ligature/yoga-yoking of religion cannot be in postmodernity what it apparently was in the Roman Empire, a tying-down to the traditional (the patriotic, even), but a patterning-seeing that remains fluid and yet grants sufficient sense of affective wholeness that we are "healthy" (from Old English hælth) in relation to that now-shattered wholeness that used to seem the epitome of Western civilization. Sexson's initial definition in the first sentences of her book guides her insightful and creative volume and provides here a summary of the position I am suggesting many of the contributors to this book would affirm: "Improvising may be the religious ritual and thought of the contemporary world. The interplay of old and new is at once iconoclastic and remythologizing. Religion—whether we choose to name the experience thus or not—is to be lured by the transitory that reveals the transcendent, to be captured by the aesthetic that discloses the divine word, and it is to mingle those categories so that, ultimately an integrative play cancels discrimination and makes obsolete or meaningless [the usual] divisions between sacred and profane" (1).

How the transitory lures the transcendent is evident today in the professional association of religious-studies teachers, the American Academy of Religion. The AAR's annual meetings now require the conference facilities of several major urban hotels and offer such a gamut of presentations as might astonish middle-American assumptions about what "religion" entails. Recently I have noted papers on spiritual aspects of male masturbation, gnostic recognition of feminine power, womanist reconstructions of African-American literature, and gay/lesbian spirituality, alongside the customary papers on the biblical traditions of several religions, and repeated studies collating contemporary critical theoretical analysis with traditional hermeneutical perspectives. At least in professional academic religious studies, the sky's the limit, and nothing remains taboo any longer.

Religion in the everyday world is likewise disparately exercised: cults proclaim new messiahs in Brooklyn (Jewish) and in Waco, Texas (Christian). New Age spiritualities rediscover the (religious) wheel yet one more time; and most of North America finds traditional religious practice less and less relevant to the century's awkward redefinitions of statehood, even while conservative/evangelical Catholic, Jewish, Mormon, and Protestant sects increase in membership geometrically. And simultaneously ethical/valuational concerns avoided by academic philosophy (the just-war doctrine, lifeboat ethics, business/medical/communications ethics) have made their way recently into the university curriculum: today national accreditation for nursing requires academic courses in medical ethics; for many business schools business ethics is required, and so forth. Denominational religious centers (simple terms like *church* or *synagogue* will no longer suffice) are sometimes blocks long and include gyms and swimming pools, daycare for children, and singles clubs. Serious, reflective books in religious analysis or constructive theology are almost never reviewed in national news media, but sales at religious bookstores break all records. Religious preference seems less influential in swaying votes for candidates than sexual preference; even while official, public, governmental religious observances become totally taboo, the key religious and nationalistic seasons continue to shape merchandising seasons from coast to coast.

In just such a multiplex context several essays here deal with images, the arts, the body, and the contemporary puzzling-through of what "the religious" looks like today. The authors work rich veins of contemporary meaning-finding, including poetry and philosophy and the mass-communications media. They understand the quantitative changes that our late-twentieth-century atmosphere demands, and they wonder how we collect and collate meanings (*religio* means "to yoke or ligature together" important guidelines of cultural significances) in a time when the many postmodern challenges to connectedness are experienced every day. [15]

Cultural Studies and the Everyday

Although nearly half of the authors in this volume teach in the academic discipline of religious studies, their perspectives are seldom "religious" in any traditional manner. These are postmodernist-posttheological essays, as it were, essays from authors who might well be ill at ease within the narrow defines of traditional theological studies, yet who refuse to despair when faced with the fragments of meaning and artistic representation that we confront daily. "Daily life" is one of the contemporary analytical constructs that has been developed (as by Henri Lefebre, see Grossberg's résumé, 1992, 148–50) to specify everyday life as it is conceived and identified as a norm, "a map of spaces and places, a structured mobility. Places are the sites of stability where people can stop and act, the markers of their affective investments. They define the possibilities of people's identifications and belongings and construct the systems of authority in which they live" (295). When one realizes just how manipulated daily life has become in an age of *Vogue*, MTV, and "Lifestyles of the Rich and Famous," the utility of the concept is self-evident.

As contributors here continue to find significance across a wide range of contemporary novels, sculptures, myths, popular religiosity, politics, poetries, and cinematic images, they are reflecting the general scope of "cultural studies" today, a discipline so new to the American scene and so inclusive of scope that the editors of an initial, massive reader (Grossberg, Nelson, and Treichler 1992) sketch its contours in a traditional introductory overview, but then provide a thematic table of contents (the primary table of contents is arranged alphabetically) that includes some sixteen overlapping concerns, ranging from "Gender and Sexuality" to "Popular Culture and Its Audience," "Identity Politics," "The Politics of Aesthetics," "The Politics of Disciplinarity," and "Global Culture in a Postmodern Age."

Popular culture looks different when treated through analytical frameworks that respect its right to exist rather than through perspectives that presume a high-culture/low-culture split, with the "low" considered as entirely inferior to the "high." Acceptance of the new perspectives is evident in John Carlos Rowe's analysis of postmodernist studies in literature: "Literary genre theory, for example, is hopelessly narrow in its disregard of television and film. And to speak of the 'literary canon' without considering the influences of popular literature, the Western film and television episode, 'I Love Lucy,' and 'Perry Mason,' is to reduce the canon to a purely academic topic" (1992, 203). The aspects of the Enframing that once seemed so restrictive seem less so in such acceptance of the full importance of popular culture "texts," although we ought not overlook the substantive changes contributed by the elements of mass communications that reshaped a values-oriented population into a market-driven situation. I cite a few examples from Rowe:

> Information must now be comprehended in terms utterly different from those of industrial societies, in which the instrumentality of language to refer either to natural or to manufactured objects seemed unquestionable. In the service- and information-oriented economy of the United States of the post–World War II era, few commodities are understandable outside the rhetoric of both their production and their consumption. . . . Today, the value of what is produced either in words or from material substances is measured by the extent of its circulation, rather than its consumption. . . . All that the early postmoderns offered as forms of resistance to a bourgeois world of automated reflexes and dehumanization is now available in the shopping mall. . . . The endless conversation and debate often cited by postmodern liberals as the ultimate morality of the textualist position has been achieved in the mass media, both on the Business Channel and the talk show. . . . Neither "Downey" [of an interview program] nor "Geraldo" is the name that matters . . . ; the actual authors are the invisible, anonymous "producers," who are today our best and most dangerous cultural critics. Analyzing, as they must, market shares and segments, they can lay claim to the concrete evidence of their accuracy in assessing cultural trends: the ratings. (202–3)

Neil Postman's point that the mass-communications takeover of public discourse has trivialized contemporary political discussion beyond (perhaps) repair, is repeated by Rowe, who notes that "one of the consequences of the Vietnam War, often termed the 'living-room war,' was the transformation of television into the principal medium of social debate" (194). Subsequently "our capacities for knowledge are conditioned by television's demand for condensed statement rather than extended debate."

Rich and complex imagery—as in the mandalas mentioned by Daniel Noel in chapter 4 here, highly elaborated symbolic figures prototypical to Tibetan Buddhism but found in many devotional designs around the world—can have a tough time of it today, as I discovered several years ago at an exclusive New England college: I brought up the room lights midway through a slide lecture on complicated drypainting designs from southwestern Navajo ceremonials only to find that a large part of the class had vanished. A sympathetic student helped me to recognize that television had so conditioned the students' receptivity that to allow a single complex image to dominate the screen for several minutes at a time made some of them so uncomfortable that they left the class. Since then I have learned that one need screen only a birds eye view, then segment each portion of a complex picture sequentially, and students have no trouble staying on board, but my experience taught me a great deal about "picturing cultural values" in the contemporary world. The Enframing is not restricted in its influence to specific values, but as part of the general communications network of a society, it influences how communications take place, and they follow no simple one-plus-one-equals-two model.

Where the values are to be sighted in our culture is perhaps less self-evident than we might assume, given our simplistic dedication to WYSIWYG (what you see is what you get)—a computer phrase that reflects our extraordinary reliance on external appearances and our parallel reluctance to consider underlayers of psychological or philosophical significance. In this volume the philosophical ethicist David Fisher explores how "images" work in ethical and moral discussions: it turns out that philosophers are sometimes as puzzled as the rest of us by the incalcitrance of models or about how particular stories come to indwell certain ethical positions. And Kochhar-Lingren picks up the influential suggestions by Martin Heidegger about the Enframing that our technological age exerts upon all of our experience and consciousness. Reflecting upon the recent work of Václav Havel and the earlier thought of Friedrich Nietzsche, he questions the ways we come to think this or that "natural"—a question complicated enormously by the careful manipulation of that term by merchandisers and advertisers ("natural granola bars" loaded with refined sugars, "natural hairstyles" achieved only by using chemical globs of styling gel)—at least it is certainly not "naturally" part of the contemporary newspaper-radio-television sphere.

Poetry certainly doesn't seem "natural" any longer either, but in addressing the perennial question, Is poetry now moribund?, Hank Lazer argues no, but then the "official" poetry of creative-writing faculties and workshops does not begin to exhaust the poetry that is significant today. He sets out to show us the importance of what is known as "Language poetry," and a particular range of writing activity represented by Jerome Rothenberg (who contributes an essay on "a poetics of the sacred" to this collection) and Rothenberg's colleague David Antin. The crucial centrality of *tradition*, of the lasting quality ("shelf-life") of poets is part of Rothenberg's attention to a wider range of human expression than that represented by modern professional poets—especially attention to anthropology and politics, to a reopening of the question of what "the modern" means. And that means especially learning how to create, how to bring about the poetry that *is* (or can be) present-day living and thinking: in my final chapter I will suggest that there is a poesis, a poetizing of the every day that ought to remain as important in picturing cultural values in postmodernist America as any official poet laureate status or number of chapbooks sold.

Our focus is not just poetics but images, representations of value-laden contexts and ideals, metaphors that establish traditions according to which a society attains or does not attain "a humane temper." Concerning the "picturing" of cultural values here, several pieces emphatically do not treat the image as "merely" illustrative, but as directly, concretely constitutive of significance: Lazer argues that nontraditional poetics provide a political confrontation of the everyday—explaining why the poet who steps outside conventional expectations is suspect today. Irena Makarushka finds even sad sack Woody Allen's films to be an important source of imperious questioning of our cultural (read "patriarchal") values, and Mark Ledbetter's analysis of the popular novel *Beloved* calls into question the very bases of racial and gender distinctions that have made white America proud of itself.

In terms of psychological reflection, Daniel Noel follows a neo- or post-Jungian perspective in suggesting that Carl Jung himself missed an artistic boat that we late-twentieth-century psychic travelers might board to our great profit. After looking at some of the details of mandalas that Jung discussed or created, Noel counterpoises Jung's strange abhorrence of Picasso's work with his longing for unconscious expressions of cultural holism; in fact, the standard treatment of the widely found image or design called the mandala as a representation of the ego's defense against the (feminine) chaos has to be rethought as a result of Noel's essay. I would love to deal with the enormous constructions (paintings—but they include straw and molten lead and eggshells, and whatever) of Anselm Kiefer: his contemporary works, or those of the earlier Joseph Beuys, cannot but baffle the modernist aesthetic dedicated to the "pure" artwork, since they load on texts and explicit references to "the real world" that modernism thought completely taboo.

And Stephen Karatheodoris and I show how the singular-perspective view of Renaissance artists—a technological adventure we have come to consider the summit of the graphic, representational arts—was itself a matter of exerting control over images of the world-at-hand (the "daily life" we looked at earlier). That we do not often bring the artistic alongside the technoeconomic is a result of the ways aesthetics and ethics are treated in our society as unrelated entities, whereas surely the designs and appearances of our lives channel the values we express through their means. Mass communication often means mass expression, which in order to be most efficient must appeal primarily to those occupying the top end of the economic spectrum of purchasers. What might "picturing cultural values" mean as a radical project for expressing democratic values today? Why is our time so fearful of the progressive leader who might change things, lead us forward into as-yet-unconceived futures?—instead of repeating the same old things that have meant privilege to a tiny segment of our population and deprivation for the vast majority of the rest of us?

In addition to tracking what has been the normative Western white male upper-class dominance of the society, contributors to this collection heed traditionally excluded voices, as in Rothenberg's attention to the sacred aspects of several obscure Christian and Jewish writings, Makarushka's attention to pseudonormative constructions of the marital ideal, and Ledbetter's study of *Beloved*. After Iraq and Desert Storm, increasingly referred to by those of us opposed to U.S. involvement as Desert Slaughter, we have to attend oh, so carefully to the excluded-other whose voices we ignore only if we dare to jeopardize further the continuing maturation of our complex social order. In this instance the lessons taught by Edward Said (in his *Orientalism*, 1979) about Western categorical negativizing of swarthy Near Easterners went unheeded by media accounts and cartoonists who ignored the long-range historical, ethical, and economic factors and treated the Arab foes as cheap, shifty, ne'er-do-wells with hooked noses, to whom life is cheap (see Sam Keen's *Faces of the Enemy*, 1986, for a review of the terrible images with which nations and ethnic groups consistently picture the projected shadow images of military or political opponents).

Beyond Cultural Binarism

So we have to attend to what are increasingly referred to as postcolonialist perspectives or multiculturalism, and to the problem of cultural binarism. Kochhar-Lindgren reflects on his experiences in international airports and while strolling through contemporary Regensburg, Germany, at a time when the West has had The Other of Eastern Europe thrust abruptly into its lap, after several generations of ignoring what was happening outside café society. Lazer discloses modes of artistic/poetic expression that we often ignore because they seem especially "other" in terms of the language of the daily newspaper or bull session. But then if you've been keeping track, you'll remember that "the other" was one of the themes with which I began this introduction, and the essays in this volume will demonstrate repeatedly that we simply cannot restrict the canon to DWEMs (Dead White Euro-American Males) and their living establishment progeny. Or at least their ongoing influence may no longer dirempt attentive regard for cultures at the growing edges of the twenty-first century world that rushes upon us. We will not be diverted back to the good ole boys' networks of Great Ideas, Great Books, and Great Capitalist (White, Male) Heroes, no matter how the neoconservative right wants us to refuse the multiculturalism (read cultural holism) that America has trumpeted always, but never honored *in fact*. To put it into effect, such cultural holism would mean that various upper-class elites would have to give up privilege and power; and simultaneously we would all have to be more extensively educated in the cultural backgrounds and the non-English languages spoken by the several component cultures that coexist today. An imperialist vision of a melting pot in which everyone comes to look and sound the same begins to fade before a more truly democratic politics. (Interesting, isn't it, how a volume of essays begins to have a political shape—but then the *polis* was originally but the city, the site wherein democratic citizens labored together to produce a community that allowed the greatest freedom for all its participants).

"The political" itself now means many different things, as Fekete (1990) shows; likewise values issues surface at many different sites, and with many different degrees of importance, in contemporary criticism (as the other essays in Kreiswirth and Cheetham 1990 indicate). In such a situation, "postmodern thought is no longer binary thought" (Owens 1991, 171, paraphrasing Lyotard), but "the *critique* of binarism . . . is . . . an intellectual imperative, since the hierarchical opposition of marked and unmarked terms . . . is the dominant form both of representing difference and justifying its subordination in our society. What we must learn, then, is *how to conceive difference without opposition*" (my emphasis). Likewise Rowe points to the necessity to deconstruct "the existing institutions of literature and its study" in order "to reveal the ways they have served to legitimate the false distinctions and dangerous hierarchies of 'high art' over popular culture and folk art; enduring classics over journalism, protest and didactic writing; the original and avant-garde over the conventional" (1992, 191; see Taylor 1992, 12 on the dangerous connections between modernism and fascism).

Looking beyond merely binary oppositions is not easy for a culture still infatuated with Enlightenment perspectives, indeed with Aristotelian logical perspectives reaching back much further: something is either A or −A (non-A, A-privative), high- or low-culture, male or not-male—and at the point of something like gendering one sees immediately how even logic has a political edge: What about the womanish man and the mannish woman, stereotypes that nonetheless portray the binary biological condition as prior to the cultural? Yet we never have the biological without the cultural; we are socialized inescapably into gender roles, and the performance of such roles guides how the physiological being actually develops. Just how extensively we are having to look at crossover cases today—the berdache or winkte of several First American tribes, for instance, a male who lives a female life, with the society's support—may indicate some of the postmodernist dimensions of something as immediate to all of us as gendering.

Elizabeth Minnich (1990) and Nancy Jay (1981) have demonstrated alternatives to gender binarism when they turn to other traditions of logic than the normative Western binarisms. They look at situations in which a given situation can be *both* A and B, and C simultaneously, or at situations in which the second term in a duo is different, yet not negatively but supplementarily different. Just asking some questions about the rhetorics of the argumentation usually prevalent helps expose some of the hidden land mines, and it may as well offer new perspectives. So Christine Downing has begun to talk about a "poetics of the body," a metaphorical way of reading Freud and other theorists: "We might then come to be able to see the anatomical members as figures of our relation to ourselves, to others, and to our surroundings" (1992, 75). Above all Downing proposes a processual model, a relational model of gendering that is both more political and more poetic, although she finds herself "more interested in the *poetics* than the *politics* of gender, in exploring the ways we humans imagine sexual difference and what longings and fears these various images betray. The hope, as I see it, is to get past our literalism around gender, to admit that 'man' and 'woman' are fictive terms, images, which hide *and* reveal. To accept gender as *made*, as a *poesis*, means seeing it as always still in the process of being made and remade" (34). Socially constructed roles can be altered, and societies can change their inculcated patterns, when they are open to learning more satisfying models of relationships from other societies, from bodily experience, or from the storehouses of traditional culture such as mythology—or even contemporary poetries and ordinary storehouses of cultural values-images.

My own conviction that poesis is not just a frill or supplement, but a necessary political critique of society, perhaps even a destabilizing agent, conflicts with the ideals of the well-crafted lyric of personal epiphany that draws audiences to poetry readings and readers to establishment journals. Lazer acknowledges here how David Antin irritates audiences and Jerome Rothenberg shamanizes, both poets performing in a liberationist mode that challenges the usual boundaries between the written-published and the oral-performed. Poetry *in* culture, *as* culture; culture happening *in* poetry, *as* poetry: yes, but this is a view of poetry as comprising confrontational narratives that refuse interpretive seizures in specified "meanings." Like other concrete images whose "pictures" we discuss here, poetic images are *embodied*; they confront us as *sounds* that matter: the physical densities of the spoken images retain their specificity, and the cultural values their *difference*, so that tradition, even religious tradition, is both affirmed and questioned and so remains a critical voice of (not just about) poetry itself. The aesthetic is the house of expression of the ethical.

Craig Owens notes that "more than the other senses, the eye objectifies and masters. It sets at a distance, maintains the distance. In our culture, the predominance of the look over smell, taste, touch, hearing, has brought about an impoverishment of bodily relations. . . . The moment the look dominates, the body loses its materiality" (1992, 178). Owens's observation clearly marks the dominance of seeing in Western culture, yet he recognizes the "impoverishment" of bodily materiality, of what Downing might have referred to as the essential *relational* factor in gender discussions. Or we might recognize that the theme of "the body" today does not just have reference to the physical, but also to the social body.

Contemporary analysis of body symbolism in anthropology, the growing recognition of the socially constructed character of culture, and the feminist emphasis on "gender as a fundamental condition of experience and as an analytic category for specifically addressing the body's relation to language and identity, writing and power" (Bell 1992, 96), all coincide in a new approach to the body, as no longer merely "the physical body." Bell writes that "it appears we are now reappropriating the image of the body: no longer the mere physical instrument of the mind, it now denotes a more complex and irreducible phenomenon, namely, the social person." The thematic recurs several times in this volume: Ledbetter speaks to the apocalyptic violent body in *Beloved*; Fisher analyzes graphic body images used by the opposed political positions with respect to abortion; Noel probes Jung's curious avoidance of the bodily artistic; and Fox reports on a revitalized version of the Christian observance of the Stations of the Cross.

Images for the Future

My own concluding critical essay explores some of the ways we think ourselves "scientific," and hence "mythless," even while reveling in mythic byforms and archetypal manifestations that have been around for eons. The ideological and commercial applications of such themes interest me, and I'm concerned with the moral aspects of learning how to recognize just where such values are expressed within cultures, how to resist their enchantment—or how to follow *appropriate* images in ethical reflection. When someone suggests that "we just know" that particular myths or images are appropriate, we have come back to the shared conscience of a period to which I referred earlier. What someone from a different Enframing "just knows" may reflect an ideology that would distress us were we to discern it surfacing in our own cultural productions. And yet discernment can be well flexed only when it is taught on the basis of careful methodological reflections upon examples that we "just know" to be *different* from those that we turn to automatically. What we need is to be located somewhere between cognition of the traditional past (the Great Ideas loudly proclaimed by the right) and the ability to strike out in new and untried ways appropriate to a constantly changing environment (the left's stress on critical thinking). The promise of liberal education is that one's tool kit comes to contain storehouses of both data and skills in order to face the future creatively and appropriately.

We are hardly prepared for many of the revisionings and reimaginings ahead of us all, probably could not be, given the modernist stress on harmony and seamless chromium surfaces that accompanied all our schooling. We all have to learn new connectives, a new patience toward the arts in the face of the lacking copulas and the onrushing scenes and sentences that make visible our psychic incoherence. There's a postmodern simultaneity, even pastiche or collage, that jerks our equipoise across the many channels of cable TV. We race through hair or clothing styles (and in recent years, political remappings of the European, Asian, and African continents) and begin to regard as important what an earlier generation found trivial or beneath the appropriate regard of polite Western high-culture critics (pop culture, rock icons, the faces of buildings on the Strip in Las Vegas or Century Center in Los Angeles).

A series of debunking hermeneutics of deceit has shifted the ground of attention. The foreground becomes the background. The blue velvet becomes almost palpable just as it represents director David Lynch's most nightmarish subthemes. We find ourselves alert to positions and hierarchies, to points of view and "the gaze," indeed to the previously excluded voices (imagine your grandparents reading *Beloved* out loud!) and the curious intonation of newscasters. Our epistemology shifts and the borderlines get redrawn constantly. Creativity seems to mean less discovering the new (perhaps we're ready to recognize that change for the sake of change can be nonprogressive) than rediscovery of what has been at hand all along, in newly envisioned perspectives, even in Rothenberg's rediscerning of the sacred that "is resonant with its own problematics."

"Every creative act involves . . . a new innocence of perception, liberated from the cataract of accepted belief" (Arthur Koestler in *The Sleepwalkers*). And that repristinized perception flows, if courageously accepted and encouraged, beyond the old hoardings of images into those few but treasured insights that light up whole new landscapes and inscapes and psychescapes. Of course it takes a certain courage to picture cultural values today, and an attentiveness to the marginal imaginal as well as the central, to the garish and ridiculous as well as the morbid and saintly (see the volumes of *Re-Search* produced by V. Vale and Andrea Juno in San Francisco: they are mapping aspects of the marginal that make the usual literary journals look like infants' pablum).

The many ironic contrasts of our day include the fact that in our cities crack- and AIDS-infested slum blocks border on closed residential enclaves with their own private police forces (indeed, there are now more private than public police employed in America!) or the fact that President Reagan's AIDS commission had less than a third the budget allocated to the Challenger mission that ended in disaster. Or that top American business executives are paid salaries *forty to fifty times* the average salary paid to their employees, while slashes in state education budgets mean that in my city broken-down school buses cannot be replaced, and my secretary sells candy bars to raise funds for basic instructional equipment in the grade schools her children attend. A culture can ignore such realia, or it can insist upon confronting them anew with a political and artistic creativity that is deeply moral and involved, self-aware and self-critical. I never tire of emphasizing the close kinship of ethics and aesthetics, and hence the interrelationships between cultural images and values.

Deconstructionist guru Jacques Derrida is but one recent theorist who would have us reexamine the ways cultural values are pictured. His own reflection takes up a simple picture postcard and spins out a theory of communication (*The Postcard*, 1980); he quotes a saying of Cézanne and shuffles it into a series of reflections on aesthetics (*The Truth in Painting*, 1978). "I do not 'concentrate'," he writes in *Limited, Inc.* (quoted by Leitch, 1979, 31, n. 10), "on those points that appear to be most 'important,' 'central,' 'crucial.' Rather I deconcentrate, and it is the secondary, eccentric, latter, marginal, parasitic, borderline cases which are 'important' to me." Not because they are eccentric, et cetera, but *because they are important—* a useful motto as we seek paths through postmodernist disparateness. Not to sew them into a new neomodernist synthesis, but to learn how to relax with their multiphrasic images; to find the repose of the sylvan pool within the reflecting sheet-glass windows of the urban skyscraper; to inculcate a responsible picturing of cultural values that doesn't trivialize the Other at the boundaries or run in panic from the shadowy, misunderstood underside, and depth dimensions, and the symbolic and philosophic-reflective.

This book begins with the poet's voice, a selection from Hank Lazer's *DOUBLESPACE*, a work that moves like the normative Western book, from the front to the right, but also turns from the back cover to move from the right to the left, honoring the Hebrew mode of writing. And in between these halves is a blank page that stands in for a series of day poems about abstract, philosophical concepts. *Picturing Cultural Values in Postmodern America* ends with the writer Lynda Sexson, in a passage that called out to me curiously—I'd read the book in vetting her professional work, but now, rereading it for a senior seminar while I was editing this volume, it was almost as if the conclusion to her book were the conclusion to ours. The magical connection of the telephone secured her permission to let it be so, and consequently the poet and the fictioner bracket the Enframing of this book as they bracket every attempt to escape meanings' claims upon good sense.

"Making order" in a stack of fried bread (Sexson); "i'm tired of the beige walls" and "the key lies in the hasidic nigun"; "pity the poor astronaut barfing in weightless space" (Lazer). Or consider the newly developed pissers for extraterrestrial flights—What else is no longer sacred? Or no longer sacred according to wornout definitions of the sacred? "The media put the famine on the back burner" just as "in this era   willing constructions   each poet enters the line's den / one two three forwards" (Lazer), we all broach ordinariness with those few creativities allotted to each of us. My third-grade neighbor: "What has been your most creative moment?" And her younger brother, almost six: "Williams [!], why do you know the birds and why aren't there hummers now in February, and did you hide the cats' mouse-toy under your T-shirt?"—merely listening/ respeaking can sometimes be enough.

"In some sense we are all captives of a reservation culture, our heirlooms lost, our own claim consumerism," and to be without pictures of ourselves means "to be, not without mere heirlooms, but without religion—the connecting, authenticating principle of human existence" (Sexson 1992, 125). Sexson states that "behind our ethics are images" (126): yes, and before, and along-with. Pictures of cultural values indeed, as in our ridiculously but admirably up-to-date times, "we must fabricate, make up our sacred stories as we go along." But then "in making ourselves, we make the universe" (129): the contention throughout this book is that we do make/create ourselves, that nilly-willy we are indeed goddesses and gods insofar as we repeatedly determine the Enframings toward which and through which everyday realities are experienced and reenvisioned.

We imagine ourselves differently as we picture our cultural values differently. We dare prophetically to challenge the status quo in a liberational pastiche of present/past/future. The postmodernist challenge to the language of values reaches beyond Nietzsche's transvaluation of all ethical values insofar as it remains "intervalic . . . stochastic . . . willing constructions . . . " (Lazer 1992b, 3), and we are all on third base, awaiting the final pitch that will homer us into survival. Beyond the Enframing, beyond the picture frames any social construction of reality throws up as the "natural" from our first day in the cradle . . . beyond the vertiginous frames of contemporary revaluations of all the received pictures we imbibed along with the nursery-school Koolaid . . . beyond usual book introductions that point index fingers and then run off to the showers, this one asks what differences it might make were each reader of the book to engage seriously the revolutionary possibilities sketched herein, and . . .

Notes

1. I do not care to paint particular authors with the tar brush of jargon, but one does have to recognize something of the history of the way values have been approached to appreciate even the title of the *Common Knowledge* symposium (1/3 [1992]), "Beyond Post-: A Revaluation of the Revaluation of All Values," that was the first sustained answer to Kermode's call for papers. The symposium title alone reflects the question of the death of the master narratives ("Beyond *Post-*," as in postmodern) and Friedrich Nietzsche's nineteenth-century call for a transvaluation of all values.

Another example would be the first sentence in *The Hysterical Male* (Kroker and Kroker 1991, ix): "The hysterical male, then, [?] as a prelude [?] to the seduction [?] of one [?] libido"; or the verbless sentence fragment that forms the entire third paragraph, "The psychoanalytics of one libido, therefore, [?] as one last [?] playing-out of old male polyester sex theory, [?] a big zero." Much more complicated sentences, full of arcane references to the contemporary algebra of critical terms, could be cited, but I'll note only one other from the same source (Andres Haase, p. 188, initially citing Klaus Theweleit) because of its similarity to themes of this volume: "Under the gaze I am 'transformed into something cold and dead.' Transformation is not without repercussions. Signification ricochets off a privileged visionary apparatus and takes its revenge: my body is mutilated."

In editing the contributions to this volume I sought to eliminate such restrictive clique-talk as much as possible, primarily in the interest of making the materials available to a wide audience who ought to be concerned with the issues discussed here. Postmodernism *means* to many persons the sort of discourse indulged in by Baudrillard or Bataille or more recently by Avital Ronell (1989 and 1992). But surely it ought to help generally to describe ordinary-language discourse of our own late-twentieth-century period. This volume looks less at the French *outré* than at materials confronting "ordinary people" daily.

Among those who have called frequently for contemporary discussion of issues of value must surely be Barbara Herrnstein Smith (especially in her *Contingencies of Value*, 1988), and in an indirect way what I learned from her at a Woodrow Wilson

Institute on the Humanities surfaces in the production of this book. Many other figures might be mentioned, but I want to highlight especially the author of one of my epigraphs, John Fekete. In his *Life After Postmodernism* (1987), Fekete begins to name his own more positive prospects for postmodernist thought.

2. My agreement with Siebers will be obvious from my own chapter below, where I argue that the insertion of myth in culture is always particular, always framed by interpretive principles that are historically specific. On the general context, Siebers notes: "What I want to propose is that the Cold War context of modern criticism provides the key to understanding many of its theoretical developments, political stances, ethical claims, and psychological attitudes. It is easy [but, Siebers will argue, inappropriate] to believe that the 'conflict of interpretations' is merely about validity in interpretation or about small academic squabbles. . . . But debates about conflict of interpretations reveal that conflict has more than a local meaning; conflict is a major theme of modern criticism because it has been the major preoccupation of the postwar era. . . . Modern criticism is a Cold War criticism" (1992, 64–65).

A similar siting of a genre will be found in Krupat 1983, where we are shown how Native American autobiographies appeared (as "as-told-to" and hence heavily adapted materials) alongside a literature of the Frontiersman—of those folks who were famous for killing Native Americans.

3. Flax 1987 was a benchmark essay that articulated eight assumptions of Western Enlightenment thought which are thrown into radical doubt by postmodernist philosophy. These include assumptions about the nature of the human self as a coherent entity, reliance on rational means of attaining universal truths, dependence on "pure science" as a nonpoliticized site of knowledge production, and the belief that languages are transparent transmitters that do not shape definitively the contents they express.

No list of elements of postmodernism will satisfy everyone, but some features traditionally assembled include (from Harvey 1989): total acceptance of the ephemerality, fragmentation, discontinuity, and the chaotic (44, 98); the impossibility of metanarrative/universal truths (45); Foucault's point about the inescapable interplay between power and knowledge, so that one cannot escape the political consequences of knowing/administrating (45); Lyotard's emphasis on the infinite number of language games in which the social subject itself seems to dissolve (cf. Wittgenstein; 46); hence the importance of interpretive communities and the autonomy of each—Foucault's "heterotopia" (47–48); focus on communication and the means of exerting power in postindustrial information-based societies (49); the link between the signified/message and the signifier/medium, which is no longer seen as singularly determined but as constantly deconstructing itself, so that cultural life can be viewed as a series of texts intersecting with others (49–50); that language speaks through us (Barthes's and Foucault's theme of the "death of the author"; 51); ethical problems arising from lacking universal standards (in Rorty's analysis one can act only locally; Habermas seeks instead to return to Enlightenment dialogue—52); generally little overt attempt to sustain continuities of values, beliefs, or even disbeliefs (56); in terms of psychological presuppositions, the centrality of schizophrenia rather than paranoia and alienation (54); in the immediacy that is the only thing left, the rule of the sensationalism of the spectacle instead of historical continuity and memory—hence we live within a pastiche of historical tidbits ("jumbling together all manner of references to past styles," 85); consequent loss of depth, emphasis on surfaces (58); happenings, media images—a collapsed sense of time in which everything is simultaneous (61; cf. 86, the recurrent nostalgic impulse; and 87, the internationalist eclecticism of culture); a complex relationship to popular culture—"postmodernism then signals nothing more than a logical extension of the power of the market over the whole range of cultural production," with advertising as the official art of postmodernism (62–63); constant play with masking and veiling, as in reflecting glass surfaces that often hide the actual geographic sites (88).

Note Craig Owens's caution about assuming that there is a single monolithic postmodernism—as is usually assumed when taking Frederic Jameson's positions as normative (Owens 1992, 298). A useful bibliography, inclusive and well subdivided (Postmodernism and Photography, Postmodern TV and Film, and so on), will be found in Connor 1989, 248–66. Aronowitz 1991 explicates features of the postmodernist climate as they are having significant consequences in the shape of higher education. Hassan 1987 surveys some of the ways postmodernism phased out of modernism, and the dialogue about what it encompasses. And Lash 1989 charts the phases and types of subdivisions in postmodernism.

4. "If objects are the ultimate reality then there's only one true intellectual construction of things: that which corresponds to the objective world. But if truth is defined as a high-quality set of intellectual value patterns, then insanity [for instance] can be defined as just a low-quality set of intellectual value patterns, and you get a whole different picture of it" (Pirsig 1991, 100).

5. The twentieth century took up the intellect rather than the community as its ideal, and Pirsig argues for a return to the question of "Good for what?" that got excluded in objectivism (a more customary appellation would be positivism): "The paralysis of America is a paralysis of moral patterns. Morals can't function normally because morals have been declared intellectually illegal by the subject-object metaphysics that dominates present social thought" (Pirsig 1991, 306).

6. In such a context one must regard carefully the revisioning of historical experiences: the Rambo and other post-Vietnam movies tried to convince Americans that they had *won*, not lost, that war. Frequently scenes of American brutality familiar from the news media were restaged in the films, so that North Vietnamese rather than American soldiers massacred women and children citizens. These observations are made by Diane Johnson, "Star," reviewing Gore Vidal, *Screening History*, and H. Bruce Franklin, *M.I.A.; or, Mythmaking in America*, in the *New York Review of Books* 40/7 (April 8, 1993): 24–25.

7. Cf. Bernstein 1987, 115–16: "Discursively, the value of art lies in its questioning

of the disciplines of discursive truth in modernity; while, practically, the arts model, albeit not univocally, a normatively constituted, non-dominating praxis. However, because art discharges this role through its truth-claims, therefore, where these claims themselves are repressed, defused, by the discursive regimes of the present, only a philosophical criticism of artworks will allow them to fulfill their discursive role and only a non-institutionally bound reception will allow them to fulfill their practical function."

8. There are curious parallels between the "demythologizing" of the first third of this century—as in deconstruction, the prefix *de-* meant not taking away but revising—and there is a valid logic to the "mythopoetic" branch of the contemporary men's movements. Mythopoesis was a function of the psyche first posited at the end of the last century by Frederick Myers, subsequently taken up for literary studies by Harry Schlochower to refer to situations in which literary meanings of legends and myths could reappear in new shapings even when the initial mythic story was no longer current.

9. See the discussion of the ironies by which elements of borderline Chicano/a culture now appear in mainstream museums, in Marcos Sanchez-Tranquilino and John Tagg, "The Pachuco's Flayed Hide: Mobility, Identity, and Buenas Garras," in Grossberg 1992, 556–70.

10. It may be noted that contemporary German uses *Gestell* in a less allusive way than Heidegger wished: it can refer to a rack, stand, or shelf; a trestle or other support; and to a frame, either in the technical sense of a bicycle's *Gestell*, or that of a person's general type or appearance: Arnold Schwarzenegger's *Gestell* is that of the muscleman.

11. "All mere chasing after the future so as to work out a picture of it through calculation in order to extend what is present and half-thought into what, now veiled, is yet to come, itself still moves within the prevailing attitude belonging to technological, calculating representation" (Heidegger 1977, 48). Bernstein lucidly follows up Heidegger's fear that we live within the presence of "the death of art," a period in which it was moved from the center to the periphery; the discussion is especially appropriate to this volume insofar as religion likewise gets peripheralized in modernism. Bernstein comments on one section of Heidegger's "On the Origin of the Work of Art": "Artworks thrive on their own essential impossibility, on their failure to be works; and they can do no other, for that is where art is at. Hence, through them we come to experience the sense of the periphery *as* a periphery, and thus the meaning of the sway of the center. The artwork solicits in remembrance *and* anticipation of a power, a potentiality of art" (1987, 105).

12. Traditional religious conservatives will surely reject such an approach, arguing from hierarchical perspectives such as medieval Christendom that only a single deity worshipped within a single parochial form of religiosity deserves worshipful attention. It ought to be obvious that, while several of us operate in parts of the country where such perspectives still represent the majority viewpoint, the editor and contributors to this volume operate out of a much more open-ended, pluralistic, even occasionally polytheistic perspective.

13. Repeated concern with boundaries may be excused in the coeditor of a volume of trickster narratives (Hynes and Doty 1993)—the trickster is precisely the character whose boundary transgressions reaffirm the importance of the boundary restrictions, the cultural definitions of identity. Stewart (1987, 175) shows how the urban graffiti artist operates at just such junctions: "The larger threat of graffiti is its violation of the careful system of delineation by which the culture articulates the proper spaces for artistic production and reproduction. . . . It is not so much that graffiti is . . . a public art; rather graffiti points to the paradox of a public space which belongs to no one, and to the paradoxes of privacy and face, presentation and display, by which surface, space, and the frontal view are gestures of respectability and respect toward a generalized order for its own sake."

14. I have discussed the changing climates and the various responses of theologies and poetries in Doty 1990.

15. Although scholars vary in their interpretations of the root of *religion*, I (and Rothenberg and Sexton) follow here the traditional unpacking as being related to ligature, binding together, as most recently traced in the etymological supplement to the third edition of the *American Heritage Dictionary* (1992, 1525, 2111, 1495). Words with the hypothetical Proto-Indo-European stem *leig-* are *league, liable, allow, ally, oblige, rely, ligature,* and *alloy.*

THE VERTIGINOUS FRAME

Václav Havel, Martin Heidegger, and Everyday Life in a Disjointed Germany

GRAY KOCHHAR-LINDGREN

In this chapter the author examines, and exemplifies in the writing itself, the intermeshing of the near and the far that marks our culture of mass communications. From sitting in an airport in front of an advertisement of the dog Snoopy to watching new buildings and politics emerge in Europe—he wrote this while teaching American Studies in Regensburg, Germany— Kochhar-Lindgren explores the nature of the postmodern self in relation to Martin Heidegger's idea of the Enframing grid of technology introduced in chapter 1, and to Václav Havel's recent call for a more ethical politics. The author wonders whether contemporary individuals can recover the all-important balance of public virtue and private integrity.

While the next chapter will look in more detail at the historical construction of the modern self (the authors argue that many of its features derive from the Renaissance development of one-point perspectivism in painting), the present chapter already attends to some of the complex issues of objectivity and persuasive rhetorics that technology and politics model before us every day. What we mean by technology is less self-evident today than it has been for some time now: Avital Ronell (1989) explores Heidegger's misunderstanding of technology as primarily a threat, but Kochhar-Lindgren brings into consideration Havel's thought as well. The primary issue for both is how a culture organizes itself around figures, images, and metaphors such as the "picture" or the "smokestack"—very much the primary issue in picturing, modeling, shaping cultural values, since it determines who gets paid how much and how one type of being (humans) treats another (nature).

While the philosophical thought of both Heidegger and Havel raises abstract questions about technology's relationship to the natural, the local, and the distant or other, Kochhar-Lindgren here relates such issues directly to his own recent experiences.

The fundamental event of the modern age is the conquest of the world as picture.
Martin Heidegger, "The Age of the World Picture"

Politics of man, not of the apparatus.
Václav Havel, "Politics and Conscience"

Heading toward the turn of the millennium, we find ourselves at an intriguing historical crossroads. Values such as "democracy," "freedom," and the "market economy" have become dominant topics of discussion in much of the post–Cold War political debate. In 1991 *Time* named Ted Turner, the founder of the Cable News Network, its Man of the Year for having enabled television viewers to see first hand the turmoil that has swept through the world in recent years. A discussion about values and a global method of picturing the world now coincide in a way never before possible. What is the relationship between "values" and the world as a "picture"? How does the individual "fit into" the picture? How is the picture "framed" and can it be "reframed" for the benefit of the human sojourn on the planet?

I will respond to these questions stereoscopically. In some sections I will act as a diarist, recording things that catch my eye or ear, trying to convey the *texture* of my personal life. In other sections I will write in the third person and discuss the philosophical implications of selected texts by Václav Havel and Martin Heidegger. I will work on the near-at-hand and on the far-away; I will compose vignettes and I will theorize.

Since I am a native of Georgia now teaching in Regensburg, a small German city located about three hours from Havel's residence in Prague— Havel was elected as the first president of the new Czech republic on January 26, 1993—the changes in "the East" very much affect my life here in "the West." But because my situation is determined by larger forces than those that manifest themselves as a whole in my daily environment, I also want to step back, to size up things as if they were enclosed in a picture standing before me, and to theorize about the cultural shift from modernity to our own age.

Havel and Heidegger, both of whom are currently surrounded by public furor,[1] are *extremely* different in their philosophical language and intentions, and yet each argues that human beings are in the midst of a profound crisis that cannot be worked through if we do not establish a different relationship with the technopolitical apparatus in/by which our lives are framed, and with that which transcends, or interrupts, that apparatus. I hope that the differences and similarities between the two writers will spark insight into "values" and "picturing" as their words clash and resonate within the frame that I establish for them.

I

Thinking about the value of the world as a picture begins with a particular picture in a particular time and place: Atlanta's Hartsfield International Airport. This airport is a working museum where icons are superimposed upon one another, and where I decided to sit at a plastic, red-checkered table to have a cup of coffee (no free refills) before catching my flight to Munich. I will arrive, completely by coincidence, on the first anniversary of German reunification. Across from me is a familiar painting.

In the scene the moon shines with a solar effulgence as a river of light sinuously flows across the night sky, modulating from yellow to white as it sweeps up the dark hillside. Lush night-grass doubles the celestial voluptuousness and a black-green cypress, a vegetative flame, leaps skyward to prick the highest star. Quietly sleeping, a village dreams of the cypress and the stars, is dreamt by the lunar sun. The world is a fiery, silent exchange between earth and sky.

Except for one thing: a fire-engine-red doghouse whose straight lines violently intrude into the curves of the night. Snoopy, lying on his back on top of the doghouse, peers contemplatively upward at the stars. He's one cool dude, happy with life. The scene is framed in ornate gold and set in the neutral light of a small electronic billboard. Beneath Snoopy's harmonious cosmos is a text: "We're the Old Masters of Financial Security." It's an insurance ad with a clear message: Buy our insurance and become a meditative beagle.

Poor Van Gogh. Not only has his masterpiece "Starry Night" become a cartoon strip serving the claims of a risk-free existence, but Van Gogh himself, burned in the Provençal sun, has been caught in the undertow of capitalism and washed back toward the Old Masters, sober Dutchmen clad in black. History has been altered; distinct periods have been melded into a single image to support late capitalism's worldview.

The airport is a polished crossroads, a place of exchange between earth and sky, between runways and flight paths. It is a humming circuit of energy and information where everyone is in transit. Money is readily available for those hooked by/into the system and possessing a Personal Identification Number, a tiny digital pin that is painlessly inserted into the veins of our lives.

Time's up. Enough of these drifting thoughts. The Enframing requires my presence at the gate.

II

Postmodernist reflection in a variety of disciplines suggests that contemporary subjectivity occurs as the subjected nexus of linguistic, familial, political, cultural, economic, and electronic grids of power that crisscross the individual at every instant. This world-system, which creates the conditions for a certain institutionalization of objectivity and subjectivity, exists in turn only because through a complex historical process the world has come to be viewed as a representation, a picture. If the world is a picture, then the subject is fixed in that picture as a wide-eyed spectator of the framed scene—apparently looking on from the outside, but actually absolutely dependent upon the determinations of the system.

In their own idioms, both Heidegger and Havel trenchantly critique the contemporary moment and intensely reflect on the long transition from the objective system of the world as a picture, founded on the subjectivity of René Descartes's *Cogito ergo sum*, into a postmodern world quite differently framed. Both write in order to turn our focus away from the abstract and inflated "I" and toward the very background that enables the "I" to be framed as a subject in the first place. Heidegger speaks of the background that enables the presencing of any being as the "clearing of Being"; Havel speaks the more traditional religious language of the Word as the natural horizon of human life that bestows meaning.

Heidegger contends that the fact that the world has become a picture is the characteristic that distinguishes modernity from the classical Greek and medieval metaphysical positions. The world can become a picturable object only when the "I" has become a picturing subject, and this event occurs only when "what-is, in its entirety, is juxtaposed as that for which man is prepared and which, correspondingly, he therefore intends to bring before himself and have before himself, and consequently intends in a decisive sense to set in place before himself" (WP, 129).

From this perspective modernity exists as a form of representation, and "to represent (vor-stellen) means to bring what is present at hand (das Vorhandene) before oneself as something standing over against" (WP, 131). The picturing subject and the pictured object mirror one another in the presumably fixed frame of the world. A perfect correlation between the two produces knowledge and truth. What, then, happens when the frame begins to crack?

III

October 8, 1991: Six o' clock. It's already dark, but outside my windows the construction work continues. Ten men swarm around on the top of the building across from mine and floodlights transform the garish scene into a piece of performance art. Concrete is being poured into the frame of the walls by the Polish crew. The crane swings a bucket toward the helmeted men, and, in the background, twin church towers rise into the blue-black sky. Night means nothing to the enterprise of technology, although winter can still assert itself. After work the men retire to their small metal trailers in the back, living on the site, ready to meet the building's demands early the next morning.

In the news there is more about the skinhead and neo-Nazi violence against asylum seekers from outside Germany. (As of November 28, 1992, seventeen people had been killed, and nineteen hundred incidents of violence had been reported.) This is more than something happening "out there" for me. I am a foreigner here, and some of my friends are seeking political asylum: Christina is a lawyer who can no longer practice; Georg, her husband, is a painter; and their son, Simon, is quickly learning German from school, friends, and the Ninja Turtles on TV. A familiar Cold War story, but the Cold War is over—except that they would still be persecuted by the "new democrats" (the "old communists") if they were to return home. The family is without citizenship, sliding between political systems, their transition blocked on every side.

The distinguished guest on the Armed Forces Network, the Tower of Power from Nürnberg, advocates Western economic assistance to the Soviet Union in order to create a "common space where trade could occur." (Since I first wrote this, the Soviet Union has ceased to exist. History is always disrupting the sealed text.) The foreman on the roof gives instructions to a man in a red sweater; the twin spires of Karthaus-Prüll have vanished in the darkness.

IV

Havel concurs with Heidegger and regards "objectivity," in both its technological and political dimensions, as a crisis through which we must pass if we are to survive.[2] Our attention, he remarks, "inevitably turns to the most essential matter: the crisis of contemporary technological society as a whole, the crisis that Heidegger describes as the ineptitude of humanity face to face with the planetary power of technology" (P, 114).

Technology is dangerous not only because of its obvious destructive powers, but because it tears us away from our natural connections to the world. Havel remembers a smokestack that he encountered as a child, which has become for him "a symbol of an epoch which denies the binding importance of personal experience—including the experience of mystery and of the absolute—and displaces the personally experienced absolute as the measure of the world with a new, man-made absolute, devoid of mystery, free of the 'whims' of subjectivity and, as such, impersonal and inhuman. It is the absolute of so-called objectivity: the objective, rational cognition of the scientific model of the world" (PC, 138). Citing the Czech philosopher Václav Belohradsky, Havel remarks that if Descartes is the philosophical father of modern philosophy, then Machiavelli is the father of modern political "objectivity."

The origin of the modern state, Havel argues, can be found in the "moment when human reason begins to 'free' itself from the human being as such, from his personal experience, personal conscience, and personal responsibility" (PC, 143). Metaphysics, defined as reason founded on the indubitability of the self-certain "I," creates science, which as it conquers the earth with its universal but abstract truths alienates human beings from their natural world and from the presencing of Being (which is *not*, as Heidegger emphasized from *Being and Time* onward, the abstract universal). Havel and Heidegger agree that reason itself, as it comes to be thought in modernity, sunders *Dasein* ("being there," experienced existence) from its connections with the local, with the world of the neighbor.

When Heidegger discusses the dominion of technology in the frame of the world-picture, he names the essence of technology as a form of revealing, *Gestell*. Translating this term as "Enframing," William Lovitt reminds us that "the reader should be careful not to interpret the word as though it simply meant a framework of some sort. Instead he should constantly remember that Enframing is fundamentally a calling-forth . . . [a claim that] enframes in that it assembles and orders . . . that it is forever restructuring anew" (QT, n. 19). "World" is assembled and ordered into a picture, but not into a static picture framed and hung on a museum wall, for the museum itself is part of the world-picture.

According to Heidegger, modernity's predominant manner of the' revealing-concealing of Being is through Enframing, a process which operates by converting what-is—the natural, given world—into a standing reserve *(Bestand)* that is always on call for human use. Nature is given the "unreasonable demand that it supply energy that can be extracted and stored as such" (QT, 14) through such technologies as airliners, sawmills, or a power plant on the Rhine. Even clearer examples of that which puts us "on call" are the databank, the beeper, and the car phone.

V

October 11: I am lonesome tonight. Outside the floodlights beat back the darkness, and the men work on in silence, silhouetted against a growing wall of metal and concrete that blocks more and more of my view. The clock on the spires has been hidden; soon I'll have only windows reflecting my own to look out upon. TVs already flicker in other living rooms; we'll have a tiny courtyard of manicured grass, planted on concrete covered with sod.

The Enframing encloses, inhibits, forces upon us a certain perspective of ourselves.

But the Enframing also gives news. The cease-fire is once again broken in what used to be Yugoslavia, about five hundred kilometers from here. People who have been neighbors for forty years are now at each other's throats. An article in the *Süddeutsche Zeitung* tells of (former) U.S. Ambassador Robert Kimmett's vision of a Euro-Atlantic society stretching from Vancouver to Vladivostok. In the magazine section of the paper there is a picture of the now dilapidated house where Margaret Mitchell wrote *Gone with the Wind*. The house stands on Peachtree Street, in Atlanta, next to a new high-rise office building. *Scarlett* is on the best-seller lists in forty countries; people love a good romance. The world whirls around.

VI

Representation of the world as a picture enacts the revealing-concealing function of the essence of technology. And yet, as the danger from technology grows, so too grows the hope of a "saving power." But, in Heidegger's poetic analytic, this power has nothing to do with *God* or *values* in the traditional humanistic sense of these words. In the ontotheological metaphysics that generates modernity—the metaphysics of Descartes huddled in his Dutch oven—God is merely a rationally necessary part of the picture, enframed by representation as a logical necessity. The Cartesian concept of God serves to reappropriate the calculability of the world, and thus the possibility of scientific truth, for the ego that ultimately grounds the search for truth.

It is not far from Descartes's usage of God to support his rational truth claims to the death of God so famously announced by Nietzsche. And even though "God" still appears in movies, on highway billboards, and in the mouths of televangelists and politicians, s/he has not left any clues to the divine disappearance in something called "values." In fact, Heidegger, during his discussion of Nietzsche's metaphysics, asserts that "thinking in terms of values is radical killing" (WN, 108). Thinking in values, in his terms, is simply a continuation of the objectifying metaphysics of the world-picture and thus keeps us imprisoned in the position of spectator/ spectacle.

The stakes in Heidegger's assertion are extraordinarily high, and this is a crossroads where he and Havel part company. Heidegger interprets Nietz-sche's work on values as culminating in the Will-to-Power, which is "the ground of the necessity of value-positing and of the origin of the possibility of value judgment" (WN, 74). The Will-to-Power posits values so that the enhancement of life can increase, and although Nietzsche sometimes seems very far away from Descartes, Heidegger sees in both thinkers the activity of the metaphysics of the subject: "*co-agitatio* is already, *in-itself, velle,* willing. In the subjectness of the subject, will comes to appearance as the essence of subjectness. Modern metaphysics, as the metaphysics of sub-jectness, thinks the Being of that which is in the sense of will" (WN, 88). Values are part of the picture-world for Heidegger because they are the means for subjects to establish their objects. Experiencing what-is as a value—or as lack of value—is to remain firmly within the frame of modern representation and therefore to obliterate the "experiencing of Being itself" (WN, 103). Metaphysics itself thinks Being as value and thus shows itself to be a nihilistic project that hides rather than reveals Being. This is why Heidegger insists that philosophy as metaphysics must end if Being is to presence itself in unconcealedness.

Havel, on the other hand, understands values in a more traditional man-ner as tokens of transcendent worth and ethical guidance embedded within the human experience of the world. "At the basis of this world are values," Havel writes, "which are simply there, perennially, before we ever speak of them" (PC, 137). Values are not manifestations of the Will-to-Power except as they were enacted in a consistent and patient resistance to the political powers that ruled Czechoslovakia until quite recently. (Czechoslovakia ceased to exist as a political entity on January 1, 1993, and was replaced by the independent Czech and Slovak republics.) The "subject," in this con-text, is not the theoretical consciousness of Descartes and modern science, but the individual human being—complete with personal history, passions, and foibles—who is subjected to the radical objectification imposed by the totalitarian State.

Speaking about the human responsibility for words, a task that is "intrin-sically ethical," Havel remarks that this responsibility is "situated beyond the horizon of the visible world, in that realm wherein dwells the Word that was in the beginning and is not the Word of Man" (WW, 8). He then refers to Kant as the thinker who has shown why this immanence of the transcen-dent must of necessity be the case. Havel positions himself directly within the ontotheological discourse of Christianity and the Enlightenment and, as such, from a Heideggerian perspective, falls within the metaphysics of nihilistic subjectivity. And yet Havel's subjectivity, unlike that of Descartes, is grounded not in the self-certainty of the "I," but in the divine otherness of the horizon of the world.

Havel's life history and writings combine a traditional language of ethics with a revolutionary enactment of a moral vision that enables him, from *within* the violence of the world constructed as a picture of technologically encased subjects and objects, to step out of (or at least to the edge of) the frame and to articulate his "anti-political politics," his politics of a "civic forum." Such a politics provides a viewpoint from which one may recognize the world as a picture, and, knowing it to be a socially constructed scenario, refuse one's role that has been assigned by the system. But as Havel has recently reminded us, it is all too easy for "anti-political politics" itself to become a part of the system that rigidly fixes people and politics in place (1992, 172).

Havel's texts, which are based on clear binary oppositions and which are therefore eminently deconstructable, and his life, which is not, seem to offer the traditional religious-philosophical interpretation of the basis of the world-picture. And yet traditional ethics have not slowed the speed with which the Enframing gathers everything into the world-system; the world is more than ever a picture-object. Cameras have photographed the earth from the moon; newspapers, printed simultaneously in several countries, carry satellite pictures of the expanding tear in the ozone; and "we" have now experienced the first war carried, almost live, on television from the Persian Gulf. The examples are endless, and, as Timothy Garton Ash reminds us, "in Europe at the end of the 20th century all revolutions are telerevolutions" (1990, 45). The Enframing both enables and inhibits action.[3]

Havel's writings from the edge of the frame depend on an experience of transcendence, but, for the modernity of the absolute subject, the ground of any possible transcendence has vanished. Nietzsche's long shadow carries the "clear and distinct ideas" of Descartes within itself, and Havel warns us that totalitarian systems are ultimately "a convex mirror of all modern civilization and a harsh, perhaps final, call for a global recasting of that civilization's self-understanding" (PC, 145). Like others during the postmodern moment, Havel faces the dilemma of thinking transcendence in the face of an enframing apparatus that tends to assimilate all forms of transcendence back into itself in a self-reflexive loop. Perhaps transcendence as a "beyond" is no longer thinkable.

VII

October 14: On the Autobahn to attend the opening of Georg's first art exhibit in Germany. I'm riding in the back with Christina and Simon; up front are a woman from San Diego, seeking work in the local opera houses, and the driver, an ex-geophysicist turned brewer and art-gallery proprietor in Eichofen, a lovely little town where on a summer hike I had met him earlier.

On the way to Heidelberg, we stop in Oberndorf to pick up an instrument case from a cello maker. He greets us at the door while his wife continues to sand and polish a beautifully curved contrabass. Explaining that he makes instruments for players in Tokyo and London as well as nearby Bamberg, he wipes his glasses and invites us upstairs. Wooden planks are neatly stacked—they must dry for five years—as are the already-cut torsos of cellos-to-be. Onions and sausages hang from the overhead beams. The craftsman expertly runs through a few chords on a cello propped against the wall, talking about the relationship between the type and age of the wood, and the tone of a cello. We descend the stairs and thank them both for their hospitality. A postcard from San Diego, the "Playground of the Nation," is tacked to the wall. Stepping back into the narrow street, we climb into the car as a fine rain begins to fall.

October 18: Situated on the Danube, Regensburg has long been a point of transit. For the legions of Marcus Aurelius it was Castra Regina, guarding the rim of the empire against the Celts and the Germanic tribes, for whom the city must have been the first threshold to the world of fortified cities and stone roads. Wotan rumbled through the forests nearby while another god, Christ, gained strength in the south. Constantine had his vision, and over time Romanesque, Gothic, and Baroque churches sprang up in Regensburg, which was eventually named the seat of the Everlasting Diet of the Holy Roman Empire. That, in turn, brought to town the family of Thurn und Taxis—of beer, postal, and Pynchonesque fame. Today, after the rather miraculous transformations in eastern Europe and Germany, Regensburg is once again at a crossroads between cultures. Back home, miracles occur as well—the Braves have won the National League pennant. (*Now* the Braves have won the pennant, and lost the series, twice in a row.)

VIII

Commenting on the madman's speech in Nietzsche's *Gay Science*, Heidegger contends that the unchaining of the sun, the drinking up of the sea, and the destruction of the horizon indicate that the "uprising of man into subjectivity transforms that which is into object. But that which is object is that which is brought to a stand through representation" (WN, 107). Humanity has murdered God in order to make secure the constant reserve by which the world is organized and mastered, a process which is "grounded in value-positing" (WN, 107). This is why, for Heidegger, Nietzsche is the "last metaphysician" in the tradition of Cartesian subjectivism and why thinking in terms of values obscures rather than illuminates Being.

But just as the death of God announces the ultimate consequence of the world as a world-picture, so, too, it announces the moment when the frame of the picture began to crack. In all of its guises, postmodernism has to do with the vertiginous falling from the frame of the world-picture of modernity. Postmodernism is the reframing of the frame, the repicturing of the Cartesian interpretation of subject and object, consciousness and world. This "unframing" holds within itself both reactionary and liberating tendencies, but in any case it dramatically reconfigures philosophy and politics.

Heidegger, following in Nietzsche's wake, worked strenuously to step outside of the cloistered texts of philosophy and its traditional discourse of argumentation. He writes of the uncanny event that ensues when Nothing befalls Being; the way Being "harbors itself safely within its truth and conceals itself in such harboring" (WN, 110); and of art as *poiēsis* that brings with it the possibility of a saving power. Each of these sayings attempts to speak Being as the world of the world-picture fades at the edges, although the picture also gains more and more power as one corner of the canvas begins to burn. At the same time that the philosophy of modernity is being radically critiqued, the picture-world explodes all around us with a barrage of powerful images. In the complexities entailed by the deconstructions of modernism, we will have to learn to think, simultaneously, the burning and the continuity of the picture.

IX

October 20: Regensburg is bursting at the seams. On my morning walk I head up the hill past the university and a new dormitory, and then up to the highest point on this side of the river. Where there used to be a lovely tree-shaded bench, earthmovers have razed the ground to prepare for the construction of an upscale apartment complex. A huge TV tower juts above everything, and it is just this net of technology that allows me to call my family, to "reach out and touch someone."

How far away is Atlanta? It depends upon which coordinates of the grid we use to measure distance; electronically, it is less than a second away. "Touching" becomes "talking" over the wireless, a digitized and disembodied voice shot through the stratosphere. What is my "natural" world of which Havel speaks so eloquently?

Aren't we in exile from the natural? Doesn't late-twentieth-century existence within the Enframing dis-orient us and overturn all reference points? Living between worlds, the near has become the far, the far the near. Family, old friends, and familiar landscapes—all are far away. And the once far away—I first learned about Germany through the television series "Combat" and "Hogan's Heroes"—is where I now wake up, work, walk, eat, and sleep. The Enframing whirls us around so swiftly that the fundamental ways by which we know where we are—far and near, north and south, right and left, east and west—disappear. No matter where we live, we live in a particle accelerator.

And yet every morning when I walk to work, my feet remain grounded on the earth. The old coordinates are in place. The sun rises and sets, the moon waxes and wanes. We age. I am in a foreign land, *ein Ausländer.* It is good to help one's neighbor; it is evil to turn away from need. The world has its reference points. The near, as it has always been, is near. This paradox of the near and far, the way in which each stays itself and at the same time becomes its opposite, marks the changing of the frame. We are waves and particles; we exist at intersections and overlaps. Newton and Einstein, Moses and Nietzsche: a plurality of visions coexisting. Thinking along the edge of the frame, we lose our bearings, our balance, but we learn something about paradox, about the this-that of metaphorical existence.

And although the Enframing may crush us with credit checks and phone sex, there is nowhere else to go. There is no Garden. Within the Enframing, along the edges and in the corners of the picture, we have no recourse but to track and retrack, think and rethink, write and revise. We must be suspicious about the whirlwind of pictures in which we live, must be vigilant as we contribute to that whirlwind.

October 31: There used to be a farm where my apartment building now stands. Smoke rose from the farmhouse on a winter's morning as the pigs swarmed to the trough, the sun whitening the fog so that smoke and fog were indistinguishable. In the back, so far overlooked by developers, are an old stone wall and an overgrown orchard. The wall, of white and dust-brown stone, is crumbling and has completely collapsed in spots. Weeds and wildflowers have already gotten a foothold on the top ledge, and they spill over into the unpruned orchard where the high grasses have begun to return. Ecosystem and culture-system border, overlap. The trees are green and gold, curled brown at the edges. Back in Georgia, our new dog, Branden, was killed by a car. No one stopped. My wife and son took the dog to the vet, laying him on a new blanket so he would be more comfortable, but nothing could be done. Sometimes, late at night after the noise from the construction has stopped, I can still hear the pigs rooting in the earth, grunting at the trough.

X

The step beyond philosophy is not a step into a new metaphysical system, but rather a form of disciplined openness to the local, a relocating of the near, of that which brings itself before us. "What is given to thinking to think is not some deeply hidden underlying meaning, but rather something lying near, that which lies nearest, which, because it is only this, we have therefore constantly already passed over" (WN, 111). Poetry, fiction, and drama are less prone to step over the near than is philosophy with its grandiose ambitions, and Havel, even as president of the new Czech republic, remains a writer oriented by literary form. In the prose of his essays, he is quite clear about the necessity of attending to the close at hand. The question, Havel remarks, is whether we shall, by whatever means, "succeed in reconstituting the natural world as the true terrain of politics, rehabilitating the personal experience of human beings as the initial measure of things, placing morality above politics and responsibility above our desires, in making human community meaningful, in returning content to human speaking, in reconstructing, as the focus of all social action, the autonomous, integral, and dignified human I, responsible for oneself because we are bound to something higher, and capable of sacrificing something for the sake of that which gives life meaning" (PC, 149).

Both Heidegger and Havel, in their very different historical circumstances and with their very different philosophies, gesture toward a ground for human meaning that arises neither from within the human subject nor from the object that the subject confronts, but from a third place. Havel speaks of "perennial values" and the "Word that is not Man's," and Heidegger of "that destining which, ever suddenly and inexplicably to all thinking, apportions itself into the revealing that brings forth and that also challenges, and which allots itself to man" (QT, 29).

Heidegger, who writes of the abolishment of Western metaphysics, and Havel, who is squarely in the theological-Enlightenment tradition, both focus on the profound political and philosophical dilemmas engendered by a certain understanding of human *reason* as it springs from a Cartesian interpretation. It is a reason which rejects the nonrational for the certain and which acts, in its habit of abstracting, to dislocate the individual from the natural world. Reason based in the metaphysics of the subject exiles human beings from themselves by eclipsing that which is near.

This question of the nature of modern rationality is at the labyrinthine core of the debates in the human sciences about ontology, the status of reason after Freud, the production of meanings, et cetera. And it occurs "now" because the world as a picture, with all of its implications, is coming apart with ever greater force—the frame is cracking from the pressure generated from within the picture. Dislodged from the focal point in the picture, exiled from our trust in the abstractions of truth, what shall we do, how shall we act?

Havel, spinning off Michael Jackson's "Thriller," argues that "when traditional myth was laid to rest, a kind of 'order' in the dark region of our being was buried along with it. And what modern reason has attempted to substitute for this order, has consistently proved erroneous, false, and disastrous, because it is always in some way deceitful, artificial, rootless, lacking in both ontology and morality" (T, 160). Myth and reason; darkness and light. The picture comes undone and continues. Havel would have us turn away from artificially imposed rationality and return to ontology, morality, and the natural world of the free and integrated individual. Heidegger—whose work radically questions ontology, the morality of humanism, and the "autonomous" individual—would have us listen to the still-distant call of Being. But both agree that we must attend to the near at hand and revise the meaning of *subjectivity* and *reason*.

XI

Regensburg is cloudy today. My life is unraveling, coming undone, and soon I'll be back living in the mountains of north Georgia. I am unsure which way we should, or can, reframe the picture, but I know that we cannot simply clamber out of the apparatus, as if it were a constructed cave, and survey the scene beneath the sun. We cannot turn the switch that will stop, even for a moment, the massive whirring of the Enframing.

We can only proceed through the shadows, slowly, our hands lightly following the rough contours of the shifting boundaries, our bodies open to the weather around us. If we are fortunate, and if we can learn to peer along the edge of the frame from somewhere other than as a monocular spectator of the world-picture, we may one day notice the glimmer of a wave of grass and recognize the brightening radiance of a starry night.

Notes

1. Václav Havel went from prison to the presidential castle in the astonishing series of events of late 1989 and early 1990. A moving account of the transition is given by Ash (1990). Martin Heidegger is surrounded by a furor of an entirely different sort, the conflict about his relationship to the Nazis. Victor Farias's book *Heidegger and Nazism* sparked the latest round of the debate. Responses from leading German and French philosophers can be found in *Die Heidegger Kontroverse* (Altwegg 1988).

2. Christa Wolf, the well-known novelist from the "eastern section" of Germany, analyzes the crisis in much the same way. I offer only two quotations from *Cassandra* (1984): "'Knowledge which has not passed through the senses can produce none but destructive truth' (Leonardo da Vinci). There would truly be a new renaissance of consciousness if this insight were to bear fruit again, after the long dangerous experiment with abstract rationality, which resulted in thinking that everything is a means to an end" (268). "What I would like is to communicate to you the feeling which has induced my restlessness—a restlessness which this letter no doubt reflects. It is the feeling that everything is fundamentally related; and that the strictly one-track-minded approach—the extraction of a single 'skein' for purposes of narration and study— damages the entire fabric, including the 'skein.' Yet to put it in simplified terms, this

one-track-minded route is the one that has been followed by Western thought: the route of segregation, of the renunciation of the manifoldness of phenomena, in favor of dualism and monism, in favor of closed systems and pictures of the world; of the renunciation of subjectivity in favor of a sealed 'objectivity'" (287).

3. The role of the fax and the phone in Boris Yeltsin's resistance to the attempted 1991 coup in Moscow provides another example.

HUMANISM AND THE BIRTH OF PERSPECTIVE IN RENAISSANCE PAINTING

Toward a Sociology of the Gaze

STEPHEN KARATHEODORIS AND WILLIAM G. DOTY

Most of us assume that folk wisdom has it right: being "objective" is a good thing. Scientists would doubtless echo "amen." Yet philosophically inclined scientists often mutter "Heisenberg!" or even "Einstein!" as a sort of inculcation against the objectivism and positivism that have been so noninvolved and ethically impartial as to give us the atomic bomb and the gas ovens at Auschwitz.

This essay[1] regards an aspect of the Enframing that seems only too "natural," namely the way in which the subject-object dichotomy frames our interactions with the world and others. It suggests that a premodern phase of such objectivism found its working papers in Renaissance painting, where the artist began to separate himself (alas, only male artists are usually remembered today) from the long tradition in religious art in which the religious image (saint or deity) was thought somehow to indwell the painting or icon.

The Western view of things—there you have it, "view" of "things"—can be contrasted with the East-

ern; in the latter case one looks more at images of participation or mutual sharing between the object and the subject. Where does "space" enter the scene? Is it merely the background? Is the "subject" the viewer or the "object" represented as a "subject" (as in "subject to the gaze of others," a theme that is developed late in the essay)? "The others" as a theme recurs in this book; here it comes to the fore in terms of "humanism," not the atheistic brand so resented by American religionists, but as the focus on the human that will mark Western secularism generally, and especially the hermeneutics of Marx, Freud, and Foucault.

Gendering issues appear here as elsewhere in this volume: Is the male "gaze" necessarily a form of domination of women? Do not some men control the gaze of other men? Or women the gaze of other women? Perspectives again, as so often in this volume! Perspectives and ways of viewing—the "natural," "the other," the contrasexual (the members of the gender other than one's own), the "canonical" literature or poetry. This essay forms another component of the book's overall emphasis upon picturing/imaging cultural values, primarily in terms of the origins of what is so easily taken for granted today, yet has—like so many other socially important orientations—specific and determinative historical roots. When postmodernist perspectives challenge the values (represented for instance in artistic styles—and we cite several examples) responses may be knee-jerk reactions to the new, or may be framed in recognition of these historical roots and the extent to which we are always revising our meaning-laden views of them.

To illustrate a text is in a sense to punctuate it, to arrest its development by the insertion of a gaze in the form of a figure or illustration—a gaze which brings the textural machine to a standstill.

—Craig Owens, *Beyond Recognition*

In the introduction to *The Protestant Ethic and the Spirit of Capitalism,* Max Weber maintains "that in Western civilization, and in Western civilization only, cultural phenomena have appeared which [because of their rationality] lie in a line of development having universal significance and value" (1984, 13). In defense of this claim, Weber enumerates a long list of cultural achievements that he regards as justifying his conviction. His list traces the process of rationalization along two paths, first that of fields of knowledge such as the natural sciences, the social sciences, the humanities, and the arts, and then the rationalization of social institutions and fields of power such as education, the state, and the economy.

The natural sciences in the West—such as astronomy, geometry, mechanics, and physics—are cited as exemplifying the spirit of rationalism. Weber concedes that some of these sciences already existed in ancient Indian, Chinese, and Babylonian civilization, but there they lacked the rigorous mathematical foundations and the experimental method that they later received in the West. Thus, although sciences of nature existed elsewhere, they remained less arbitrarily "rational" than their Western counterparts, reflecting, for instance, religious or aesthetic systems rather than the abstract mathematical physics of the West. Weber also argues that the human (social) sciences—history, political science, sociology, economics, and psychology—develop a higher degree of rationality in Western civilization than elsewhere. And finally his insistence on the rationality of Western civilization extends even beyond his evaluation of Western scientific achievements, since he claims that Western art is more rational than art elsewhere. He notes that the rational tone intervals of music have been known elsewhere but that "rational harmonic music and the formation of tone material on the basis of three triads with the harmonic third" has existed only since the Renaissance (Weber 1984, 15).[2]

What specifically concerns us here are the views that Weber expressed on painting and architecture: "The technical basis of [Western] architecture came from the Orient. But the Orient lacked that solution of the problem of the dome and that type of classical rationalization of all art—in painting by the rational utilization of lines and spatial perspective—which the Renaissance created for us" (1984, 15). The views that Weber first expressed in 1920 have become firmly rooted in cultural scholarship and in scholarly discussions of the significance of Renaissance painting.

H. W. Janson, in his *History of Art and Music*, a textbook intended to introduce American secondary school students to the history of art (Janson 1968—the same author's *History of Art* is probably the most frequently assigned textbook in college art-history courses), writes of Masaccio's *Trinity with the Virgin, Saint John, and Donors* (a fresco painted a year or two before the artist's death in 1428 and reflecting Brunelleschi's recent experiments with one-point linear perspective): "And—*for the first time in his-*

tory—we are given all the needed data to measure the depth of this painted interior, to draw its plan, and duplicate the structure in three dimensions. [Masaccio's *Trinity*] is, in a word, the *earliest* example of a rational picture space" (Janson 1968, 101). Janson stresses the replicable and rational character of the newly invented picture space, although Masaccio is also famous for indicating the viewing perspective of the artist, the gaze with which the viewer is invited to identify as artist and viewer stand on the same picture plane. Visual distortion is normal, but the artistic viewpoint regularizes it in particular "gazes" that are related, as we will see below, to particular ideologies of masculine domination and patriarchal control.

One need only look at nonperspectival materials to see how discomforting it can feel to have another reference system employed: an excellent example from New Mexico is documented by Steele (1982), who shows how artists in the backcountry Hispanic areas have continued to employ pre-Renaissance, Baroque artistic conventions that were nonrealistic and nonrepresentational, but marvelously suited to represent ethereal, spiritual, nonearthly realities. And a Westerner may feel nervous before the restrained, almost-hidden representation of human beings in Chinese landscape paintings—easily contrasted with the many snapshots of Niagara Falls in which the photographer's companion predominates over the backgrounded falls. Or we may remember Egyptian artistic canons by which only rulers are full size, all their court being reduced to rows of miniature bodies.

The example of Masaccio helps us develop a consciousness of the gaze as being determined by particular social habits that are instilled in us from the cradle. We idolize "realistic portrayal," yet actually realism itself is only one of the recent modernist conventions now naturalized in our culture to the extent that already cubism seemed atheistic if not inhuman. In addition to his development of perspectival representations, another of Masaccio's achievements was just as striking at the time, that of having divine figures perambulate the same temporal spaces that are trod by mere mortals. In such an instance one sees the human self and the divine less dualistically opposed, as the Renaissance confidence in human abilities grew stronger. But even in something like Masaccio's *Tribute Money* (ca. 1425–28) there is a formal constructedness that belies any virtual bodies or geography. We are on our way to full-bodied figures whose fleshly weight will occupy measurable volume, and whose feet will leave footprints across the spaces of the paintings, but the influence of the frontal, planar icon or wall mosaic is still strong.

Between 1400 and the seventeenth century the concept of space underwent drastic changes not only in painting, in which these changes first appeared, but in physics, mechanics, and astronomy as well (see Koyré 1968). The philosopher and historian of science Edwin Burtt (1954, 93; see also Cassirer 1972, 181) describes the changes in the Western conception of space as follows: "According to Aristotle space is not something underlying all objects so far as they are extended, something *occupied* by them; it is the boundary between any object and those which enclose it. The object itself was a qualitative substance rather than a geometrical thing. The habits of thinking encouraged by this aspect of Aristotelian physics could be overcome only slowly by the new science; people could not accustom themselves to the thought that objects and their relations were fundamentally mathematical." This rational conception of space as an underlying, infinite, and homogeneous medium in which subjects live in mathematical relations with one another first appeared in painting, and eventually spread to physics and astronomy.

Space and the Subjects of Painting

These views of Weber and Janson concerning the significance of the picture space produced by Western painting are shared not only by many art historians but also by many painters. For example, in his Norton Lectures, the American painter Frank Stella says: "But, after all, the aim of art is to create space—space that is not compromised by decoration or illustration, space in which the subjects of the painting can live" (1986, 5). Stella defines picture space as a surface unstained by decoration or illustration. He views the aim of art, in the sense of its *telos* or end, as the creation of space. In order to reach this *telos*, however, painting must exclude decoration and illustration from the picture surface and replace them with a space "in which the subjects of the painting can live." And, as we have seen, Janson's comments on Masaccio's *Trinity* celebrate the first historical appearance of this interior and imaginary space. Janson's choice of the term *rational* to describe this picture space reminds us of the procedures that Masaccio used to resist illustration and secure a replicable geometrical and physiological structure. The *subjects* of painting first appeared in a *"rational* picture space" produced with the help of one-point linear perspective.

We may trace the newly emerging phenomenon of "the subject" to the innovations in visual representation that occurred in the Renaissance, but the expression "the subject" itself is ambiguous. When Frank Stella claims that "the aim of art is to create space . . . in which the subjects of the painting can live" he is using the term "subjects" to refer to those who live in the imaginary space created by painting. But who are the subjects whose very life is sustained by illusion? Who inhabits the imaginary spaces created by Renaissance painting? "The subjects of painting" refers not only to those who are depicted by the painter but also to the spectators who are drawn into the picture's imaginary space. The expression "the subjects of painting" refers to those whose features are inscribed on the picture plane (the subjects who are painted) and also to those who are addressed by the painting and drawn into its interior spaces (the viewing subjects).

A critical difference between mere illustration and the technique that Masaccio used is the power of the latter to situate the viewing subject in a field that is not only contiguous with but also continuous and homogeneous with that of the painted subject. Thus, the viewing subject must take up a position in the imaginary space created by linear perspective and the term "subject" is overdetermined, multiply determined: it now refers not only to the viewer and the viewed, but to the reciprocity between these positions established in Renaissance painting. Viewer and viewed stand in a symmetrical relation mediated by the invisible mechanisms of linear perspective. Thus the term *subject* also refers to the reciprocity that underlies the Cartesian ego—self-reflection is what uniquely characterizes human rationality. "Subject" refers as well to the experience of an inner, self-reflective subjectivity that grounds the possibility of *épistème*—the choices available in the culture, from which one develops a sense of authentic "selfhood," and to the subject of humanism, Man, who was born in the imaginary space created by illusionism in Renaissance painting.

Frank Stella's insistence that the *telos* of art is to create space is linked to his conviction that Man—the subject of painting—needs space in which to live. *Rational picture space* is the original habitat of the newly emerging subject. How is the subject linked to the imaginary or virtual space produced by one-point linear perspective? Why does "illustration" threaten the life of this subject? If space is a necessary condition of the life of the subject, then before the invention of linear perspective there were no subjects, but only illustrations. The subject, if it existed at all, existed elsewhere. Stella links the appearance of the subject to the production of space, but people were not always conceived as "subjects." What we may track further here is the relation between *rational picture space* and the emergence of the subject.

Stella may be pointing especially to Masaccio's achievement of helping the viewer enter the painting: it is no longer a curious window in time that opens to archetypal forms but represents in a more problematic manner the world in which the viewer, too, is involved daily. For Stella that world remains a world of abstraction, in an almost pre-Masaccian, Baroque timelessness. Its rationality is far removed from the subjectivity of the Renaissance assertions of human primacy over nature, and it is a rationality now developing, in Stella's most recent paintings, a constitutionality and embodiment that might represent his own renaissance or development from the abstractionism to greater concretion, just as at a much later point in the Renaissance Velázquez's *Las Meninas*, to be discussed below, represents the artist himself physically embodied in the picture, and the question of the viewing-gaze itself becomes problematical in ways that would doubtless have astonished Masaccio.

Humanism, Man, Self-Reflection

Despite the fact that the humanist conception of Man[3] has come under attack by structuralist, poststructuralist, and feminist thinking, it remains the ideological linchpin of the social sciences and humanities, where many still believe in Man, that there is such a thing as *the* Human Condition. Humanism maintains that man is at the center of his own history and of himself; he is a free subject who chooses the meanings to assign to his own actions, as opposed to the positions of linguistics or Marxian criticism, namely that none of our own choices can be fully disentangled from the cultural systems in which they appear. It also assumes that the concept of man is universal and that there is a human essence. Humanism ascribes to man innate drives and needs that transcend the historical and social conditions in which people find themselves, and assumes that man has the capacity to satisfy his own needs, as well as the ability to reason and to communicate.

What we have said thus far about humanism is offered not as a description but as an ideal toward which various humanist movements converge. Humanism recognizes that man is only more or less in control of his actions and utterances, and that he is able to satisfy his needs only more or less. It even concedes that man is constantly in jeopardy of "losing control" of himself. However, these concessions do not conflict with *the ideal* of man to which it subscribes, since humanism's response to man's loss of control has been to help him regain control ("Learn to be a man!"). Its response to man's frustration is to help reeducate him so that he may satisfy his needs and fulfill himself. Its response to man's alienation, to his loss of authenticity, and to his loss of a stable sense of identity is to seek to help man restore or beef up his self-image.

The discourse of Renaissance humanism and its subsequent transformations is intermixed today with antihumanisms. For instance, there is a humanist Marxism, associated with the work of George Lukacs, Eric Fromm, and Herbert Marcuse, alongside an antihumanist Marxism associated with structuralists such as Louis Althusser. Similarly there is a humanist psychoanalysis associated with ego-psychology, and an antihumanist psychoanalysis identified with the *école freudienne* and Jacques Lacan. In philosophy there is both a humanist phenomenology, associated with existentialism and the writings of Jean-Paul Sartre, and an antihumanist phenomenology developed from Martin Heidegger's fundamental ontology. We identify these binary oppositions within Marxism, psychoanalysis, and phenomenology not in order to provide an orderly classification of these complex positions along the lines of humanisms and antihumanisms, but as a heuristic device for the purposes of this particular study, whose theme we will now introduce.

Since its inception in the second half of the fourteenth century, humanism has not only been an *épistème* that takes man as its topic, but it has also been a cultural movement associated with the arts. Humanism contains three distinct but related aspects. First, it is an *épistème*, or inquiry that takes human nature, its limits, and its interests as its theme. Second, humanism is a pedagogy, a cultivation of the soul; *humanitas* expresses a cultural ideal much as Plato's *dialektikē* expressed in fourth-century Athens. And finally, humanism is an artistic movement whose goal is to represent what is universal in the human condition.

Here we explore the relationship between these three aspects of humanism, its *épistème*, its *paideia*, and its aesthetics, emphasizing the impact of visual representation on the formation of the humanist subject and reading humanist texts of the Renaissance with the assistance of certain anti-humanist texts of the twentieth century. We hope that this discussion will clarify aspects of the interrelationship between the humanist subject and the birth of perspective in Renaissance painting that have only been intimated but never explicated.

Optical Apparatus, Labyrinth, Machine, Discourse

One-point linear perspective functions as an optical apparatus, not unlike devices such as the telescope that appeared alongside it. Like any other machine, it is used to produce something; it produces certain kinds of images. While art historians and theorists of visual representation have been preoccupied with describing and analyzing the kinds of images produced by one-point linear perspective, we would like to reverse that gesture and instead of gazing *out* through the optical apparatus of linear perspective, look *in* to the spectatorship produced by linear perspective. In fact, we can imagine that the optical apparatus is an instrument at one of whose ends an image is made and at whose other end a subject is produced: one-point linear perspective is a two-ended optical instrument that projects the painted images of the Renaissance out of one end, and the subject of humanism out of the other.

One-point linear perspective is a mechanical invention or perhaps a reinvention of the Renaissance. Samuel Edgerton (1975, 5), the art historian whose monograph *The Renaissance Rediscovery of Linear Perspective* remains the definitive English treatment of the subject, writes: "So far as we have been able to ascertain, no civilization in the history of the world prior to the time of the ancient Greeks and the Romans ever made pictures according to this procedure. There is even some doubt as to whether these classical artists themselves knew perspective rules as such. We do know that certain of the classical mathematicians, in particular Ptolemy (Claudius Ptolemaeus) of Alexandria in the second century A.D., knew about geometric perspective, although they apparently applied their formulations only to practical maps and stage designs." While the technique may have been present, its application was to geographical or theatrical designs, not to the representation of human beings. It was not yet a proper way of seeing for the artist.

Edgerton's speculation on the historical origins of linear perspective is informative because of its similarity to other discussions concerning mechanical inventions which first appeared in classical antiquity. Although the prototypes of certain mechanical devices that play an important role in modern industrial economies were present in antiquity, they had the status of, at most, toys or amusements. The Greeks had a model of the steam engine, the water wheel, and other Archimedian devices, but these were not yet machines in our sense of this term. They were not articulated in a *system* of mechanical reproduction. These mechanical devices, which in modern times came to be regarded as world-shattering technological innovations, were for the Greeks amusements. Technically they existed *in* the Greek world but they were not *of* that world, as Peter Green's essay (1986) on the negative attitudes toward technology in the Hellenistic world illustrates. Similarly, as Edgerton points out, linear perspective was present in antiquity, but it was not a part of the Greek world, it was not articulated in a technological system of mechanical reproduction.

The notion of mechanical reproduction is borrowed from Walter Benjamin, to whom we are indebted: see "The Work of Art in the Age of Mechanical Reproduction" (in Benjamin 1969), an influential essay on what happens to the "aura" of an "original" work of art when contemporary reproductive techniques are so good that copies can be indistinguishable from the originals.[4] Benjamin romanticizes Renaissance painting and sees it as a bastion of resistance to capitalism's mechanized leveling and mediocritization of the world. But at the same time Renaissance painting is a necessary precondition of the very mechanical reproduction that Benjamin deplores.

To return to the idea of one-point linear perspective as an optical apparatus invented in the Renaissance, we note that one-point linear perspective functions like a labyrinth that disarms and charms those who enter its doors. Most important, Western painting is a machinery of *erasure*, in that both Renaissance painting and modern mechanical forms of visual representation are based on the same optical machinery that underlies modern graphics, printmaking, photography, and cinema. It is a machinery that may be said to represent a device for extracting and capturing the soul of the spectator and erasing something of the soul of the subject; subsequently the soul captured by this device experiences *aporia* (doubts or objections) and disorientation. In short, the machine of one-point linear perspective is an optical apparatus that displaces people as it situates them in the position of spectators. Its product is the imaginary space occupied by the humanist subject.

We would describe this machinery as a *discourse*, although it is painting and visual representation that we seek to describe with this term. It is in verbal discourse that we gain sight of the term *subject* and its relation to the humanist conception of man. The subject of a sentence, in a purely grammatical sense of this term, is the person or thing about which an assertion is made. For example, in the sentence, "The dog sees the man," we are told that the word *dog* functions as a subject because it answers to the question, Who or what "sees"? But the meaning of the term *subject* is not exhausted by the notion that it is something about which something is asserted. From the point of view of the grammatically complete sentence, the action or state of affairs described by the sentence is something that is performed by or that belongs to the subject. So when we say "The dog barked," the word *dog* can be viewed as possessing a double function: first it is that about which I, the speaker, am making an assertion about a subject; it is *subjected* to my sovereign power to assert. Secondly, as it were, "the dog" "sees"; by virtue of its position in the sentence, it is the subject that performs (the verb) an action. Thus the dog in this account receives the action of the speaker—it is the subject of the assertion, and it acts on its own—it sees.

Let us now take a second sentence similar to the first, but in which the two senses of the term *subject* coincide, a sentence in which the speaker and the one spoken about are one and the same person: "The dog sees the man." In this sentence the dog has ceased barking and is quiet, but that is no longer what is being asserted by the sentence. Now the sentence asserts that the speaker hears something; the sentence is making an assertion about what the speaker hears. In this assertion it is the speaker of the sentence—the asserter—who is asserting something about herself. "I hear the dog barking" is structurally quite different from the "The dog is barking at the man." In the latter sentence the subject that is spoken about and the subject that speaks are not identical. Thus although the first sentence contains a subject—the dog—this is not yet the subject of humanism. It is only in the second sentence, "I hear the dog barking," that the subject of humanism—man, properly speaking—is born. It is only when the speaking subject is also the subject spoken about that we enter the world that properly belongs to humanism's self-consciously perceived subject and its conception of the dual subject, man.

To summarize: the grammatical subject of a sentence is always in a double relationship: it receives the accusations of a speaker—you were barking—and it performs an action—it barks. Although grammars tend to stress one or the other of these two functions of the grammatical subject, its definition is nevertheless always split between them. The rift between the one who speaks and the one who is spoken about is spanned by the notion of man—the subject of humanism. Humanistic discourse is born of a "self-reflective gesture" in which the speaker reflects on the necessary conditions of speaking, just as the perspectivism of Renaissance painting situates the self-conscious viewer (subject) over against the object (subject in the other sense) of the painting.

We use masculine pronouns and the term *man* when speaking of the self-reflective speaker in deference to Luce Irigaray's contention that "any theory of the 'subject' [that emanates from humanism] has always been appropriated by the 'masculine'" (1985, 133). Thus the subject of humanism and the self-reflective speaker who emerges as the hero of the Renaissance is certainly Man in the fullest sense of this word. We place woman in opposition to the "Assent of Man," paraphrasing Bronkowski's *Ascent of Man*, because *the subject position* in discourse, representation, and desire is always appropriated by the masculine, which *at once* seeks to be called the whole and to exclude woman. Just as the grammars or the technological machines of a society may appear genderless, so the Western humanist subject and the patriarchal domination and control of ways of seeing, as well as the assumption that humankind had spoken when males had their say, easily came to replace more diffuse, less structured, more "feminine" modes of perceiving and speaking.

Las Meninas

To conclude by re-iterating how two seemingly disparate worlds—painting and human discourse—are mutually illuminating, our frame of reference is the idea that painting is a practice that interpolates subjects. Painting acts as an ideological apparatus in the sense of ideology first developed by Louis Althusser in his influential essay "Ideology and Ideological State Apparatuses" (1984; see Eagleton 1990, esp. 387, 391). Painting is a discourse that situates observer and observed (subjects and objects) in an imaginary space (produced by optics and fantasy) in which desire and power cooperate (see Mulvey 1975; Foucault 1980). Perspective is a method for the production of subjects and objects. Such an argument is similar to that first proposed by Emile Benveniste (1971) in his treatment of personal pronouns, further developed by Althusser in his discussion of ideological apparatuses, and first applied to painting by Michel Foucault in his philosophical discussion of Velázquez's *Las Meninas* in the first chapter of *The Order of Things* (1970, 3–16).

Leon Battista Alberti's fifteenth-century discussions of painting and perspective, in his treatise on painting (Alberti 1966), and Leonardo da Vinci's remarks about painting and the other arts, in his *Paragone* (Leonardo da Vinci 1949), have been helpful to unravel some of the connections between the invention of perspective in Renaissance painting, the ascendance of vision over the other senses, and the humanist notion of man. Perspective is a socially organized practice, similar to the notion of "sensuous practice" that Marx discusses in his *Theses on Feuerbach*, or as Max Weber would put it, seeing is "a social action" oriented to a normative order of perspective. It is subjectively meaningful for the one who engages in it, while simultaneously it takes into account the behavior of others, as we saw in the instance of the grammar of the barking dog.

Seeing also encodes power relations between the viewing subject and the viewed object. The subject of the gaze and its object occupy positions in the discourse of perspective that have formative effects on the psyche of anyone who occupies them, since the control of appearances through the use of perspective is intrinsically related to political authority (Bryson 1983; Berger 1972). *Subjects and objects are figured by perspective,* a point that brings out clearly the connections between the invention of perspective, the humanist conception of man, and the politics of the gaze. The posthumanist discussions of pleasure, image, and subjectivity as social constructions develop some of the sociological implications of what the art theorist Norman Bryson (1983) calls "the logic of the gaze." Even gendering, we begin to realize, is not something "innate" so much as it is a constituent of a social system wherein one or the other gender is assumed to have "natural" dominance, so that historically female nudes as the object of the desiring gaze of males have been legitimate objects for painting, but not male nudes (although that convention has begun to crumble during the last two decades). Femininity and masculinity are seldom described in contemporary gender studies from biological perspectives, but they are treated as constructions of social/ethnic/national groups with historical limits. How one "sees" masculinity or femininity will then depend upon a historically bounded discourse in which the self and the other have roles assigned automatically.

The discourse of Renaissance painting causes one within its discourse of perspective to conclude that the world of appearances turns a face to the other that it does not turn to him/her. Perspective implies that the eye of the other is an invisible point in my world through which all of my wealth and strength can be drained off, "erased" by the extractive gaze of the optical apparatuses developed in the Renaissance and in modern art reproduction. Perspective teaches me that I cannot visualize this focal point but that I can *feel* the effects of the other's gaze as it snatches everything within my reach, even my inner subjectivity, and carries it into its vortex.

Freud's "pleasure in viewing others erotically" (scopophilia) becomes a sign of neurosis, a sign that in another culture such as Tantric Buddhism might be aestheticized in a religious erotics. But having been inscribed within the perspectival *épistème* of post-Renaissance Western humanism, my desires have already been constrained before I have them, they are already vanishing from my subjective intuition as they become the objects of the other's controlling gaze. We might say that in Renaissance painting and the humanist perspective that it shaped, the eye of the viewing subject is the center of a hemorrhage that leaves my world lifeless and silent. The eye of the other functions at the boundary between two worlds. It separates the world of appearances from the world of the self-conscious subject and teaches me how to be a subject, how to recognize boundaries between the inside and the outside—between healthy and infirm self-consciousness. The eye has become the passage into the consciousness of the other; the "I" (Freud's *das Ich,* Latinized as *ego*) has *become* the site where the other views my subjectivity in its objectivizing gaze.

Self-consciousness in the Hegelian sense is a condition of the possibility of perspective. In fact, we can deconstruct the socially organized practices of seeing (the construction of the eye of the other—which is also its dissection, an experiment such as that which Descartes performed on the eye of a dead man) as a material practice of self-consciousness. Descartes wanted to see the world from the dead man's perspective. Perspective provides a narrative of consciousness by showing us how our world can turn its face to the eye of the other while concealing from us what it shows the other. The only way Descartes can "see" what the dead man saw is to evacuate the man's brain from behind his eyeball. Thus Descartes views his world through the eye of a dead man; he only can accomplish the feat by displacing the man's subjectivity and figuratively occupying the position that the man's subjectivity formerly occupied.

Of course we image the other, the self, the subject-object differently according to the perspective underlying the various cultural sites we occupy. Avoiding Descartes's metaphorical dead-person's eye-view, a postrationalist, posthumanist, now even postmodernist "I"-view seeks nonmediated vision, experiential seeing unfettered by the masculinist hierarchies typified by and reinforced by the Renaissance development of perspectivism. This chapter has exposited (ex-position-ed) the gazing machinery of perspectivism that we take so for granted that the postmodernist novelists' multiperspectivalism inflames and outrages us: the heroine either did or did not perform a certain act, let's not reverse in chapter 2 what was narrated in chapter 1. Or we are troubled by the Escher-like curiosities of multilinear perspectivism that keeps us turning the print this way and then that, the eye never satisfied that the object of its gaze is truly the subject of the drawing. Or the simultaneity of aural references in contemporary electronic music: we have been taught that one ought to be able to recognize the central theme or leitmotif, and not have to endure the clashing, overlapping chords of several marching bands (Ives's "The Fourth of July") or of several waltz themes competing (Ravel's echoic tribute to the Strauss waltz kings, "La Valse"). Such instances now are posthumanist in that they postdate the assurances of masculinist control derived from one-point perspective and the promise that ultimately, by a deity's design, it will all cohere in the end—but before that point it seems more likely today that we may well disintegrate into a nuclear apocalypse of barely imagined furor.

The clamoring confusion of competing voices/views may even be antihumanist, as we demand to hear the many unspoken voices as well, to see the many "I"s of others' cultural values mapped today more by electronic pulses than bourgeois chromolithographs or modernist views of Parisian boulevards—see Gustave Caillebotte's *Paris, A Rainy Day* (1877), with its coy gazings and perspectival ploys; or Barbara Kruger's message-laden texts infringing upon the visual image; or Anselm Kiefer's recovery in molten lead and straw (!) of subjects such as the Exodus or Yggdrasil: it would be hard to picture them all strolling hand in hand, yet each demands that we reopen locked houses of imagery, resee from no single vantage point, but from several post/antihumanist positions simultaneously.

Post- or antihumanist not as a rejection of every post-Renaissance value, but as a negating challenge to particular aspects of perspectival domination that have long been assumed to be "natural": postmodernist revisionings begin from a depth of historical reconstruction such as we have attempted here, heeding the historical/aesthetic traditions, yet also honoring the creative revisionings evoked by each new generation. No "I" is self-generative, but is in part a construction of the "eyes" of others (a lesson that developmental and Lacanian psychologists never tire of repeating). Hence the importance of the gaze, of the moral perspective from which the "I" is seen, the "eye" admonished to view or not to view in a singular or multiple perspective, from within only one dominating hierarchy of regard, or from all the rich panoplies of hypertextual vision that our twentieth-century communications media can make available to us. The "rational" itself is no longer as clearly self-evident as it was to the art historian Janson, let alone the sociologist Weber; and the conceiving of subjecthood (the I or the It or the Other) likewise becomes obscured as we recognize increasingly volatile challenges to the WDWM (White Dead Western Male) authors of the perspectives through which aesthetic values no less than economic systems have been determined and enforced. And yet an artist, DWEM such as Picasso, can so *reconceive* a classic that one's breath is taken away by having learned to see *the* original anew: see the side-by-side comparison of Velázquez's *Las Meninas* (1636) and Picasso's *Las Meninas* (1957) in Bal and Bryson (1991, 198).

In this chapter we have looked first at one constitutive aspect of the reality-structuring viewpoint according to which we've learned to identify the limits of the I (the subject) and disengage ourselves from the other (the object) by heeding only the "rational" as defined by the Euro-American philosophical, sociological, and aesthetic traditions (the other is non-white, nonmale, nonhegemonic, noncapitalist, et cetera). Secondly, we have touched upon the pedagogy of the soul according to which the I/self is made to feel rich and full or meager and empty, according to which we are subject or object, and from which perspective. And thirdly we have explored the Renaissance mechanization of the arts by which even our aesthetic experiences were to be projected onto a painter's grid, so that each line out there (in the object) would be made parallel to its simulacrum in here (in the subject)—a process detailed repeatedly by painters such as Albrecht Dürer, whose works repeatedly show the object of the painter's gaze being viewed through a framework strung with wires to make a cross-hatched grid.

However, our century developed not in terms of the precise rational grid of square blocks and boulevards that earlier city planners always tried to realize, but rather polymorphically along the lines of the hologram in which each tiniest part is a microcosmic reproduction of the whole, a dense crystalline armature in which no single perspective is allowed to determine the subjective position. We've yet to imagine what the twenty-first-century self will look like, how we will configure the cultural gaze that eventually replaces the social tyranny of one-point perspectivism. We've recommended proceeding cautiously, because as popular wisdom puts it, "it's just a matter of how you look at it." Yes and no. It is a matter of how you look at it, within the long-range predominance of Western visual metaphors that couldn't even be charted here. But it's not "just" such a matter, not "just" in the sense of "merely," which is a derived secondary meaning, but "just" in the sense of the Latin *iustus*, that which is proper or fitting. "It all depends upon how you see it": yes, and here we've shown the importance of remaining self-conscious about that way of seeing, lest we merely perpetuate tradition-hardened views of the subject that do nothing but objectify it in a matrix that no longer reflects our lived subjective realities or our projected moral ideals for changing them.

Craig Owens's posthumous collection *Beyond Recognition* (1992) returns repeatedly to the third thematic of that collection, representation, but especially in the chapter entitled "Posing," where he moves with his usual brilliance from a specific art exhibit across the range of psychoanalytic criticism. Owens saw clearly that "to represent is to subjugate," and the editors of his essays recognize clearly that such an argument "required the rejection of earlier twentieth-century notions of artistic value, in which images were considered to 'represent' truthfully the position and interests of subjugated groups *outside* the arena of representation" (xiv). Owens advocated teaching much greater consciousness about "the ways in which we are recruited to identify with images that appear to be natural, inevitable, universal, immutable." What we have sought to do in this essay is precisely to develop such teaching.

Notes

1. The germ of this paper is a presentation that Karatheodoris made to the Sixth Annual New College Conference on Medieval and Renaissance Studies, March 10–12, 1988, in Sarasota, Florida. In this second major posthumous essay of his that I (Doty) have composed out of leftover segments, I found myself entering into the text so frequently that the work became *our* work, and it wouldn't be right to say this is "SK

edited by WGD," as I did in the prize-winning essay "Male Desire in the Political Economy of Sexual Difference" (Karatheodoris, n.d. [1993]): while the initial impulse was Stephen's, the working out of the essay, and many additions and changes, are my own. The work has been improved by comments by Eloise Angiola, Ute Winston, and Mathew Winston, and especially by the engaged struggling with the text of Virginia Rembert, professor emeritus of art.

2. Dr. Rembert reminds us that Weber's point may be a bit overdrawn here: there is "rationality" already in Roman painting, certainly in (Doty's examples) Byzantine apse mosaics with their elongated figures meant to be foreshortened when seen from the floor, even in the manner in which Greek temple columns were tapered so as to *appear* parallel to the viewer.

3. *Man* and *man* are used here ironically and self-consciously in a feminist mode, in order to call into question precisely the *"man*kind" that has been the dominant way of naming humankind throughout much of Western intellectual history. "Humanism" is likewise one of those slogans we were brought up on, which nonetheless is repeatedly challenged today as yet another of the masculinist projects that has suppressed the voices of women and others. For all its contributions to the development of the Western mindset, the Renaissance across Europe was, from our contemporary perspectives, sexist as hell, and hardly inclined to admit women's perspectives. Which in turn implicates "perspectives," as we begin to see that apparently neutral artistic developments lode classist, racist, sexist ideologies as well—the work of John Berger (1972), to name just one debunking writer, points out precisely how the bourgeois burgher's possessions and values were replicated in the artworks, how attending to otherness came to mean merely objectifying them as "different," and reinforcing a mechanizing perspectivism that established the rapid turn in the modern world toward positivistic modes of knowing.

There are a number of punches to the cultural solar plexus that Michel Foucault might well have landed. I have emphasized the term *realism*, because "one-point linear perspective" is a convention of realistic painting. *Las Meninas*, the "subject" of the fifth part of this essay, is the "realistic" painting that Michel Foucault highlights as he begins in *The Order of Things* (1970) to call into question our received modes of perceiving and valuing particular bundles of conventional perceptions, calling each an *épistème* reflective of the values of a particular period.

Without going into the technical literature on "the gaze" in feminist writings; without explicating Foucault's obsession with the "seeing" of the human "subject"; without exercising the massive antihumanistic splay that some contemporary critics such as Jacques Lacan have performed: avoiding those sleights of hand, we hope here to have exploded some of the central Western chestnuts about naturalistic painting, realism, perspectivism, and the privilege we give to the ocular mode of seeing.

4. Parallels to Heidegger's negative attitude toward technology, discussed in chapter 1, will be obvious. Our use of "mechanical reproduction" applies it to a wider range of visual representation and artistic activity than that Benjamin treated.

4 JUNG'S ANTI-MODERN ART OF THE MANDALA

DANIEL C. NOEL

Few contemporary psychiatrists have had as wide an influence as Carl Jung. His name pops up in literary contexts, mythological critiques, and even with respect to lie-detector examinations (his work on the association between certain stimulus words and physiological reactions provided the initial parameters for subsequent developments). Repeatedly, psychoanalysts and culture critics find Jung's astonishing intellectual oeuvre fruitful, and anyone working with the "world picture" concepts that are the basic motif of this volume must confront Jung's system.

But once again we have a figure whose life was caught up in the transition from the modern to the postmodern. Jung seems conservative from some of the perspectives of recent analysis, yet radical indeed within his own lifeworld. Noel's explorations here treat the "pictures" of the contemporary soul that Jung developed. Such pictures or cultural images as the mandala (a figure of a square within a circle) characterize certain aspects of Jungian theorizing. Noel proposes that Jung himself might have gone in different directions had he been analyzed by a Jungian therapist!

Particularly post-Jungian, Noel does a Jungian analysis of Jung. No simple cop-out, stating that something of psychological interest must indeed have been derived from patients' materials, Jung's own approach to the artistic has to be studied. Noel finds that Jung was curiously unable to extend the creative expansions of one's life-projections and imaginings to his own self-story. Hardly a "postmodernist," Jung's own artistic endeavors were suspect within his own framework. Ought they be to his postmodernist successors?

During the years after his break with Freud in 1912–13, Carl Jung experienced and wrote down—and eventually drew or painted—what he described as "an incessant stream of fantasies." His autobiography recounts what happened when, at a certain point, he asked himself what this disturbing process was all about:

> "What am I really doing? Certainly this has nothing to do with science. But then what is it?" Whereupon a voice within me said, "It is art." . . . I knew for a certainty that the voice had come from a woman. I recognized it as the voice of a patient, a talented psychopath who had a strong transference to me. She had become a living voice within my own mind.
>
> Obviously what I was doing wasn't science. What then could it be but art? It was as though these were the only two alternatives in the world. That is the way a woman's mind works. (Jung 1961, 176)

After reaching this dubious inference Jung continues his memory of the episode by describing his repeated refusal to accept the judgment of the woman's voice: "I said very emphatically to this voice that my fantasies had nothing to do with art, and I felt a great inner resistance. . . . Then came the next assault, and again the assertion: 'That is art.' This time I caught her and said 'No, it is not art! On the contrary, it is nature.'" He says he was "greatly intrigued that a woman should interfere with [him] from within," going on to report the following conclusion: "She must be the 'soul' in the primitive sense, and I began to speculate on the reasons why the name 'anima' was given to the soul. Why was it thought of as feminine? Later I came to see that this inner feminine figure plays a typical, or archetypal, role in the unconscious of a man, and I called her the 'anima.' The corresponding figure in the un-conscious of woman I called the 'animus'" (185–86).

This long passage suggests that what his autobiography recalls as the very first identification of the anima with soul in modern psychology came, for Jung, out of an incident in which the message of soul or psyche was *refused*. Why this refusal? What does it imply about Jung's lifework, so concerned to assist "modern man in search of a soul"? What, indeed, does it imply about soul itself within this psychological context? And what does it imply about the role of the aesthetic in each? Finally, what might all this imply about cultural values as we move from "modern man" to post-modern persons engaged in their own search, still reliant in many ways upon Freudian and Jungian resources?

The following essay addresses these questions from the standpoint of images drawn from—and more directly drawn or painted *by*—Jung, images that reflect a tangled but connected thread of preoccupations.

Jung Against the Anima

At the outset it can be observed that Jung's characterization of women's thinking as rigidly oppositional tells us more about *his* mind than any woman's. It was, after all, Jung's own oppositional schema that posited the anima as a component of male psychology only, visiting upon women the vexed contrasexual baggage of the animus.

We know from recent "post-Jungian" works by James Hillman and De-maris Wehr that the anima can be seen as an autonomous personification of soul for women as well as men, and that she represents less a set of either-or alternatives than a shifting kaleidoscope of enticements to the ego (cf. Hillman 1985; Wehr 1987). Moreover, there are reasons for supposing that art as much as science is the proper mode of response to soul's entice-ments. In Jung's confrontation with her, of course, she was herself offering this very advice about how to engage with her. But Jung rejected it—and rejected her, at least in the curious encounter I have rehearsed.

My intention here is not primarily to speculate on the underlying causes in Jung's own personality development for this refusal. I wish, rather, to probe its wider ramifications as a possibly representative picturing of cer-tain cultural values. What Jung himself says in explanation of his refusal, while not to be taken at face value, is a place to begin exploring ramifica-tions. Again in the autobiography he recounts that "what the anima said seemed to me to be full of a deep cunning. If I had taken these fantasies of the unconscious as art, they would have carried no more conviction than visual perceptions, as if I were watching a movie. I would have felt no moral obligation toward them. The anima might then have seduced me into believing that I was a misunderstood artist, and that my so-called artistic nature gave me the right to neglect reality. If I followed her voice, she would in all probability have said to me one day, 'Do you imagine the nonsense you're engaged in is really art? Not a bit.' Thus the insinuations of the anima, the mouthpiece of the unconscious, can utterly destroy a man" (187).

Once more we find Jung's response to be suspiciously projective, expressing a misogynist hostility toward this soul-woman whom he has called a "talented psychopath" and now finds deeply cunning, an insinuating and untrustworthy seductress. Notice also that, for all we know, the voice of the anima has never called him a *misunderstood* artist; he supplies that adjective himself, projecting upon artists as well as women—perhaps upon artists *as* women, as effeminate. And to these negative qualities he opposes the morality of the ego, the male, "scientifically" controlling and controlled ego. This is the conscious center that takes up a "responsible" attitude toward the natural images produced by the unconscious, unlike either the artist or Jung's inner woman, the very voice of the unconscious psyche. "In the final analysis," he stresses, "the decisive factor is always consciousness, which can understand the manifestations of the unconscious and take up a position toward them" (187). No doubt such a verdict is true of psychological development generally. But what a *fearful* and *oddly defended* ego-consciousness he seems to be championing here!

After his declaration of allegiance to the ego Jung recalls how his fantasy writings from the period of his encounter with the anima-voice were collected in "the Black Book," then transferred to "the Red Book" and "embellished with drawings": "It contains most of my mandala drawings. In the Red Book I tried an esthetic elaboration of my fantasies, but never finished it. I became aware that I had not yet found the right language, that I still had to translate it into something else. Therefore I gave up this estheticizing tendency in good time, in favor of a rigorous process of *understanding*. I saw that so much fantasy needed firm ground underfoot, and that I must first return wholly to reality. For me, reality meant scientific comprehension" (188).[1]

Clearly this passage not only describes Jung's "esthetic elaboration" of the fantasy material but also constitutes an elaboration of his refusal of the anima and her recommendation. The ego-consciousness that must "understand" the unconscious responsibly is a scientifically comprehending ego as contrasted with a spontaneously responding "estheticizing tendency"—the tendency his soul-voice had told him to follow. His "mandala" drawings in the Red Book, collected chiefly during his difficult divorce from Freud (which helped provoke the fantasies) but produced until as late as 1927, manifest visually Jung's attraction to artistic media in engaging the unconscious psyche. At the same time, however, they reflect his rejection of the full psychological value of these media.

How should Jung's ambivalent investment in the mandala form—a form which he presumably continued to use with his patients even beyond the late 1920s, and which Jungian psychotherapy continues to sponsor in the culture to this day—how should his investment inform our larger inferences from the refusal we have charted? We will need to attend more closely to the details of his creation and interpretation of the mandala pictures.

"That Esthetic Lady" and the Emergence of the Mandala

Jung proceeds with his recollections of the 'teens with an account of how he "successfully" concluded his time of inner turmoil: "Two events," he notes, "contributed to this. The first was that I broke with the woman who was determined to convince me that my fantasies had artistic value; the second and principal event was that I began to understand mandala drawings" (195). Having painted his first mandala spontaneously in 1916 without having "understood" it in the required scientific fashion, he is saying, two or three years later he did achieve the desired comprehension, thereby commencing an emergence from his "creative breakdown."

But it is Jung's inner anima-woman—here identified with the concrete person of the "talented psychopath" and called "that esthetic lady" (195), the female patient he has identified as the external source of the anima's specific voice—who first precipitates the requisite understanding. Or perhaps we should say that Jung's response to the anima by way of a break with her outer embodiment was itself *tantamount to* the achievement of scientific understanding. "My science," he testifies in this regard, "was the only way I had of extricating myself from that chaos. Otherwise the material would have trapped me in its thicket, strangled me like jungle creepers" (192).

When Jung's patient wrote to him in 1918–19 reiterating, as had her voice in his mind, that "the fantasies arising from [his] unconscious had artistic value and should be considered art," he was irritated. Her letter, he observes, "was far from stupid, and therefore dangerously persuasive. The modern artist, after all, seeks to create art out of the unconscious. The utilitarianism and self-importance concealed behind this thesis touched a doubt in myself, namely, my uncertainty as to whether the fantasies I was producing were really spontaneous and natural, and not ultimately my own arbitrary inventions" (195).

Here, in a crucial move for our explorations, Jung expresses a decidedly contemptuous estimation of the artist—more particularly, the *modern* artist. He finds a hubris in modern art because of what he sees as its presuming to appropriate and manipulate the spontaneously "natural" outpouring of unconscious images. By the same token, he worries that his own dealings with fantasy material are in line with this supposed process of the modern artist: arbitrary invention that is neither spontaneous nor, in any adequate sense, drawn from the unconscious at all. After this remarkably insensitive judgment on modern art, to which we shall return, he relates a further step, which took him to the sort of understanding he felt was his sole means of release from the chaos of the fantasies. "Out of this irritation and disharmony within myself," he states, "there proceeded, the following day, a changed mandala: part of the periphery had burst open and the symmetry was destroyed" (195).

Jung's own assessment of how this step happened is not spelled out: Was his irritation only with the woman patient's urgings? Or was its source the unconscious itself, whose chaotic fantasies had assailed his harmonious functioning even before the arrival of the anima-voice? Was he upset because he thought his "estheticizing tendency," his "inner modern artist," was mishandling the unconscious material? Or was he bothered—consciously or otherwise—by the fear that pursuing an artistic mode as he had been urged to do by the unconscious psyche herself would in fact precisely *reveal* a truth about the soul that his scientifically comprehending ego was unwilling, in this instance, to confront?

Whatever the root *cause* of his irritation, in any case, on the basis of the factors we have probed thus far we can say that the symmetry of his mandala had been destroyed by the anima herself, "that esthetic lady," the unconscious soul whose female voice Jung had refused to heed. And symmetry, we are told by Jung's psychology generally, is what mandalas present when all goes well with the developing ("individuating") self. This is because mandalas, as Jung says of these centered and foursquare visual productions, are "cryptograms concerning the state of the self"—"the wholeness of the personality, which if all goes well is harmonious, but which cannot tolerate self-deceptions" (196).

This is a formulation that raises some further as well as familiar questions regarding the autobiographical preoccupations we are probing. How can Jung's retrospective notion of the self as he reviews this critical period, a period which in most respects was characterized by great *openness* to what James Hillman has called "the pandaemonium of images" (cf. Hillman 1983), contain such strong resistance to the voice of those very images? Did Jung discover, in this sense of self with its bias in favor of mandalic harmony, a device to distance himself from—and dominate—the welter of fantasy images which were finally intolerable to ego-consciousness? Did Jung develop his concept of the centered, holistic self in part as a *defense,* a safe enclosure created by scientific comprehension? And what are the implications for contemporary cultural valuing of the oppositions emerging in our survey of Jung's perceptions: ego *vs.* anima, self *vs.* soul, science *vs.* art, centered harmony *vs.* decentered fragmentation?

As already suggested by the background discussion above, Jung's attitude toward the value of aesthetic factors in psyche and modern society—starting with what we may term his own "anti-modern art" of the mandala—can help us with all the questions collected thus far, from the specifically biographical and Jungian to the more broadly cultural. To this end we turn now directly to the particulars of Jung's dealings with the mandala.

Jung's Mandalas: Protective Circle and Triangular Fragments

We know that *mandala* is Sanskrit for "circle" and that the mandala has its own rather different function in Buddhist meditation. But Jung also calls it a "protective circle" (1972, vi), and the adjective is worth pondering as we consider the visual elements of Jung's personal mandala creations. These begin with one eventually acknowledged to be his first, the 1916 picture called *Mandala of a Modern Man* which he executed just after writing down his enigmatic Gnostic vision, *Septem Sermones ad Mortuos* or *Seven Sermons to the Dead* (cf. Jung 1961, 195).[2] The arrangement of the visual components in this picture accords with the general meanings of the mandala given above: we see the definitive circular configuration repeated as a concentric series with the images from the *Seven Sermons* grouped along four arms radiating in a cross from the center. A feature that might escape notice in this symmetrical design is the three bands of zigzag lines representing the rays of an "inner sun" at the middle of the entire composition. These solar rays are in each case a circle of blue triangles with red ones showing through between them from behind.

In a popular essay on the mandala, Jung refers to Western versions as typically including a "central point to which everything is related." Since the essay also speaks of these mandalas' "concentric arrangement of the disordered multiplicity" (1972, 4), the *Mandala of a Modern Man* seems a most successful instance of harmonious selfhood in the making, a well-guarded growth toward wholeness. But another ingredient may lurk in those jagged rays of the solar microcosm, the inner sun at the center. Curiously enough, the rays immediately surrounding the central sun, like the rays in the other two concentric bands farther out, are not themselves red or orange, yellow or white as we might expect. Instead, the most prominent of these triangular rays are blue: The solar core of Jungian selfhood glows with—or is it struggles with?—jagged blue flames. The blue triangles forming the microcosmic sun's rays recur in a second of Jung's mandalas (fig. 1). It is presumably also from around 1916, for like the first it is influenced by the *Seven Sermons:* a small darkish shield to the right of center contains words not easily visible in a reproduction: "VII Sermones ad Mortuos."[3]

In the upper right of an Arabian Nights–like scene, a robed and turbaned figure, possibly a young boy, sits cross-legged on a cushion observing what is below. At the bottom three similarly attired adult figures are kneeling as they elevate a serving plate or monstrance above which floats, in the center of the picture, a radiant circle quartered by an inner cross. Overall there is the sense of a ritual achievement of wholeness, with the four figures and quartered circle expressing what was to become the classic Jungian emphasis upon quaternity as a sign of centered selfhood with strong religious overtones. The pictorial background for this scene, on the other hand, is less reverentially harmonious. The triangular rays or flames of the first mandala have returned as blue tiles or fragments, an array of shattered shards upon which the scenario of mandalic serenity is superimposed.

Two mandalas from the late twenties present clearly "successful" orderings of triangular elements: "Window on Eternity," as he called it, is based

The Baynes Mandala by C. G. Jung (By permission of the H. G. Baynes Estate,
Courtesy of Diana Crockford-Jansen)

on a 1927 dream and shows an aerial view of symmetrical city streets and plazas with a glowing magnolia tree residing, lotuslike, at the center. A second, "The Castle," from 1927, depicts a walled fortress town from above: it is arranged concentrically around circular moats with a cross-shaped structure in the middle (cf. Jaffé 1983, 90–94). Yet another, not clearly dated, places a collection of circles or globes in a four-armed shape around a central circular "firmament" containing a blue-and-white-rayed star in the midst of floating brown clouds of clods (cf. Jaffé 1983, 94–95).

Of the pictures from Jung's Red Book to which we have access, four can be called mandalas (cf. Jaffé 1983, 70–73). In each case the triangles reappear—visual intimations, it may be surmised, of what he was refusing to give positive place to both in his experience and in his theory of the mandalic self. First in sequence (Red Book no. 54; Jaffé 1983, 72) is a picture showing an uplifted serpent surrounded by a large red-orange triangle, possibly of flames, against a darker background of black and gray swirls. Rising out of the snake's open mouth toward the top of the painting is a multibranched brown and purple tongue bordered by lighter blue and gray swirls. The triangular fragments manifest themselves in this instance as geometrical green diamond shapes on the snake's back, while the Sanskrit name below the bottom left border of the picture and verses in German across its top indicate, according to Aniela Jaffé, a divine forerunner of Brahman pronouncing an invocation to the rising sun (1983, 68).

Another Red Book painting (no. 115; Jaffé 1983, 70) features a room with a floor, three walls, and a ceiling. The floor is covered with solid black and pale yellow squares, while the walls and ceiling are filled with orange and red squares and rectangles, except that in the back wall is a subtle circle. Above and below it, widening to the ceiling and floor, there is a band of rays composed of more irregular triangles and parallelograms, establishing the circle as a solar disk. Against the back right corner of the room is a large dark figure wearing a black top hat and layered greatcoat or cloak in black tinged at the edges with the orange of the walls. Jaffé merely calls the picture *Meeting with the Shadow* (68).

The next painting (Red Book no. 125; Jaffé 1983, 73) is very similar to the second one stemming from the *Seven Sermons* vision discussed above, at least as regards its upper half. This portion of the picture contains a large yellow quartered circle bordered by a band of red. It is enclosed in white and red flames on a background of small triangular fragments, red and orange where they are closest to the flames but including light and dark blue ones farther away. Centered below the sunburst a figure sits cross-legged, as in the earlier painting, facing the viewer and the scene in the bottom part of the picture. There we see a panorama of industrial bustle and war-making activity in a seacoast town, perhaps an outer political expression, drawing on World War I events, of the inner disintegration threatened by the fragments.

The fourth and final Red Book mandala (no. 129; Jaffé 1983, 71) shows a huge fire-breathing diamond-backed snake coiled around a small multicolored sphere with an inner cross the arms of which extend slightly beyond the outer circumference and also meet at an inner center of tightly packed concentric circles. This more complex spherical design has in addition outer rays, triangles of white pointing outward in star fashion behind the coils of the serpent and fading into blue where they almost merge into a dark blue-black background. This background includes a night view of a cityscape with a few dim lights as well as the faint visual suggestion that some of the bottom sections of the triangular star rays have broken off, like glass, and fallen to the bottom of the picture or beyond. Jaffé names this painting *The Light at the Core of Darkness* (68).[4]

Jung's Mandalas: Shards/Serpents/Suns/Centers

Two other mandalas by Jung, apparently not from the Red Book, also require brief description along with a consideration of his related comments. According to his note on the back of a canvas in the Jung Foundation offices in New York City, he painted one in 1920. Again a serpent with reticulated markings hovers near a floating sphere, and again there are triangular tiles involved, this time as a dull gray-blue background. While there is nothing published specifically about this picture, it resembles paintings in a series by one of Jung's female patients for which we do have his commentary.

These paintings, from 1927, include interactions between a black snake and a colorful mandalic sphere, with one picture featuring wavy lines or layers near the sphere's outer edge.[5] This feature Jung calls "a regular rind or 'hide' " that provides "protection against outside influences." He then makes a provocative connection to the triangular rays or tiles by speculating that these protective layers may flake off as "the cortices or *putamina* ('shards') mentioned in [the Jewish mystical system known as] the cabala"

(Jung 1972, 44 and n. 115). He makes an equally pertinent reference to the drawings of a second patient in the notes to his 1934–39 seminar on Nietzsche's *Zarathustra*. Having alluded to the medieval alchemists' idea of chaos as "a multitude of fragments of units" (Jung 1988, 1404), he finds the same representation in two of this second patient's pictures:

> In the first, one gets the impression of a terribly cut-up condition: it looks like sort of spiders' webs. This is a state of complete chaos, with many splits in it. . . . It is as if those sharp splits, like splitting wood or ice with sharp edges, might eventually cut the whole human being into fragments. Then the next stage is the big snake, and here we see the close association. She herself is almost crushed in the coils of an enormous serpent. This is again chaos but in the form of the great leviathan. . . . This was a great advance, for the chaos was then in a form and the splits had disappeared; that sort of dead chaos became vivified in the form of the great original serpent. In other words, the chaos lost its multitudinous quality and became, as it were, personified; it was gathered together and shaped into one being. (1409–11)[6]

Jung never refers to these two drawings of his patient as mandalas; they have apparently not yet achieved that honorific status, which would entail a *unifying* and, thereby, a simultaneous *banishing* of the chaotic fragments or splits. That these latter constitute the sort of images by which soul seems to announce herself—as suggested by our explorations in part 1—is an issue to which we will want to return in concluding. For Jung the antiartist of the mandala, in any case, the chaotic multitude must be reduced to oneness: the serpent supersedes the shards by embodying them, with the centered circle of the true Jungian mandala about to appear like a rising sun.

And that is exactly what does appear in the final example of Jung's own mandalas. It is of indeterminate date, but it is reproduced with Jung's commentary in a collection of his essays entitled *Mandala Symbolism* (1972).[7] Of this picture he says "the centre is symbolized by a star," or the sun as a star, adding that "the picture shows the self appearing as a star out of chaos. . . . it sets the structure of the self as a principle of order against chaos" (90–91). Actually, in concrete visual terms the star image is to the right of center, straining Jung's symbology somewhat (or being strained *by* that symbology's relentless centrism). As another multicolored sphere, the star has an inner cross dividing it into the usual quaternity as well as outer triangular rays of white fading into blue at the edges. Behind this floating body, as we might expect, is a field of blue fragments, here mixed with brown ones.

Yoking the Kleshas: Privileging "The Way of Understanding"

Jung's discussion of this mandala brings in the East Indian concept of the "kleshas," which he had treated in a separate essay on Eastern meditation. There he describes the kleshas as "the disorderly and chaotic forces which yoga proposes to yoke" (1978, 171) and identifies them with the repressed contents of the "personal unconscious." Since one of the yoga meditations he is dealing with employs the image of consciousness as a translucent lapis lazuli "floor" through which lower depths can be glimpsed, Jung's correlations here to his own psychology reverberate with the familiar presence of the blue shards. The yoga text under review refers to a symmetrical eight-rayed design with the Buddha seated on a lotus blossom in the center, which Jung says "symbolizes the all-embracing unity of the *bodhimandala,* the magic circle of enlightenment" showing through the blue translucent floor from what Jung would see as the "collective unconscious" below. This latter vision is then said to supplant "the chaotic disorder of the kleshas" (173).

The blue shards and other fragments of Jung's mandalas, as he created and "scientifically comprehended" them, first embodied and unified by the serpents and then superseded or vanquished by the rising solar spheres or stars, resemble the threatening kleshas discerned beneath the lapis lazuli threshold of consciousness and then positively undermined, so to speak, by an even deeper principle of centered unity. "The mythological motifs whose presence has been demonstrated by the exploration of the unconscious," he concludes, "form in themselves a multiplicity, but this culminates in a concentric or radial order which constitutes the true center or essence of the collective unconscious" (173).

We have seen that in his retrospective reflections about the urgings of the anima-voice during the period after the break from Freud, Jung was dismissive of modern art, declaring that it was a matter of arbitrary invention as contrasted with the spontaneous natural outpourings of the unconscious, best understood not through his own "estheticizing tendency" (as the "mouthpiece" of the unconscious had herself insisted) but through scientific comprehension. During this period he wrote down his fantasies—including the Gnostic vision he called the *Seven Sermons to the Dead*—and drew or painted his mandalas as he built a theory of how the mandala helps in the individuation of the self.

From 1916, the year of the *Seven Sermons* and his first mandala, we have in fact one of Jung's few "scientific" writings of this turbulent period of his so-called "confrontation with the unconscious." "The Transcendent Function" (1960/69) is an essay that directly pertains to the artistic status of the mandala while pointing also to Jung's regard for modern art and, beyond this, to cultural values concerning modernity implied by Jung's own strained relation to his personal art experience. The essay proposes a two-sided approach to the interpretation of fantasy materials, the choice of approach being dependent upon which of two tendencies predominates in a given analysand. "One," says Jung, "is the way of *creative formulation*, the other the way of *understanding*." The first of these, he goes on, "leads to the aesthetic problem of artistic formulation" and harbors the danger of "overvaluation of the formal or 'artistic' worth of the fantasy-productions" (84). As an alternative to the method of intellectual clarification, "patients who possess some talent for drawing or painting can give expression to their mood by means of a picture. It is not important," he hastens to add, "for the picture to be technically or aesthetically satisfying, but merely for the fantasy to have free play and for the whole thing to be done as well as possible" (82–83).

Jung's orientation here clearly echoes his own process in starting to create mandalas the same year. It may even be that, given the timing of the essay's composition, his creative process *followed* this schematic conception and was to some extent dictated by it, that on some level the supposed spontaneous process was already "understood"—perhaps oppressively so— in 1916 (not two or three years later, as Jung recalled in old age). It is obvious that he had more than a little technical competence as a painter or illustrator: "the whole thing" is indeed "done as well as possible," and his fantasy productions are often formally quite satisfying. This is what "that esthetic lady" tried to make Jung see. Yet with him the second tendency, the way of scientific understanding he favored for his personal individuation, came to take precedence. And where this is the case, he says of his patients, "the aesthetic aspect is of relatively little interest and may occasionally be felt as a hindrance" (84).

The two approaches to fantasy material outlined in this 1916 essay, in other words, are not actually given equal value. The way of understanding is privileged clinically and theoretically as much as it was personally. Even in this public statement of the scientific psychologist, Jung worries, with a projective affect we have noted earlier, that an aesthetic predilection will lead patients "to fancy themselves artists—misunderstood ones, naturally" (87). Likewise, the essay closes with a plea for the ego to "take the lead" (87) and to "seize the initiative" (89) in its engagement with the unconscious.

For all his courageous proclamations that the standard of selfhood must entail a carefully balanced equality between ego and unconscious, when it came to the role of art Jung's new psychology—one which in clinical application has often promised analysands the liberation of their "artist within"—this psychology favored the ego's need for ordered intellectual comprehension over an aesthetic attentiveness to the multitudinous forms arising from the deep psyche in fantasy and dream. Thus the undervaluation of the aesthetic in Jung's own remembered experience can be taken to imply, in this context, the comparative denial of the unconscious psyche in his concept of the self. Furthermore, the focus in this concept on harmonious meaning, the overreliance on a controlling scientific understanding of the order in the pandaemonium of anima's unconscious contents (or such understanding as the ego's *superimposition* of the order), is precisely what characterizes the pictorial details of Jung's own mandala art.

Jung on Modern Art: Picasso's "Lines of Fracture"

Based on all the foregoing questions, conjectures, and claims, and in order to venture some concluding inferences, we can envision a line connecting three factors: first, Jung's refusal to accept the artistic status of his own dealings with fantasy material (even when expressed with considerable pictorial skill); second, his psychotherapeutic devaluation of an aesthetic approach to such material; and, third, his dismissive attitude toward "the modern artist." Leaving aside speculations as to the personal causes for such attitudes and behavior, we can nevertheless imagine this line pointing both "inward" to a problem for Jung's psychological theory—his self-contradictory disregard for the "unconscious psyche" when it was voiced by an anima figure who was also an apologist for art—and "outward" to a problem of cultural values. While all three factors can be seen to contribute to each problem, the second of these two problems, that of cultural values, is most directly related to the third factor: Jung's stance toward modern art and artists.

In our first part above we noted Jung's judgment that the modern artist's attempt to "create art out of the unconscious" actually "concealed" a "utilitarianism and self-importance" (Jung 1961, 195). The context for this strangely intemperate remark, we recall, was the issue of the opposition, as Jung saw it, between spontaneity (nature) and "arbitrary inventions" (modern art). Although this reading of a nature-art tension is consistent with Jung's stated reason for refusing to consider his own fantasy-generated pictures as art—and, more subtly, with the interpretive priorities surrounding his work on the mandala—it can scarcely be allowed to stand as an assessment of modern art. His encounter with Pablo Picasso, the quintessential modern artist, is accordingly the place to question Jung's attitude and to follow it, finally, into the more general picturing of the modern that it exemplifies.

We know that Jung's one published article on Picasso was occasioned by an exhibition of 460 of the artist's works at the Kunsthaus in Zurich in the fall of 1932. The piece opens with his insistence that he will deal only with "the psychology underlying this kind of artistic creativeness," leaving "the aesthetic problem to the art critics" (Jung 1966, 135). As with his own artistic creativeness, this latter problem is not so easily separated from the underlying psychology, and despite his disavowal, formal compositional elements play an important role in Jung's approach to Picasso's paintings.

This approach also includes another claim that he immediately contradicts: Jung says that the inner states manifested in Picasso's art are "strictly analogous" (135) to those of his analysands in therapy. And yet he goes on to admit that "because of their lack of artistic imagination the pictures of patients are generally clearer and simpler, and therefore easier to understand, than those of modern artists" (136–37). Undaunted, he proceeds to psychoanalyze Picasso's work as he would were it produced by his least imaginative patients, dividing these into neurotics and schizophrenics. He then describes, in self-contradictorily aesthetic terms, a typical picture created by an analysand in the second category: "From a formal point of view, the main characteristic is one of fragmentation, which expresses itself in the so-called 'lines of fracture'—that is, a series of 'faults' (in the geological sense) which run right through the picture. . . . This," he quickly adds, "is the group to which Picasso belongs" (137).

While a note explains that in a later version of the article Jung responded to letters challenging his diagnosis here by softening the ascription of schizophrenia to Picasso—Jung elaborates that he finds only this "disposition" in the artist's painting (137 n. 3)—the main body of the essay nevertheless continues along on the same excessive course. Jung observes, for instance, that unlike the neurotic, whose pictures are accessibly unified and meaningful, the schizophrenic is disinclined to communicate any meaning to the beholder. Instead, "it is as though he had been overwhelmed and swallowed up by it, and had been dissolved into all those elements which the neurotic at least tries to master" (137–38).

We have already found that Jung's ideal in regard to his and his patients' mandala pictures favored integrative patterns and an ego-mastery that strains even his own general goal of balance between ego and unconscious. But we have not until now seen how drastically his psychologically vexed interpretation of visual products shapes his denigration of modern art and of the modern more broadly. In fulminating about the modernity represented by Picasso's art, Jung is also railing against what he most resisted in himself when it surfaced in the urgings of "that esthetic lady" or in the background fragments that his mandalas sought to master. He speaks of the personality in Picasso that "follows not the accepted ideals of goodness and beauty, but the demoniacal attraction of ugliness and evil," after which his attack becomes an explicit indictment of the modern: "It is these anti-christian and Luciferian forces that well up in modern man and engender an all-pervasive sense of doom, veiling the bright world of day with the mists of Hades, infecting it with deadly decay, and finally, like an earthquake, dissolving it into fragments, fractures, discarded remnants, debris, shreds, and disorganized units. Picasso and his exhibition are a sign of the times, just as much as the twenty-eight thousand people who came to look at his pictures" (138–39).

Two decades later, in response to an interviewer's inquiry whether he would ever write about other modern artists, he echoed his 1932 vilification more mildly by way of declining: "Art is, after all, intimately connected with the spirit of the times, and there is a great deal in just this spirit of the times to which one could take exception" (1977, 221 n. 3).

Conclusion: Picturing the Modern

With Picasso as with Nietzsche and Joyce, two other representative modernists he similarly excoriated, Jung could find no positive contribution, only a kind of morbid and, indeed, frightening posturing prone to psychic and social dissolution. Although it is only fair to reiterate that in important respects his psychology honors the anima, with her eccentric moods and imagery, as an equal partner in the development of a flexible selfhood, when her inner multivalence presented itself pictorially, a defensive psychic monocentrism was elicited which Picasso's cubism in particular must have exacerbated. He almost admits as much himself to his 1952 interviewer: "At one time I took a great interest in art. I painted myself, sculpted and did wood carving. I have a certain sense of color. When modern art came on the scene, it presented a great psychological problem for me. Then I wrote about Picasso" (221). The language of this statement actually reveals more than Jung intended; the context makes it clear that he meant the difficulty was with the art in its resemblance to the disordered pictures of his patients.

But in having a personal problem with the art of modernism he was certainly not alone. Nor does this necessarily make Jung, who entitled his first mandala painting in 1916 *Mandala of a Modern Man* (Jung 1972, ix), any less a figure of his times than Picasso, Nietzsche, or Joyce. Modernity was always a contested ground, and if the latter figures now seem more congruent with recent intellectual conventions than does Jung in his aesthetic anti-modernism, there are nonetheless many today in the culture (though usually outside the academy) who value what they take to be Jung's hopeful holism as an improvement on what they take to be nihilistic versions of the modern.

In 1952 he told his interviewer that "a new revelation from within, one that will enable us to see behind the shattered fragments . . . one in which the true image appears, one that is constructive—that is what I am waiting for" (Jung 1977, 223). Jung wanted the constructive revelation to come naturally, in the spontaneous image. The year before his death in 1961 he wrote to the art critic Sir Herbert Read, personifying as an "awe-inspiring guest" this natural revelation of wholeness and reiterating his denunciation of Picasso as the arch-exemplar of the modern artist's "willful mind" (Jung 1975, 590). He further proclaimed to Read that "nature has a *horror vacui* and does not believe in shard heaps and decay, but grass and flowers cover all ruins inasmuch as the rains of heaven reach them" (590). Once more— and finally—he felt that he and his vision stood for nature, which was responsible for "the objective manifestation of the psyche" (590). In opposing this vision to the work of the artist, however, Jung caught himself in a contradiction—one that, ironically enough, resulted in perhaps his greatest contribution to the shaping of cultural values.

We have explored this major inconsistency in considerable detail. It began in the 'teens with his rejection of the anima-voice and continued to the
end of his life with his refusal of Picasso's modern art. It was pictured in the
mandalas he and his patients were led to create. It concerned the imposition
of the ego's scientific understanding as a defensive reaction to the naturally
decentered imagery of both the anima and the artist. Even Jung's own
mandalas, where centered harmony seems more often invented than discovered, manifest the spontaneous imagery of fragmentation at their pe-
ripheries, as if to hint that the artist whom the anima spoke of in Jung
himself could not be totally suppressed. The anima and the spontaneous
artistry she urges provide the true imaginal revelation, to which the formal
craft of the artist responds supportively.

A close inspection of Jung's own language shows us the conflict between
the formulations surrounding his anti-modern art and his actual experience
of the fantasy material following the falling out with Freud in 1912–13. He
had then complained, for example, that the anima's alluring images were
like a "thicket" of strangling "jungle creepers" (Jung 1961, 192). Now,
some forty-five years later in the letter to Read, he objects to Picasso's "field
of ever so attractive-looking and alluring shards" (Jung 1975, 590). He
evidently could not see that like the thicket the field is a natural image,
and that the "shard heaps and decay" he found in Picasso are likewise as
natural—they are equivalent to the jungle creepers—as the grass and
flowers he said would cover them.[8]

While the experiential state of affairs he recalled in his autobiography
contradicts his pronouncements on both mandalas and modern art, render-
ing them false to the data they address—and false as well to the insights of
the "other" Jung I have been implying exists as a champion of the anima's
imaginings[9]—the irony is that these pronouncements have largely carried
the day in the current popular culture of personal growth. The values
pictured by the Jungian mandala manifestly participate in the irony: they
are the values not of the spontaneously imagining psyche, expressed and
espoused by the anima, but rather those of scientific comprehension employed by the ego as apotropaic protection against that imagining. Such
values are also the ones to which those of us who are uncomfortable with
the decentering forces of modernity will want to repair. Hence Jung's popularity among people for whom the only acceptable *post*-modernism is a
well-defended *anti*-modernism.

Jung, the Jung who inscribed his wishful scenario of centered harmony upon the psyche's welter, contributed an ideal to a future populated by modern men and women many of whom, like him in these contexts, take exception to the spirit of modernism. For such people this Jung, the anti-modern artist of the mandala, has himself become the "awe-inspiring guest" he awaited. He has arrived to defend them against the fragmentation they fear in psyche and art alike.[10]

Notes

1. None of the Black Book material has, to my knowledge, been published. Illustrations from the Red Book are available in black and white in the cloth edition of Jung 1961 and in color in Jaffé 1983. Permission was not obtainable to include these illustrations here.

2. Permission was not obtainable to include this illustration here. It appears as the frontispiece to Jung 1972 and is also reproduced in Jaffé 1983.

3. I was allowed to photograph this unpublished mandala in 1979 at the home of Mrs. Anne Baynes in West Byfleet, Surrey, UK. Jung had given the painting to her late husband, H. G. Baynes, an English psychiatrist who had been his assistant in Zurich and had translated the *Seven Sermons* into English. I include an illustration and my discussion of the mandala with the generous permission of Mrs. Baynes's daughter Diana Crockford-Jansen. The *Seven Sermons* are published as Appendix V to the paperback edition of Jung 1961, 378–90.

4. Permission was not obtainable to include these three illustrations here. They also appear with Jung's discussion in Jung 1972.

5. Permission was not obtainable to include these illustrations here. They appear with Jung's discussion in Jung 1972.

6. Permission was not obtainable to include these illustrations here. They appear with Jung's discussion in Jung 1988.

7. Permission was not obtainable to include this illustration here. It appears with Jung's discussion in Jung 1972 and is reproduced in Jaffé 1983.

8. For a different reading of Jung's letter to Read, see Lockhart 1987.

9. Essays by David Miller and Edward Casey and a discussion among Miller, Casey, Paul Kugler, and James Hillman in Barnaby and D'Acierno 1990 argue persuasively that this "other" Jung is a proto-postmodernist.

10. Coming from a different direction from my analysis in the current essay, D. W. Winnicott's review of Jung's autobiography nevertheless offers a similar critique of Jung's notions of a "centered" self expressed in the mandala: "He was preoccupied with the mandala, which from my point of view is a defensive construct, a defence against that spontaneity which has destruction as its next-door neighbor. . . . It is an obsessional flight from disintegration" (1989, 491).

A POETICS OF THE SACRED

5

JEROME ROTHENBERG

The remarks in this chapter are revised from a keynote speech delivered in September 1990 to a conference on "poetry and the transcendent" held at Fu Jen University in Taipei. The participants included Gary Snyder and Wai-lim Yip, along with an audience of other poets and of religious and literary scholars assembled from many different places. Rothenberg states: "My intention throughout was to keep these observations informal in tone, to present them as a range of topics to be filled in only later. In speaking of myself as part of a larger, pluralized group, I had in mind a particular but widespread 'community' of poets and of kindred spirits."

Where does the postmodern begin in poetry? With dadaist writers? With Pound? Or is the point of origination that moment of pastiche, word collage that began already in modernist experimentation with concrete poetry? Or the exposing of the poetic structures themselves, in analogy to the exposed structures and heating ducts in a classic building such as the Centre Georges Pompidou in Paris?

Wherever the "first" be located, it is clear that signs

are already visible in the work of Rothenberg, in his recourse to dada in his poetry and essays, in his turn away from the modernist isolated poet manqué to the community, especially to the implied community of religionists, to poetry in life rather than abstracted in books—hence his "readings" are performances and include chanting and other sounds, sometimes even elaborately staged representations of shamanism.

Rothenberg's interest in the deep mythological and ritualistic aspects of "primitive" materials from around the world, his wrestling with his own Jewish tradition (and especially its Polish remnants, and the Holocaust), and his dedication to the process of translation all reflect this burly poet's concern with religion, with the sacred. Not necessarily with the traditionally defined religious: in writing about two major translations in progress (Frederico García Lorca's Suites *and Kurt Schwitters's selected poetry) Rothenberg states that "Lorca and Schwitters are as sacred to me— as near to the sources of poetry and speech—as any more religiously specific poetry; and it is this sense of the numinous or sacred that forms a common thread, for me, between the poets and the shamans" (1992, 65).*

Likewise in referring to his massive A Big Jewish Book *(1978), Rothenberg notes that "the crux of the Jewish work for me is that of a disengaged engagement." The sense of the sacred as "the word-come-alive" "should be at the heart" of what poets do (1992, 66). Finally, it is Rothenberg's hope, expressed in the concluding part of this essay, that "poetry—wherever found—may act as a vehicle for enhancing our sense of the human and other-than-human, their convergence in the sacred." Rothenberg refers to the famous statement of Tertullian, "Credo quia absurdum," I believe because it (the Christian faith) is absurd (or nonlogical), a seeming slam against the intellectualizing rejection of metaphysics characteristic of school philosophy, with its demands for logical/positive/material consistency, and consequent bias against the religiopoetic.*

Blessed art thou, O Lord our God, King of the Universe, who permittest that which is forbidden.

—Personal prayer of Sabbatai Zevi, seventeenth-century
Jewish messiah and mystic

The strange thing about it, for many of us, is that we so clearly recognize the origins of poetry in states of mind and in forms of behavior that we think of as religious in nature. And yet, speaking for myself at least and for many like me, our tendency has been to pull away from religion as such. It is a tension that I feel in whatever I've done as a poet, and it's a tension that I'd like to address on this occasion: *what a concern with the sacred might mean in an age of secular thinking and being in which many of us share.*

The Sacred

The *sacred* rather than the *transcendent,* because the transcendent, however generously defined in the prospectus for the present conference, implies for me too great a denial of the *here and now;* and the source of poetry, as I understand it, is deeply rooted in the world around us: doesn't deny it so much as brings it back to life. "Eternity is in love with the productions of time," wrote William Blake, who in the later eighteenth century was our first great poet of the here and now. It is in *time* that I engage myself, and it is to the productions of time that I look with some fascination, to discover or create the sense of a life that can energize the common world we share.

In that energizing—that first, deceptively simple, act of poesis—something strange happens, whether to the world at large or to our sense of it. Remaining here-and-now, the world begins to lure us with a feeling, an intuition, of what the poet Robert Kelly speaks of as the not-here/not-now. Poetry, like religion, has always been filled with such "extraordinary manifestations" ("coincidence, chance, odd happenings, large rocks, hailstorms, talking animals, two-headed cows," and so on), but for those of us for whom poetry in some sense takes religion's place (albeit as a religion without assurances), those manifestations aren't bound or fixed but open-ended, different (we would like to think) each time we go at them.

On God

If this implies a yearning for what the surrealists—radical modernists of an earlier time—called the "marvelous" and "wonderful," I would be careful not to play down the risks involved—the dark side of the picture. "The world is charg'd with the grandeur of God" begins the great sonnet by the nineteenth-century Catholic poet Gerard Manley Hopkins, not as an image of transcendence but of immanence. I respond still to what he writes, but I can't speak of God myself without a sense too of negation and rejection. After Auschwitz and Hiroshima, the line comes back to me distorted: "The world is charged with the terror of God," it says.

Here I report my intuition, but it is an intuition curiously reinforced by a form of hermeneutic numerology from the tradition of Jewish kabbala. There, since every letter of the Hebrew alphabet was also a number, words of sacred scripture whose letters added up to the same sum were treated as being in significant relation to each other. This way of linking words was used, not surprisingly, to substantiate accepted religious "truths," although there were times when the system (called *gematria* from the Greek *geo-metria*, "geometry") was used by the more heretical and heterodox of the Jewish practitioners to call the others into question.

In following that system, then, I found that the letters in the Hebrew god-name, *eloha*, aleph-lamed-vav-hey add up numerically [= 42] to the Hebrew word *behalah*, bet-hey-lamed-heh, "terror [panic, alarm]." That they also add up to *kvodi*, "my glory," only intensifies the problematic. In short, a form of correspondence or collage that many poets in this century have viewed as crucial to their art.

So, take it any way you choose. *Where God breaks into what I write or think, it is the terror that admits him.*

The "Other" Traditions

There is accordingly a string of words with which we work with some degree of caution—the sacred, the holy, the numinous, the spiritual—and others that we shy away from even more—the supernatural, the pious, the divine, the transcendent. Even the sacred for me depends on how and why I'm using it; is resonant therefore with its own problematics. When the contemporary American poet David Antin, reacting against the easy—and popular—view of the sacred, says, "I reject the idea of a sacred language," I understand his objection even before he completes it: "For me, poetry is a mental act, not work which will become the object of a specialized cult." But I also understand the mental as the *spiritual* (another danger word) and that there are times, for Antin as for me, when the language of the mental act of poetry becomes itself what the surrealist master André Breton called "a sacred action."

It is largely a question of where we locate these words—in what context or tradition. Antin's rejection of the "cult" reflects a distrust of institutional and pietistic forms, of orthodoxies and closed systems, wherever found. In my own generation, both in America and Europe, this has meant a turning away from a Western and Judeo-Christian view of mores and religion—in contrast, say, to the rush into Christian orthodoxy of the generation of the 1940s, led by poets such as T. S. Eliot and W. H. Auden. What *we* came to identify with, beyond our own mental acts, was what the poet Gary Snyder has spoken of as a subterranean and very ancient tradition—or a series of such—that has manifested throughout history in movements antithetical to established governments and religions. Such a tradition, as Snyder describes it, carries with it a poetics of the open as against the closed, the free against the fettered, the transgressive and forbidden against the settled. Its poetic shibboleths—coming closer to our time—are terms like *"free* verse" and *"open* form"; the cry of the Dada poets of the 1920s "to liberate the creative forces from the tutelage of the advocates of power"; and the earlier political-poetic assertion by William Blake that "poetry fetter'd, fetters the human race."

The Spiritual in Art

It is so easy to lose sight of all of this; so easy, say, for an academic formalism to obscure the understanding of a great modernist artist like Vasilly Kandinsky that the work in which he was engaged in the first decade of this century was not merely "modern" but was directed toward a renewal of the "spiritual in art." So too—in its own way—was Guillaume Apollinaire's call for a "new spirit" in poetry and art. Or Tristan Tzara's insistence that the Dada poetry and art which he was fostering at the end of the First World War weren't based on a new method or technique but on a profoundly altered state of mind *(esprit)*—something like "an ancient buddhist spirit of indifference" he also called it. This insistence on a spiritual/mental component may seem curious from a man who was also, politically and philosophically, a (dialectical) materialist, but such a dichotomy turns up again and again as a defining issue within the twentieth-century avant-garde. It's there—as search, as dark-&-doubtful-presentiment—in Breton's contentions for surrealism that "existence is elsewhere" and that, at the end of the surrealist search, "the mysteries which are not will give way at last to the Great Mystery." And for the American poet, Ezra Pound, that kind of emphasis was the mark of a yearning that transcended the trap of the political (that which led him to fascism and a World War II indictment as a traitor) and that brought him at last to the sense of his own (and possibly *necessary*) failure:

> I have brought the great ball of crystal;
> who can lift it?
> Can you enter the great acorn of light?
>   But the beauty is not the madness
> Tho' my errors and wrecks lie about me.
> And I am not a demigod,
> I cannot make it cohere. (Canto 116)

A coherence constantly lost sight of and constantly recovered.

There are times too when the search has issued in a struggle with Western science and materialism (Kandinsky and a multitude of other artists could provide the case in point), but it would be a mistake not to recognize that religion—Western religion certainly—has also been at issue. For some this has meant a rethinking, a re-viewing of Christian and Jewish ties and sources, some of it extreme, rejectional, embattled, openly transgressive, but unwilling in general to stray far outside what Robert Kelly has called "the through-the-west-inherited gnosis." This would range from the foregrounding of metaphysical but recognizably Christian poets of an earlier era—Donne or Gongora or Angelus Silesius—to the fascination in our time with gnostic traditions outside the normative religious orders. There is already an "othering" at work here—more exactly a sense that our own singleness is more akin to what was silenced and made other in an alliance of church and state that may now be coming to an end. (Or that may, conversely, be returning once again to haunt us.)

New Archaeologies, etc.

The freedom to think outside those long-established orders—a spiritual gift of the eighteenth-century Enlightenment, for which religion (even where most rejected) was in fact a central issue—has allowed us to move radically beyond the Christian and the Western. The connection of poetry to pre-Christian and pagan sources goes very deep into Western history, moving into radical new territories and archaeologies from the eighteenth century on. A form of such a pagan-Christian linkage is familiar enough from T. S. Eliot's use of classically oriented anthropologists such as James G. Frazer and Jane Harrison to provide the mythological underpinnings for the sterility and religious/psychic vacuum of his 1920s poem *The Waste Land*, although his intellectual conservatism (both in religion and in poetry) kept him from a fuller exploration of the possibilities that this kind of move had opened up. With other of Eliot's contemporaries—Ezra Pound, for example—the normative Christian gave way substantially to the force of the non-Christian and non-European past and present.

But the alternative past—even where it keeps, roughly, within the boundaries of Europe or of Asia Minor—can take still more extreme forms. I'm thinking here of twentieth-century poets like Robert Graves, whose image of the White Goddess (in the book of that title [1966]) drew largely from the bardic taxonomies of the pagan North; of Charles Olson, who explored a pre-Hellenic "archaeology of morning" in the Sumerian and Hittite past; of Clayton Eshleman with his direct entry into the paleolithic caves and imageries of ancient Europe; of the Russian "futurist" poet Velimir Khlebnikov, who found a primal "beyondsense" language, matching his own experiments, among Slavic peasants and central Asian shamans; of the French poet Edmond Jabès, who in his extensive *Book of Questions* reshaped a kabbalistic literature into a new mental landscape of endlessly discoursing rabbis. It is precisely in mappings and remappings of this kind that one begins to sense the ongoing power of any Western-centered modernism that we would still be willing to inherit.

Such a "modernism"—pushing as well into the "post"modern present—has often enough left Europe far behind it. If this connects in some sense to terms like the critic Edward Said's "orientalism" (1978) or to "primitivism" as we've often had it used against us, it's also, I would insist, a part of what Gary Snyder, echoing Walt Whitman's poem title from a century ago, once called a "passage to *more than* India." For Europeans and Americans who have used it sensibly, it is a project of the immediate present, not of the exotic and romantic past. And it is a project intended—above all—to question and disrupt the power of the dominant European discourse.

Pound's *Cathay*

Take Pound's *Cathay*—his early modernist translations from the ancient Chinese—as a primary example. Rather than a capsule glimpse at an archaic—and from a Western perspective, exotic—poetry, it represented Pound's sense of what it was to be alive and writing poetry in 1915, in the midst of the First World War. "Largely a war book," the critic Hugh Kenner describes it in *The Pound Era* (1971); "its exiled bowmen, deserted women, leveled dynasties, departures for far places, lonely frontier guardsmen, and glories remembered from afar, were selected from the diverse wealth in the notebooks [of the sinologist Ernest Fennollosa from which Pound was working] by a sensibility responsive to torn Belgium and disrupted London." Pound's writing, then, came at a moment in history when a debased poetry, an unanchored language of transcendence, had separated us from the immediacies of our experience (debilitating as that experience may have been) and when a new sacralization (the renewal of the spiritual-in-art) depended on connecting to the concrete particulars of the world around us. For this, which was the objective of Pound's "imagism(e)" (his 1913 literary movement) and of that version of it "in motion" that he called Vorticism, something in Chinese language and culture served as both a model and a confirmation.

In his repeated three-point directive for Imagism, two of Pound's imperatives spoke clearly to and from the ways of poetry he thought he found in China: "direct treatment of the 'thing,' whether subjective or objective," and "using absolutely no word that did not contribute to the presentation." The third—"as regarding rhythm: to compose in the sequence of the musical phrase, not in the sequence of a metronome"—was a necessary part of his modernist package but had a more ambiguous relation to Chinese practice as such than he might then have thought. It was a package, circa 1913, without reference to the sacred or transcendent or religious, but in the aftermath Pound himself would move toward the intellectual worlds of Kung Fu-tze [Confucius] and of the Tao, say, and would relate them also (as with the poetry of Li Po or the still more ancient *Book of Songs*) to contemporary circumstance and praxis. All that as a starter for the century at large: a through-the-*East*-inherited gnosis that would, particularly on its Buddhist side, have a fundamental impact on later American poets like Snyder and Allen Ginsberg and a host of others. Snyder's attempt, as I see it, to write an American poetry unencumbered by reference to a traditional Christian and European past, is an immediate example of how such an experiment in gnosis can take shape. And this is true also, although much less often recognized, for the radical experiments with systematic chance that underpin the projects over the last four decades of a John Cage and a Jackson Mac Low.

Toward a Primal Poetics

The idea of a concrete language dominated both American experiments with image and surrealist, largely European explorations of an oneiro-poetics, a poetics of the dream. In either case the orientation was toward the thing—the object sighted, sensed, "directly" treated—with an insistence on the closeness between thing and word ("signified" and "signifier," for those who prefer the abstract counterparts as given by French "theory"). "We have lived too long in a generalizing time," Charles Olson wrote in his essay "Human Universe," as he too turned away from it, aiming (while bound to fail) to heal the break between reality and language. Some such aim has been a central project of our work as poets; it has been a key both to our search for a primal poetics and to our search for the sacred. And it was this idea—that a sacralized view of the world was tied, somehow, to a clear sharp language of names and nouns, dream names included—that led us into the depths of our own cultures and into cultures far distant from our own. As Gertrude Stein wrote, who was surely our greatest experimental modernist: "Poetry is really loving the name of anything. . . . It is a state of knowing and feeling a name." And George Oppen, American "objectiv-ist" poet, based a poetics on

> The small nouns
> Crying faith
> In this in which the wild deer
> Startle, and stare out.

It was this, or something very close to it, that I tried to put forward in *Technicians of the Sacred* (1968, 1985), the global anthology of tribal and oral poetries that I fashioned in the 1960s as a series of connections between two mythic poles: a "present" and a "past." *Sacred*, of course, was one of the two key words in that title, and behind it was Mircea Eliade's authoritative description of the shamans (religious figures rooted in our deepest human past) as masters of the techniques of ecstasy (the journey *out*) and enstasy (the journey *in*) and of the means to bring those into language. If this sometimes implies a poetics of transcendence, I would be careful not to place it "beyond experience" as did the organizers of this conference in their description of its theme, but to remember, for example, how Snyder locates the shaman's work in the experience of those who have "seen the glint in the eye of an eagle or the way a lizard's ribs quake when he does pushups"—and from that as a base, "have stepped outside the social nexus to . . . make contact with a totally nonhuman other" from which the poem, as inspired voice, arises. The source of a contemporary poetry of similar intensity may shift the area of experience—the place in which it happens, even the objects of the search—but the source and the experience can never be wholly separated from each other. And the poet's work, like the shaman's, may be carried on primarily through language— may start with language and use that as the vehicle with which to drive toward meaning, toward a (re)uniting with the world.

And having gotten this far, I would point out—if it isn't needless to do so—that the etymological meaning of *religion* carries with it the sense of a "reconnecting" or a "binding up." Its use in an expression like "nature religion" may be what's at stake here—as a reconnecting (not a separation) from the world. The binding to an orthodoxy or to a settled version of the real is of course another reading.

The idea that we could learn about such things from a wide range of cultures—some more advanced in them than our own—triggered the move in our time to a new poetics grounded in an *ethno*poetics. Such an ethnopoetics—my coinage, in what seemed a fairly obvious way, circa 1967—refers to an attempt to investigate on a transcultural scale the range of possible poetries that have not only been imagined but put into practice by other human beings. It was premised on the perception that Western definitions of poetry and art were no longer, indeed had never been, sufficient and that our continued reliance on them was distorting our view both of the larger human experience and of our own possibilities within it. The focus of our ethnopoetics as such was not so much inter*national* as inter*cultural*, with a stress on those stateless and classless societies that an earlier ethnology had classified as "primitive."

A Poetics of the Sacred

Behind this search for origins—for what would allow us to begin again, to break free from the past even as we reclaimed it—was the trauma of the Second World War, when "man" (Charles Olson wrote for all of us ["The Resistance," circa 1950]) "had been reduced to so much fat for soap, super-phosphate for soil, fillings and shoes for sale." It was against the back-ground of this crisis—of the mind, the spirit—that the work we were engaged in first revealed its meaning. So, if Gary Snyder, say, spoke of that work—"the real work of modern man"—as "[the] uncover[ing of] the inner structure and actual boundaries of the mind," the urgency of his statement related to the time in which it was spoken. If mind is its own mystery, so are the objects that the mind uncovers or conceals: in short, the world. So is that language which is both mind's vehicle and its prison.

In writing of those poetries (traditional/oral/tribal) that filled the first part of *Technicians of the Sacred*, I underscored first off my sense that they were (like the languages in which they were framed) complex rather than simple. This was reinforced by seeing the words as part of larger ritual and mythic wholes and served me further as a way of undermining the notion that complexity and intelligence were all on "our" side, minimalism and a kind of naked energy on theirs. Rather, I suggested, poetry both then and now (here and there) was a juncture of intelligence *and* energy that I equated with (another poet's code word) "imagination." And from that juncture—which was what the gathering was really about—emerged the idea, but more so the experience, of what we've sometimes called "the sacred."

In Lieu of a Conclusion

With an eye then, on both the here and there of it, it was my hope that the poems and juxtapositions in *Technicians of the Sacred* would illuminate the ways in which poetry—wherever found—may act as a vehicle for enhancing our sense of the human and other-than-human, their con-vergence in the sacred. If we don't etherealize or abstract this process, it can of course be read as an equivalent to that definition of transcendence that the organizers of this conference gave us to work with: as "a function or a being that transcends [that goes beyond or through] the possibilities of

experience and yet is necessary to give meaning to the data of experience."
Such a search for meaning will take us into dangerous areas as well as safe
ones, "blinding images" (in the formulation of the modern Chinese poet
Wai-lim Yip) as well as illuminating ones; and its effectiveness will be
proven in some sense by the degree to which it remains problematic and
resistant to our attempts to evade or to resolve it.

As a function of our *un*belief, it may then resemble that absurdity—that
doubting of the sensible and probable—on which the early Christian
thinker Tertullian once rested his *belief.*

THINKING MADE IN THE MOUTH

The Cultural Poetics of David Antin and Jerome Rothenberg

HANK LAZER

Earlier generations turned to poetry automatically to find expressions of cultural values—and many persons eager to display their education still sprinkle their speech with references to Shakespeare or Milton. Only during brief bursts of aestheticism has poetic writing been considered the work of an effete professional class composed of persons generally removed from the political and environmental concerns of the everyday.

But on the other hand Hank Lazer, a professor of poetry, graphs one of the reasons the average reader today knows little about the wide range of contemporary poetry making: it has become a specialty like any other in the academic marketplace, and one particular style of intensely personal, self-revelatory lyric is what the professional poet writes—if she or he is to get a job or find a publisher other than the tiny poetry presses with their chapbook series. My concern is not to sponsor this or that sort of poetry, but to indicate that there is a whole realm of "poetry" that does not fit the personal lyric genre, does not treat poetry as a sort of emotional ornament to the inner life, is not repre-

sented widely in poetry workshops, but is regarded in literature courses, if at all, as "experimental."

Lazer shows that much of the latter type of writing is too well established to be termed experimental any longer, and proposes that readers will find in the work of writers he cites a lean and mean type of writing that does not avoid tough-headed thinking, philosophical reflection, even the sorts of puzzling through of cultural imagery we are engaged in in this volume as a whole. The focus here is upon Jerome Rothenberg and David Antin, whose works direct us "toward sources and disciplines beyond what are conventionally considered to be 'literary' and 'poetic,' including anthropology, archaeology, linguistics, philosophy, and mythography." Poetizing is not in these materials an act remote from criticizing, but both are considered creative modes of thinking; nor is it something done in a quiet attic, but as a matter of inshaping performances and talkpoems that often "destabilize cultural values . . . in part through the disruptive powers of song and speech."

Here, then, is a poetry that does not hesitate to be pedagogical, shamanic, community building, liberational; the poet shares the making of the poem as a making of sense, finding meaning in our time. And we come to see that this has always been a feature of poetry, whether "primitive" or "modern," because its essence is dialogic, not monologic; its function is less to sanctify things as usual as to question their sway over us and to stimulate ongoing inquiry about ethical, religious, and philosophical foundations.

For at least ten years we have seen a barrage of essays and books lamenting the sad state of contemporary American poetry. In spite of accurate laments—about the sameness of mainstream poetry's product, a lack of intellectual ambition, a narcissistic and limited version of self-expression, the taming effects of poetry's almost absolute institutionalization—such evaluations are almost guaranteed by narrow reading habits and conservative institutional practices that limit the field of consideration.[1] The latest and best of these myopic complaints is Dana Gioia's argument (in "Can Poetry Matter?" [1991]) that in spite of the boom in poetry-writing programs, poetry publications in books and magazines, and the proliferation of poetry writing grants, prizes, and readings, "the energy of American poetry, which once was directed outward, is now increasingly focused inward. . . . Moreover, the engines that have driven poetry's institutional success—the explosion of academic writing programs, the proliferation of subsidized magazines and presses, the emergence of a creative-writing career track, and migration of American literary culture to the university—have unwittingly contributed to its disappearance from public view" (95). Or, as another recent critic suggests, "Verse writing in the postmodern era . . . is less a visionary or sacramental art than a highly competitive industry" (Kalaidjian 1989, 15).

But such characterizations depend on a limited and limiting exposure to contemporary American poetry. To put it simply, there are many fine, important, and challenging poetries being written today, though most of them are inaudible in mainstream critical analyses, in the models used in creative-writing courses, and in the "major" American literature and contemporary poetry anthologies. Cary Nelson, in analyzing the peculiarities of erasure in prevailing histories of modern American poetry, argues that "indeed, we tend to be unaware of how or why such a process of literary forgetfulness occurs, let alone why it occurs among the very people who consider themselves the custodians of our literary heritage. Custodians, of course, concern themselves not only with conserving the past but also with selectively disposing of much of it, though the two impulses become deceptively conflated in the imagination of academic disciplines—so that a self-congratulatory process of conservation remains primarily in view" (1989, 4). Such remarks apply to current custodial actions with regard to the preservation and presentation of *contemporary* writing as well. The two examples which I examine in this essay—the work of David Antin and Jerome Rothenberg—are but two of *many* that point to the health, intelligence, and range of contemporary poetry. In these two cases, I am dealing with a range of activity that has established itself over the past thirty-five years but whose work is absolutely unrepresented and unacknowledged in the *Norton Anthology* used in most universities, indeed in all other "major" anthologies of American literature and modern poetry.

Perhaps such exclusions can be explained, in part, by developments in academic specializations—that is, in recent disciplinary formations. Over the past thirty years, "creative-writing" programs have separated themselves out from "academic" literary programs. Even though most creative-writing programs require a substantial component of academic literary courses, already the very distinction contrasts creative writing with other forms of writing. More important, the ideology of most creative-writing programs promotes an identity built on a hostility toward the so-called "abstractness" of theory. It may also be true that the popularity (and professional necessity) of training in theory has indeed taken away from an interest in contemporary poetry. Such a lack of interest is understandable when the complexity, stylistic adventurousness, and intellectual excitement of many forms of theory are placed beside the too often accepted, but erroneous, characterization of contemporary poetry as a somewhat feeble-minded and nostalgic lyricism of outmoded self-expression. I'll argue that the writings of Antin and Rothenberg (as well as a host of emerging writers such as Charles Bernstein, Susan Howe, Lyn Hejinian, Ron Silliman, Alan Davies, Barrett Watten, and Bruce Andrews) demonstrate convincingly the aberrant and deleterious nature of such institutional disciplinary divisions. Thus the poet/writer who writes in opposition to divisive disciplinary professionalisms, according to Rothenberg, stands in a position similar to that of the native informant who opposes a distanced version of the anthropologist: "The antagonism to literature and to criticism is, for the poet and artist, no different from that to anthropology, say, on the part of the Native American militant. It is a question in short of the right to self-definition" (Rothenberg 1981, 171).

Antin and Rothenberg, both prolific discursive writers as well as poets, do not reject the value of critical writing and thinking. Indirectly, they critique the institutional separation of those activities and the added implicit claim of professionalized critics to have the right to define the nature of "important" poetry. Rothenberg proposes "that poetry is not simply what is called 'poetry,' which usually refers to a semi-professional literary activity. I think poetry is involved with the creation of meaning through language. There are a lot of boundaries which get crossed here. Poetry is attempting to discover the otherwise unknowable" (1981, 222–23).

Whatever the precise root causes of the institutionalized divisions critiqued by Antin and Rothenberg, we find ourselves in a situation best described by Ron Silliman: "The stereotypic figure of the artist unrecognized in her or his own time who emerges decades or centuries later to become one of the building blocks of western civilization is really the reverse side of a more ominous token: our society discards enormous quantities of that which it could benefit from, and this includes poetry. The shelf life of a good poet may be something less than the half-life of a styrofoam cup" (1990, 150). One result is that often "poetry, particularly in the United States, is a *profoundly amnesiac discourse*" (150; my emphasis). Many poets today, with little or no "shelf life," offer important information to us, including the kind of personal guidance and essential pedagogy that is often cited as a function of myth and ritual, namely "educating the imaginative function that must assemble the possibilities for acting" (Doty 1986, 33).

For Jerome Rothenberg, such an assembly begins with an act of conservation and reinhabitation, principally in new anthologies and translations which provide a means of recovery: "The matters that touch on the 'recovery' are, first, the idea of poesis as a primary human process; second, the primacy of the 'oral tradition' in poesis; third, the reinvigoration of the bond between ourselves & other living beings; fourth, the exploration of a common ground for 'history' & 'dream-time' (myth); & fifth, the 're-invention of human liberty' (S. Diamond) in the shadow of the total state" (1981, 120).

The activity of recovery, shared by Antin and Rothenberg (who have worked together for some thirty-five years as editors, friends, collaborators, and now as professional/academic colleagues), involves a broadening and inclusive notion of poetry, one which directs us toward sources and disciplines beyond what are conventionally considered to be "literary" and "poetic," including anthropology, archaeology, linguistics, philosophy, and mythography. As the title of one of Rothenberg's many anthologies has it, we are directed toward *A Symposium of the Whole* (Rothenberg and Rothenberg 1983).

One aspect of such a project is a radical rethinking of the relationships between the modern and the primitive, a rethinking that causes Rothenberg to leave "open the question of whether the 'primitive' is influencing the 'modern' or the 'modern' is directing our attention to forms we may now recognize as poems in tribal/oral cultures" (1981, 20). Antin's rethinking of the modern undermines our current, glib, "postmodern" sense that modernism is somehow distant and finished. In his astonishing essay "Modernism and Postmodernism: Approaching the Present in American Poetry," published some twelve years before Frederic Jameson's supposedly seminal essay on postmodernism (and written with a range of understanding of poetry and the visual and plastic arts that puts Jameson to shame), Antin argues, "Clearly the sense that such a thing as a 'postmodern' sensibility exists and should be defined is wrapped up with the conviction that what we have called 'modern' for so long is thoroughly over. If we are capable of imagining the 'modern' as a closed set of stylistic features, 'modern' can no longer mean present. For it is precisely the distinctive feature of the present that, in spite of any strong sense of its coherence, it is always open on its forward side" (1972, 98–99).

Antin wonders, "When and to whom did the career of 'modern' American poetry appear to be over and what did this mean?" (1972, 100). For Antin, and for a wide range of other innovative contemporary poets (including Rothenberg, John Cage, Charles Bernstein, Ron Silliman, Lyn Hejinian, and Susan Howe), the modern *is not over:* the innovations and generative possibilities of artists such as Duchamp and Stein are not mastered, understood, assimilated, and, therefore, "over with." Perhaps one academicized version of the modern—mainly a limited narrative of high modernism and subsequent conservative retellings by T. S. Eliot and others—has reached completion, but as many recent critical writings demonstrate, one of the most exciting and invigorating tasks today is to reinvestigate the modern.[2] A rethinking of the modern has to do with a fundamental grasp of the possibilities for innovation put forward by a broad range of twentieth-century artists.

Rothenberg and Antin, in their complementary explorations of the primitive and the modern, are involved in an important political project. I find affirmation of my point in Sherman Paul's reflecting on the meanings of the primitive in the work of Antin, Rothenberg, and Gary Snyder. Paul claims that if any particular aspect of the primitive "is focal, perhaps it is the political, for the good reason that these poets, dedicated to *poesis,* have entered the public realm and, to that extent, reclaimed the *polis,* the place of speech and act, that Plato tried to abolish. Plato also tried to banish the poets, and with this, the abolition of the *polis,* is a direct attack on the primitive, on the *muthologos,* as Olson says in The Maximus Poems, on the shaman, on the trickster. Politics, as we have come to know it, follows Plato in wishing to be rid of contradiction, opposing voices; and the poet, who by virtue of his vocation never loses connection with the primitive, is of necessity often at war with the state" (1986, viii).

Precisely such a broadened *anthropological* orientation toward poetry— which is distinctly opposed to the more institutionally entrenched model of the personal lyric, or the monovoiced personal narrative, each of which is taught on the basis of craft, repetition, and eventual mastery marked by "finding one's voice"—provides for a radically different answer to the question, What is poetry for? In opposition to mainstream academic poets who take pride in the "well-crafted" poem, Rothenberg rejects "the notion of poetry as elegance of expression" in favor of poetry as "newness of thought" (1981, 223). For reasons that are implicitly political and social, Rothenberg puts forward poetic practices that may in fact be immodest and contradictory: "Poets are not necessarily modest in what they set out to do, nor are mystics. I'm amused by this. I think it's absolutely wonderful and crazy that people should try to know the unknowable. (Not the unknown, by the way, which is a very different matter.) I think what happens is that you get a lot of contradictory propositions . . . and that helps to thwart the monoculture and single-minded total state. At the same time, my own approach is increasingly comic" (1981, 223).

In opposition to more commonly held (and taught) academic approaches to poetry, Rothenberg contends that

> poetry has rarely been composed as an occasion for criticism (the "New Critical" poets may here be an exception). It has other, very different functions for those who make it, & may (as a process) appear in situations that aren't easy to define within the framework of "literature." When it does, all kinds of factors "outside" the poem—the intention of the poet, his relation to a community, the conditions of his life & time, his politics, the claims he makes to vision or experience, & so on—all these (& more) become important, even central. And the "criticism" that doesn't recognize them, that can't, with Cage, reverse the roles of life & art (& share that life, at least by way of challenge), can only obscure the function, push the poem into a different realm, one with far less at stake. (1981, 35)

Rather than an institutional model where literary practitioners take pride in juridical acts of judgment, valuation, and ranking, Rothenberg pulls apart the academic Fred-and-Ginger dance team—that is, the poetry-and-criticism team (remember Eliot's pronouncement that "criticism is as natural as breathing"!)—in order to enact poetry as a putting into being of a present-day living and thinking. In this sense, Rothenberg and Antin treat poetry with Emerson's expectation that holds the highest function of art to be *generative.*

Rothenberg advocates "a move away from the idea of 'masterpiece' to one of the transientness and self-obsolescence of the art-work" (1981, 168). Creation leads to further creation; reading inspires writing. And for Antin, Rothenberg, and Snyder, life should be lived in consonance with one's aesthetics. On the one hand, such poesis confirms the more explicitly political utopianism of Ron Silliman, who claims that "among the several social functions of poetry is that of posing a model of unalienated work: it stands in relation to the rest of society both as utopian possibility and constant reminder of just how bad things are" (1987, 61). And on the other hand such poesis affirms the inextricable relationship found in the story about John Cage's response to an annoyed listener to Cage's composition without musical notes, 4'33". The listener says, with considerable impatience verging on anger, "I could do that." Cage responds, "But you won't." And the reason the listener won't is that composition, as Cage, Antin, Rothenberg, and others show us, is inseparable from living and from the governing models of consciousness that determine who teaches what in which venue and how "creative" writing differs from "criticism."

Even in an age that tends to discount the relevance and impact of poetry, the poetic practices of Antin (particularly in his talk-poems of the last twenty years) and Rothenberg (perhaps most dramatically in his "total translations," his readings, and his anthologies) inhabit a charged and important cultural site. As Cary Nelson reminds us, "Poetry is the literary genre that is most consistently, thoroughly, and unreflectively idealized" and "literary idealization is thus necessarily in dialogue with, and embedded in, all the other idealizations by which our culture sustains and justifies itself" (1989, 245–46, 130). In one of the most insightful statements articulated recently, Nelson warns us that

> in the competition to define and dominate our sense of what poetry is and can be, quite different notions of what poetry can do within the culture are validated and rejected. In the dominant mode of literary history, such issues are suppressed in favor of a narrowly aesthetic history of the conflicts between different kinds of poetry. We need to recognize that poetry throughout the twentieth century is the site of a much broader cultural struggle. It is a struggle over whether poetry can be an effective and distinctive site for cultural critique, over whether poetry will offer readers subject positions that are reflective and self-critical, over whether poetry can be a force for social change, over what discourses poetry can plausibly integrate or juxtapose, over what groups of readers will be considered valid audiences for poetry, over what role poetry and interpretation of poetry can play in stabilizing or destabilizing the dominant values and existing power relations in the culture as a whole. (1989, 245)

Rothenberg and Antin destabilize dominant cultural values, and they do so in part through the disruptive powers of song and speech. For Rothenberg, as in "Old Man Beaver's Blessing Song," or in his "total translations" of the Navajo Horse Songs of Frank Mitchell, the primacy of sound is the principal force for disrupting the ordinary business-at-hand that rules our lives. He enacts and prizes magic, spirit, and ecstasy, realms that practical Republicans teach us to ignore. And Antin's talk-poems enact thinking in a public domain. Instead of the sentimentalized intensification of poetic thinking as *recollection* or as a philosophy that shields itself from the grit of vernacular speech, Antin's talk-poems offer an instance of poesis as present-being.[3] Both Antin's talk-poems, made up on the spot and spoken in relation to a specific audience, and Rothenberg's sound-poems share in and extend a twentieth-century innovative tradition that includes Stein, Duchamp, and Cage, art works that have a disruptive, disconcerting immediacy.

In his essay included in this volume, "A Poetics of the Sacred," Rothenberg affirms "the cry of the Dada poets of the 1920s to 'liberate the creative forces from the tutelage of the advocates of power'; and the earlier political-poetic assertion by William Blake that 'poetry fetter'd, fetters the human race.'"

Charles Bernstein contends that

> . . . official verse culture
> of the last 25 years has engaged in militant
> (that is to say ungenerously uniformitarian)
> campaigns to "restrict the subversive,
> independent-of-things nature of the language"
> in the name of the common voice, clarity, sincerity,
> or the directness of the poem. (1992, 46)

Although formal innovation and eccentric language-enactments are often assailed as elitist or antidemocratic, in fact such criticisms mask a desire to impose a rather uniform version of self-representation:[4]

> Too often, the works selected to represent cultural diversity are those that accept the model of representation assumed by the dominant culture in the first place. "I see grandpa on the hill / next to the memories I can never recapture" is the base line against which other versions play: "I see my yiddishe mama on Hester street / next to the pushcarts I can no longer peddle" or "I see my grandmother on the hill / next to all the mothers whose lives can never be recaptured" or "I can't touch my Iron Father / who never canoed with me / on the prairies of my masculine epiphany." Works that challenge these models of representation run the risk of becoming more inaudible than ever within mainstream culture. (6)

In a tremendously effective introduction to his talk-poem "talking at the boundaries," a piece which keeps returning to and considering the nature and effect of obstacles, David Antin says

> i had tried out the idea of the artist as
> obstacle   how perhaps instead of giving a more precise
>   or glamorous form to the platitudes of the culture
>   the artist might propose himself as a sort of impedi-
> ment like sticking out a foot in a corridor and chang-
> ing the direction of the traffic. (1976, 52)

Antin is well aware that "the effect of an obstacle depends on its placement and direction of traffic" (1976, 52). Antin's talk-poems conflict with the ideal of the well-crafted lyric. In a (poetry) culture dominated by the ideals of the well-crafted lyric of personal epiphany and of the poetry reading as an occasion for recollection which erases process, Antin's talk-poems themselves provide a readily audible obstacle, even after twenty years of such activity.[5] And were we to look today for poetry's place as reenforcer of cultural platitudes, I would suggest magazines like the *New Yorker*, where even poetry declaring empathy for the hard lives of common people appears in a small box (on a page along with a sophisticated cartoon, some more centrally prominent prose writing, and advertisements for furs, jewelry, fine foods, and exotic vacation spots). In such a context, the poem in no way disrupts the surrounding and predominating cultural advertising métier. Indeed, the poet and the poem submit to and re-enforce the cultural priorities reflected in the layout of the page.

Sherman Paul observes that the cultural position of Antin and Rothenberg is akin to that of the shaman, whose role of vision and healing inspires Rothenberg's version of the poet to take "on the necessary work of *turning the mind upside down*" (1986, 99). For Antin, the thinking enacted in his talk-poems bears a strong resemblance to William Doty's description of a critical engaged version of mythography: "Mythography, critically pursued, may function as a curettage device, scalpeling away debris (from our present perspective) that should have been removed long ago. But it also may provide us with some of the tools for making moral choices among the vast range of myths that are available to us; it should provide us with a heightened dedication to forge the best possible personal and cultural mythostories, the stories that can serve as symbolic constructions of reality leading to individual freedom and social growth rather than a retreat into an automatically repeated and uncritical view of historical events that now may need to be drastically reshaped" (1986, 19).[6]

Rothenberg's "A Personal Manifesto" (1966) begins with the declaration "I will change your mind," and that manifesto ends with a provocative recasting of Jesus: " '& if thou wdst understand that wch is me, know this: all that I have sd I have uttered playfully—& I was by no means ashamed of it.' (J.C. to disciples, The Acts of St. John)" (1981, 51). Rothenberg's own reading/chantings confirm Doty's observation that "myths provide opportunities 'to perform the world,' that is, to engage in sacred play by reciting them or by ritually enacting them" (1986, 15). While Rothenberg's assertion of Christ's essential playfulness links Jesus to a long line of (sacred) tricksters, such a characterization (along with Doty's phrase "sacred play") places the poetic activities of both Antin and Rothenberg squarely within the anthropological framework posited by Victor Turner, who regards liminal situations "as the settings in which new models, symbols, paradigms, etc., arise—as the seedbeds of cultural creativity" (1982, 28).

Antin's talk-poems present an irritation that is an occasion (both for Antin and for members of the audience) for questioning and/as thinking:

> because the one who comes there and has
> been thinking of talking is a kind of agent provocateur   he is
> the one who comes bringing the troubles and has been preparing
> to unpack his pandoras box of them and leave them with you
> for your   entertainment. (1984, 220)

Antin's performance is fundamentally pedagogical, though not especially didactic. Rather, it is a process of withdrawing certainties. In its often rambling form, with starts and stops, misdirections, cul-de-sacs and avenues, there is a Thoreauvian productive idling at work (and at play) in an Antin talk-poem. First-time listeners often wonder about *the point* of his rambling stories and conjectures. Such a reaction might be juxtaposed with Turner's observation: "Dumazdier thinks that it is significant that the Greek word for having nothing to do *(schole)* also meant 'school'" (1982, 36).

Antin's form of talk is intentionally "sacred play," provocation, and unprofessional conduct:

                              he had not
          had a good career and he wound up on a crucifix   and it is not
             the aim of the ministry to wind up on a crucifix   its not
             professional   there is no profession in being crucified
             because one of the things about being a professional is you
          assume there is a body of doctrine that can be taught and learned
             that you can have a tradition   and it is not good to have a
             tradition that puts itself to an end   you dont hope to educate
             people to do this and say the first step is here   this is the next
          and then you can look forward finally to that   which is your
             end   they dont intend to teach that in the church as a
             profession   because thats intended to create chaos   which
             no profession   wants and the intention of jesus was to provoke
             chaos it was not to produce peace on earth and the continuity of
          life   jesus said i bring not peace but a sword   and he meant
             it   he got himself crucified in order to cause a great deal of
                trouble   it was supposed to put an end to an untenable world
                as i remember   which is why he sent his apostles around
             to say that "the end of the world is at hand"   and he meant
             right away   im going to produce it by getting myself crucified
                                             now as i said
          thats not a professional position because a profession assumes
       a world that you want to continue   and behave more or less
          appropriately within. (1984, 227)

Antin's principal allegiance in such "unprofessional conduct" is to radical philosophical inquiry—a questioning and questing by means of language theory, by narratives, and by the presentation of unsettling and unresolvable situations.

On the other hand, Rothenberg's principal (though, as I will suggest later, not absolute) identification is with the shaman:

The act of the shaman—& his poetry—is like a public madness. It is like what the Senecas, in their great dream ceremony now obsolete, called "turning the mind upside down." It shows itself as a release of alternative possibilities. "What do they want?" the poet wonders of   those who watch him in his role of innocent, sometimes reluctant performer. But what? To know that madness is possible & that the contradictions can be sustained. (1981, 134)

Either route, the shamanic or the Socratic, unsettles "natural" or habitual modes of thinking. Each encourages and makes appealing subversion and questioning.

In that encouragement—in the commonality of that enterprise—there is a solidarity, a *communitas*, that complicates what I have rather mono-lithically been describing as *the poet's function as obstacle*. A communal vision of artistic activity involves a rejection of linear models of artistic genius and progress. Such a version of literary or artistic history posits a series of great accomplishments that are out of the reach of other artists and that serve as (proprietary) barriers. But the experience and writing of both Antin and Rothenberg contradict any such narration; each makes substantial and free use of previous artistic activity. Each of them experiences the work of predecessors as either irrelevant or generative, but not, as in Harold Bloom's model of manly contestation, a father figure's deed which unmans one until the father is overcome. It is a communal version of the avant-garde which Antin posits,

> and thats what
> i told this man in washington   or something to that effect
> and what i realized as i said it then   and realize as
> i say it now   there is something of an idea of the avant-
>   garde in harold bloom   however inverted   and even
>   he seems more at home with than i am   a notion of first
> comers whose achievements were new and blocked the way to
>   further achievements along the same path   an idea of
>   patented inventions   each one acting as a roadblock
> and the tradition as a series of bitterly fought retreats till
>   the last "strong" poet finds himself like kafkas rodent
> or a beckett character backed into the last corner of the
>   room   it is a funny view of a tradition having it back
> you into a corner   and comically a little like clement
> greenbergs versions of modernist painting   in which the
>   brilliant achievement of one artist closes an avenue to
> the next. (1985, 62)[7]

Likewise, Rothenberg has little use for a conceptualizing of the avant-garde that relies on closure and unapproachability. His own participation in the avant-garde defies linear models in favor of the making of breadth and open-ended opportunities: "If there's still any sense in talking of an avant-garde, then that must be it for me: an insistence that the work deny itself the last word, because the consequences of closure & closed mind have been & continue to be horrendous in the world we know. . . . We must no longer think in terms of a single 'great tradition' but can open to the possibility of getting at the widest range of human experience" (1981, 4). Rather than poesis as an attempt to put a form of artistic activity out of the reach of other artists, Antin's version of accomplishment is, like Rothenberg's critique of "masterpiece" art, contingent and social, directed in part at other artists who might be able to make use of it:

> and i did the best i could   under the
> circumstances   of being there   then   which is my
>   image of what an artist does and is   somebody who does
> the best he can   under the circumstances   not about
>   making it new or shocking   because the best you can do
> depends upon what you have to do and where   and if you have
>   to invent something new to do the work at hand you will   but
>   not if you have a ready-made that will work and is close at
>   hand and you want to get on with the rest of the business
>
>   then
>   youll pick up the thing thats there   a tool that somebody
> else has made   that will work   and youll lean on it and
>   feel grateful   when its good to you for somebody
> elses work   and think of him as a friend who would borrow
> as freely from you if he thought of it or needed to   because
> there is a community of artists. (1972, 58)

Rothenberg suggests that "the function of poetry isn't to impose a single vision or consciousness but to liberate similar processes in others" (1981, 105)—an essentially communal, generative, and Emersonian definition of poetry. For Antin, that shared activity also constitutes the basis by which an artist establishes his contemporaneity, "mainly because the truly contemporaneous artists of our time are known primarily to a community consisting of themselves. In a sense it is this capacity of the contemporary artist to recognize his contemporaries that is the essential feature of his contemporaneity" (1972, 99).

As I have found in my own twenty years of activity as a poet, Antin is exactly right: through work, effort, attentiveness, play, and more important through generative affinities with fellow artists, one approaches the present. Residing in present artistic activity as an opportunity for renewal and innovation is not given to one by virtue of a birthdate. As earlier portions of my essay indicate, in my characterizations of mainstream poetry the dominant stories do not offer an artist the chance to approach the present moment except in a narrowly professionalized sense.

For Antin, that issue of approaching the present, how to live in it and how to make art that is of it, guides the methodology of the talk-poem as he finds himself

> going to places   to improvise something   because as a poet i
>   was getting extremely tired of   what i considered an unnatural
> language act   going into a closet   so to speak   sitting in
> front of a typewriter   because   anything is possible in a closet
> in front of a typewriter and nothing is necessary   a closet is no
> place to address anybody   or anything   and its so unnatural
>   sitting in front of a typewriter   that you dont address any-
>   one   what you do is you sit at the typewriter and you bang out
>   the anticipated in front of the unanticipated. (1976, 56)

Indeed, for Antin, the rejection of poetry composed in a closet comes from a recognition of a reading as an occasion that has the capacity to re-enforce, rather than to negate, inherently social and interactive dimensions of enunciation.

Discomfort with the premises of standardized, "natural" poetry writing constitutes a principal affinity between Antin and Rothenberg. Ultimately, for each, a reinvestigation of the potentials and practices of an oral-based poetry unsettles habitual assumptions about both the value of writing and the nature of the book:

> the whole problem of our literate and literal culture has
> been   to some extent   the problem of the totally dislocated
> occasion   that is in this case the book   which goes out into a
> distributional system unknown to us. (1976, 56)

There are different possible solutions to this vexing problem of distribution, which is one aspect of the commodification of the work of art. Poets can confederate and take over much of the process of publication and distribution, as the Segue Foundation and other similar organizations have demonstrated. And by virtue of their immediacy, Antin's talk-poems constitute an ingenious solution to potentially alienating distribution methods, in that Antin's talk-poems are simultaneously the creation of the works of art and their distribution and circulation.

In critiquing the "naturalness" of the book (as the best container of knowledge), both Rothenberg and Antin reassert and reinscribe the importance of an oral poetics. Antin, in the talk-poem "how long is the present," recounts some of his own ambivalences and his own gradual movement toward the form of the talk-poem:

> since i knew that i was coming to a bookfair i brought along a book
> i dont know a lot about bookfairs and i didnt know much
> about what people do there   but i thought it might be
> appropriate to read here   i dont get invited to read anywhere
> anymore   i get invited to talk because thats what i do
> talk   and this time i was extraordinarily tempted to produce
> a violation of my   form   and read a talk piece or part
> of a talk piece   or moderately tempted   i was not
> sufficiently tempted but i brought a book   specifically this
> book   my book   so that i could have done it   read
> out of it   and i brought it not specifically because it was
> my book and i was at a bookfair and wanted to advertise it
> but mainly because i was curious to find out if i had any
> temptation to read
> and i dont   not at all   and the
> reason i dont have any temptation to read or no sufficient
> temptation has often been mistaken by others   that is
> there is a kind of discourse   of which i am a part   about
> whether poetry is inherently oral   made in the mouth
> or whether it takes its definitive shape in writing   and when
> i say poetry i mean poetry in the large sense   i hope nobody
> takes me for someone who composes quatrains while
> either speaking or writing   or even in lines because for years
> i havent uttered anything that approached a line in any way
> but i mean poetry in the large sense that sir walter raleighs
> history of the world is poetry or   kafkas castle is
> poetry   or any work that one can think of as a significant
> attempt to take possession of the world   or some part of the
> world   for experience through language
> but the reason

       im not tempted to read is different i think than most people
    suppose   the reason   my reason   is the sense that i
    have in looking at a book   my book   not somebody
 elses book   but in looking at my own book and feeling
       that as i look i lose my sense of the present   my sense
    of the present disintegrates for me as i read. (1984, 84)

For Antin, the movement toward and into an oral poetics, a poetry of talk, has to do with the fundamental issue of how best to inhabit the present. (I cannot help but emphasize the importance of Antin's rejection of the line as the fundamental unit of poetic construction; indeed, his poetry, and perhaps most of the innovative poetry of this century, may very well depend on the consideration of other units of construction—the page, a unit of performance—time, prose blocks—as fair game for poetry.) Antin's affirmation of orality is not without ambivalences. After all, in "how long is the present" Antin carries a book with him (his own book): he writes books, and he speaks to an audience at a bookfair. But in rejecting the "natural" assumption that at a poetry reading he should read from a book he has already composed, Antin offers and explores an alternative set of preferences (which, by contrast, may serve to expose our more habitual assumptions about appropriate behavior in such a context):[8]

                    i have a taste
          for the present   which i imagine you can forgive me
          if you dont forgive me im sorry   its a strong and peculiar
       taste   and the present is a difficult thing to have a taste
    for   its very difficult because   in satisfying it the question
          i always have to ask myself is   what is the present and
          how long is it?   how long is the present?
                    thats a question
 i take very seriously as a poet   i have a very strong commitment
          to the idea of the present   and at various times i have
          had different attitudes toward what i thought it was   and
          i thought if i came to a place   and had no words in my
 hand or mouth   but only my historical disposition to speak
             in a particular way   out of whatever particular background
             i had   that whatever i said and did would have to relate
    to this place   and so in a sense i prepared to come
          unprepared to this place. (1984, 84–85)

Such an activity, as Antin stresses, is not some deed of "purity" and "innocence" that somehow manages to evade contingency and historical determinations. Quite the opposite: Antin acknowledges the particularity of his development of the talk-poem. Such a development is historically and personally governed. In Antin's case, perhaps such a form of poesis may come out of his own brooklyn-new york-jewish-artistic cultural milieu, of storytelling and a principally Jewish tradition of seriocomic standup routines, or even out of a nineteenth-century American intellectual tradition of the lecture, as well as Antin's own activities as an art critic. Antin acknowledges as well, in an earlier talk-poem, that his talking is also a means of self-disclosure (though by means of, in Antin's case, relatively impersonal acts of storytelling):

> the only way
> that   i can conceive of myself   as a personality   is by
> an act   of memory   by an act of interrogation of my memory
> which is   also talking   the self   itself   is emergent
> in discourse. (1976, 10)

Together with the translations, poems, and anthologies of Rothenberg, Antin's talk-poems provide a crucial reconsideration of the value of orality to poetry. Antin "hate[s] being the servant of a previous impulse" (1984, 148), a declaration which has important formal consequences for his composition and presentation of poetry.[9] But Antin's oral-based investigation of the present comes at a cost, which he openly acknowledges. What he does in a talk-poem, given its improvisatory nature, may well, Antin states, "violate my sense of good design":

> this problem of the
> present tense   and this is very awkward   for me
> because   whatever im doing   i want to be doing it now
> at whatever cost   and there is always a cost. (1984, 150)

But that cost is not just one of shapeliness or design. In fact, Antin's talk-poems tend to be very well designed and carefully constructed, depending, as I hear them, upon a series of off-rhymed (or, roughly homeomorphic) stories leading toward not resolution but a confrontation with an underlying question or conflict. What Antin "pays" in lost form, he gains back in restructuring and calling into question the nature of a poetry reading. Instead of the recitation of a prior act of poesis (modestly reinvigorated by a "live" reading), Antin's talk-poems expose and disclose his labors. Rather than erasing or making secondary a prior act of (written) composition in favor of making present a labor of *recitation* (as a poet does in a typical poetry reading), Antin's talk-poems allow a listener to witness much more of the poem's *making*.[10]

By contrast, the more standardized and university-accredited poetry reading features other priorities and values. If we examine the ritual of the poetry reading from some of the available ethnographic and anthro- pological perspectives, the oppositional nature of Antin's talk-poems be- comes a bit clearer. If we assume, as in Victor Turner's mode of thinking, that a poetry reading is a ritual designed to affirm and to do certain things, several features are *irrelevant* to Antin's type of performance. Given the hegemonic value of the poetry reading, as an institutional prop for given ideologies and aesthetics, the poetry reading in its more "natural" (that is to say, *customary*) form re-enforces a dominant version of the careerist poet as the maker of "well-crafted" lyrics of accessible, clear, personal expression. It re-enforces culturally approved models of sensitivity and creativity, and a sanctioned but limited realm of acceptable poetic rhetoric and discourse. And it re-enforces a notion of a unified subjectivity/voice.[11]

Antin, by contrast, gives a much greater emphasis to talking as a mode of exploratory, heuristic thinking and questioning; Rothenberg's readings take up the site of the poetry reading as a place to enact shamanic impulses by means of magical properties of sound. As Turner observes of similar cultural and ritualistic relationships to dominant institutions and values: "I see the 'liminoid' as an independent and critical source" (1982, 33). In this sense, the versions of orality put forward by Rothenberg and Antin inter- rupt business-as-usual, calling into question key elements of what we have come to recognize as a poet's professionalized behavior. These poets of a more oral emphasis function heuristically to disclose some of the simply *assumed* aspects of being a professional (university-employed) poet today.

The oral poetics of Antin and Rothenberg go to the heart (and ety- mology) of myth: "*Myth / muthos.* Jane Harrison: 'A *mythos* to the Greek was primarily just a thing spoken, uttered by the *mouth.*' I take this from Olson, *The Special View of History*, where he reminds us that both *muthos* and *logos* mean 'what is said,' and that the poet, the *muthologos*, under- takes 'the practice of life as story'" (Paul 1986, 48). Such a poetics is not a rejection of the written in favor of a simplistic idealization of the oral, but a reemphasis and reinvestigation of the situation of orality within the professionalized domain of the "literary." Rothenberg responds "to a conventional & deeply entrenched view of poetry that excludes or minimizes the oral; & I'm saying that the domain of poetry includes both oral & written forms, that poetry goes back to a pre-literate situation & would survive a post-literate situation, that human speech is a near-endless source of poetic forms, that there has *always* been more oral than written poetry, & that we can no longer pretend to a knowledge of poetry if we deny its oral dimension" (1981, 11).[12]

The range of such a broadened version of poetics is impressive: "I would say that I'm speaking of THE TRADITION WHICH TAKES VISION & CONFLICT AS THE ESSENTIAL CHARACTERISTICS OF POETRY; SEES THESE AS BOUND TO THE STRUCTURES OF THE POEM & THE DYNAMICS OF ACTUAL SPEECH; & TRACES A 'LINE' FROM THE INNOVATORS OF OUR OWN TIME & THE CENTURIES IMMEDIATELY PRECEDING, BACK BY WHATEVER ROUTES, TO REACH THE FIRST MYTHOLOGIZED SHAMANS OF THE LATER PALEOLITHIC CULTURES" (1981, 33).

Obviously such a broadened poetics has fundamental curricular implications which go far beyond current anthology and canon debates. The inclusiveness of Rothenberg's poetics—as his many anthologies have demonstrated, particularly *Technicians of the Sacred* (1985) and *America a Prophecy: A New Reading of American Poetry from Pre-Columbian Times to the Present* (Quasha and Rothenberg 1973)—make even the more praiseworthy of recently reconceived American literature anthologies such as the celebrated D. C. Heath collections seem tame, narrow, and inadequate.

The cooperative working relationship between Antin and Rothenberg is such that their poetic projects have reciprocal effects that invigorate our sense of the modern as well as the primitive. The interaction and reinvestigation of the two poetries, principally by means of a renewed attention to the possibilities of speech and song, leads to fundamental redefinitions of poetry and of poet: "The range of the tribal poets was even more impressive if one avoided a close, European definition of 'poem' & worked empirically or by analogy to contemporary, limit-smashing experiments (as with concrete poetry, sound poetry, intermedia, happenings, etc.). Since tribal poetry was almost always of a larger situation (i.e. was truly intermedia), there was no more reason to present the words or the pictographs arising from the same source. Where possible, in fact, one might present or translate all elements connected with the total 'poem' " (Rothenberg 1981, 96). Such re-search, by means of comparison and translation, leaves us open to consider that therefore "the modern poem is open to everything; that it becomes the vehicle for 'anything the mind can think' " (106). Of equally fundamental importance, such a view of poem and poet implies a self-resistant means of anticommodification and a healthy antiprofessionalism: "With such means at his disposal, the poet can enter on a career as a prophet & revolutionary, a cultist or a populist by turns. Or he can, in a more profound sense, become the person who keeps raising alternative propositions, eluding the trap of his own vision as he goes" (106). Rather than advocating the currently entrenched institutional model of the poet— where the developing writer is encouraged to "find his voice," to make a series of poems that show some range but a consistent and recognizable (professional) identity—Rothenberg and Antin point toward a career of poesis as a process of thinking and investigating possibilities, a process that is intentionally self-evading. The contemporary institutional model of craft-training rests upon the commercial visual arts model: an artist succeeds in commodifying his or her work by creating a recognizable (and thus privatized and commodified) style. That is, the commodified work of art has a certain signature to it that marks it as saleable private property. But Antin and Rothenberg urge a career in poetry where such self-imitation is one of the traps to be avoided.

In a shared resistance to some forms of poetry's commodification, Antin and Rothenberg each (differently) present an interesting critique of writing and the book. Antin argues that

> writing is a form of fossilized talking   which gets put
> inside of a can   called a book   and i respect that can   its a
> means of preservation   or maybe we should say in a frozen food
> container called a book   but on the other hand if you dont know
> how to handle that frozen food container that icy block will never
> turn back into talking   and if it will never turn back into talking
> it will never be of any use to you again. (1976, 45–46)[13]

Similarly, Rothenberg suggests, "writing, that strange aid to memory, eventually becomes its surrogate, displaces memory itself—the first, great Muse" (1981, 131). As a history of scripture, Rothenberg notes that this displacement "follows roughly the stages (torah, mishna, kabbal, magic &

folklore, etc.) by which the 'oral tradition' ('torah of the mouth') was narrowed and superseded by the written" (121).

Their critique of the written, as in Antin's remaking of the site and activity of the poetry reading, depends on a preference for process over product:

> its harder to understand what an oral culture is doing when its
> making art   say   and easy enough to understand about stories
> and talking   but you want to know what about pots?
>   because pot making is one of the things they do in oral cultures
>   some of them   and some people call those pots art   if
> this pot making is art   its the art of making pots   its not the
> pots that are the art   pots are the outcome of the art. (1976, 192)

Antin makes such an assertion precisely because, as he notes, it is far too easy to "convert the act of meaning into the object of meaning" (202). Thus Antin emphasizes process over product,[14] and he proposes a distinction between making and distributing poetry:

> when
>   i went somewhere i wanted to make things happen   because
> it seemed to me that the art of poetry was the act of making
> poetry not distributing it   and the act of going around reading
> from a book id already written seemed to be the act of a publisher
>   more than a poet   though it may be basically useful to us as
>   poets   and there is a sense in which we all have to distribute
> our lives to make them effective. (1984, 151)

Antin acknowledges the necessity and desirability of the work's distribution—indeed his talk-poems merge the activity of making and distributing.

While speech itself is Antin's medium, he is not naive about its limitations. Books as such have many of the limitations that Antin and Rothenberg (each the author of many books) point out; but then

> everything has its problem   talking also
>   has its inherent difficulties   there is no such thing as a
>   perfect medium   thats why they call it a medium   because
>   its in the middle   so to speak   its between   it mediates. (1984, 56)

In his transcription of a talk-poem, Antin transforms a speech-event by placing it in another medium. He transcribes it

> in the hope of finding what in it was the real thing
> the real action   and i try to get it into the book in such a
> way that its still intelligible when it goes into this rectangular
> object with covers that you open   like this   and which
> is partitioned arbitrarily by those things they call pages
> there are
> no pages when i talk   you dont turn anything at   all that
> is   i turn you turn but we dont turn pages. (56)

Such a play on "turning" plays off of poetry's misidentification with verse, which literally means a turning. Antin's talk-poems *do* focus on turning; they offer a listener an occasion to turn his or her thinking in other directions.

Antin's talk-poems, then, place him in a kind of existential crisis, but one that he approaches with humor and with the resources of an improvisatory vernacular. Admittedly, Antin's is a broad vernacular, including the discourses of linguistics, philosophy, Yiddish, anthropology, poetry, art, art criticism, and so forth. Antin's talk-poems put him on the spot; each one—and this is the tension built into such a performance—holds him accountable before an audience, accountable to make something then and there, and to answer certain fundamental questions:

> we come back again to   "what am i doing here?"
> what is it that im doing here?   im trying to find out   how i
> could find out   and what im trying to find out is by
> essentially doing what i think talking does   that is
> talking and thinking may not be the same thing   but i see
> thinking as talking   i see it as talking   to a question   which
> may give rise to another question. (1976, 20)

Of course, that is what professionalized activity *never* does: put itself into question. A "regular" poetry reading does not overtly call into question the value of honoring a previous impulse and a preestablished script. In a sense, Antin's version of the poet bears a strong relationship to the work of the ironist as put forward by Kierkegaard in *The Concept of Irony*, where master-ironists such as Socrates and Christ are marked by their ability to challenge fundamental assumptions by questions that gradually withdraw the content from no-longer-tenable assumptions.

In his introduction to the first talk-poem in *Talking at the Boundaries*, Antin makes a similarly audacious suggestion, one that flies in the face of "correct" professional behavior for a poet:

> i had suggested that i had always had mixed feelings
> about being considered a poet   "if robert lowell is a
> poet i dont want to be a poet   if robert frost was a
> poet i dont want to be a poet   if socrates was a poet
> ill consider it." (1)

For Antin, then, there is a close identification among talking, thinking, and questioning. Such linkages help to explain his rather complex and unusual theory of narrative, a theory that emphasizes questions, problems, and knots. An investigation of narrative lies at the heart of Antin's considerations of what it means to be a poet. Narrative involves processes of remembering, and often Antin's talk-poems both present narratives and reflect on the nature of such narratives. Antin's presentation of narrative is distinctly social as the narratives and other elements of a talk-poem become a medium through which Antin and an audience become attuned to one another:

> now the point of doing these pieces
> for me   is that it gives me a chance   by a kind of subtle but
> ordinary human concentration   to get a sense of where youre
> coming from and how   and to allow that sense to put some
> pressure on my own way of moving. (1984, 167)

Antin's knowing emphasizes movement: "my knowing which is really a way of going not of standing" (168). As a social interaction, his public thinking relies on processes of tuning (which is the title of his 1984 collection of talk-poems). Such tunings, or attunings, involve resistances between listener and speaker, as well as internal resistances within Antin's own presentation and consideration of unresolvable narratives. Antin counts on these internalized responses as part of what energizes his public process of thinking aloud. Our relationship to an Antin talk-poem thus enacts metaphorically a whole range of other tunings, such as our relationship to one another, to works of art, and to the ecosystem we live in.

Antin's talk-poems put us (and him) in a place that poses a problem. One of Antin's terms for such a place is a dialogue, as in the talk-poem "dialogue" where he asserts, for example, that "the collision of the idea of christ and the idea of jesus was the dialogue of christianity its basic problem framed as a dialogue and a severe one between a man called jesus and a god called the christ" (224). At the center of such dialogue is a paradox or a conceptual knot: " 'a crucified god' it fits all right in your mouth but you cant quite think it" (1984, 224). In narrating the difficulties of a Lutheran friend who questions his calling to the ministry, Antin points toward his own concern with a particular version of narrative. Antin's friend, who contemplates the jesus/christ paradox, is troubled in part because for such a problem "he couldnt extract its root" and he ends up "despising and loving himself despising himself for his doubt and loving himself for his doubt and for despising himself for his doubt" (224). Antin's talk-poems are extended instances of what fits "in your mouth" but what cannot be thought through to conclusion.

Antin's narratives, as in "The Price," delivered in 1986,[15] point toward unresolvable questions. Antin begins "The Price" by proposing, seemingly casually, the principle conceptual nexus that will concern him:

when i thought about doing this piece i intended to call it
"where are you?"   because i wanted to think through some ideas i had
about the self   and because thinking for me means asking questions to
   which at the start i dont have answers   this title took the form of a
question addressed as much to myself as to you and was i suppose something
of an answer or at least a response to a review of a talk i gave in new york the
year before   in which someone complained that i suffered from a belief in
the unitary self and had not enjoyed the benefit of french deconstruction
   which should have disabused me of this illusion
   now even i have felt the french breath of deconstruction
unimpressed with it as i am   but i am still interested in the self though i
never thought i believed in its unity in so flatfooted a way as all that   i always
   thought the idea of the self was surrounded by questions and in fact what i was
interested in were precisely those questions   and those were questions i spent
   a lot of time asking because i didnt know the answers   for if i knew the
answers i wouldnt have any reason to ask the questions   and one of the
questions i'm interested in asking is what is the locus of the source or ground of
the self. (1989, 14)

Antin's talk-poems are both about his relationship to narrative and an enactment or present-being of that relationship. Antin's theory is that "the self   however you may define it   is entirely constructed out of the collision of the sense of identity with the issues of narrative" (15). For Antin, it seems fairly evident "that the self could not exist without narrative" (15).

"The Price" represents Antin's most sustained attempt to explain his theory of narrative:

> now this may seem purely theoretical but i'm not interested in it in
> a purely theoretical way   yet i would still like to distinguish in my own mind
> what i mean by narrative
>   i dont mean story   everybody generally means story
> when they say narrative   but i would like to distinguish between two things
>   one i would call narrative and the other story   and as i see it theyre
> related but not the same   story is a configuration of events or parts of events
>   that shape some transformation   but narrative   or so it seems to me   is
>   a sort of psychic function   part of the human psychic economy and probably
>   a human universal   at least we identify it with being human   and it
>   involves a particular paradoxical confrontation. (15–16).

Antin's initial effort to describe narrative gets deferred in "The Price," though Antin is already identifying (in the overlap of story and narrative) a crucial undercurrent of his most successful talk-poems: they offer us (as well as Antin) an occasion or a place in which to undergo transformation. For me, the experience (though not the rhetorical strategy) is like reading the best writing of Thoreau; the reader/listener is called upon to question deeply held assumptions about thinking, making, and valuing. Though Thoreau is much more accusatory and bullying in tone, using sarcasm much more than Antin, in each case we are confronted by an act of poesis that calls us (in)to account.

As confrontation is essential to my experience of Antin's talk-poems, so confrontation is essential to Antin's emerging definition of narrative:

> now my sense is that the center of narrative is the confrontation of
> experience   an experiencing subject with the possibility of transformation
>   the threat of transformation or the promise of transformation   these two
> possibilities adjust it a little differently   in terms of desire   and without
>   desire there can be no narrative   but one of the fundamental things we
> desire   is to continue to be. (1989, 16)

At the heart of narrative lies a double desire: "we want to be different but we want to be us" (16). Though we seek transformation, which entails self-difference (since we wish to become something other than what we are before the transformation), "at bottom nobody wants to become something totally other" (16).[16] This knot of untenable self-opposition is the energy source for Antin's narratives.

Beneath narrative configurations that we experience as story, Antin claims that "it is the engagement with the possibility of change that is the fundamental issue" (18). The construction of a self occurs on a site—analogous to the site of Antin's talk-poems, which exists at an intersection of language, talking, thinking, and questioning—which is marked by various resistances, exclusions, and inclusions, "because every self holds itself together   to the degree that it holds its self together   at a price" (19). For Antin, "what narrative at its core celebrates or ritually reenacts is this grounding of self" (18). This difficult choice of self-consolidation and/or self-dissolution rhymes with similar choices for poesis, in which an artist must choose between competing claims of consolidation/conformity (of genre, career, profession, and acceptability of artistic activity) as opposed to actions that resist, oppose, and interrogate preexisting choices. Though Antin's own practices align much more thoroughly with the latter option, he too is aware, for self and implicitly for poesis, that pure potential and pure resistance, "this unlimited and indistinct consciousness is a delusive and socially useless system" (18). Which may be why as interrogating as Antin's talk-poems are, they are also formally coherent and carefully (if spontaneously) constructed. Narrative, as Antin describes it, is that conflicting energy/desire that underlies the spewing forth of story. The particularity of a given self and consciousness is formed, says Antin, by the interaction of that consciousness with its troubling narratives:

and ultimately it is a matter of whether that
consciousness perceives an impending event as a threatening transformation
that determines whether or not we are dealing with narrative   so that a
particular consciousness chooses its narratives   though it may feel as though
certain narratives choose you   but they choose you by the character of
your   consciousness to begin with   which is to say that by the grain of your
consciousness your narratives are chosen   and by what they do to your
consciousness your self is formed. (1989, 23)

At the end of an Antin talk-poem, we are offered not a moment of closure (which is one of my chief criticisms of monologues like Garrison Keillor's: they end with a manipulative moment of sentimentalized wonder, and thus they evaporate and have no ability to bring about transformation; they remain merely consoling forms of entertainment), but a final story that ends in an enigma specific to the concerns that have energized that particular meditative occasion. As with the story of Harry at the end of "The Price," or the story of Antin's Uncle Irving at the end of "what it means to be avant-garde," or the story of the marine at the end of "talking at the boundaries," the conclusion to an Antin talk-poem plunges us further into the complexities and irreconcilable demands of an issue that has called for his thinking and ours. At their best, as in the end of "what it means to be avant-garde," we are placed between competing demands made on us by the emotional immediacy of a story and by a (rhyming) conceptual engagement that arises from the talk-poem's framing conceptual issues: "and it seems to me that if you cant respond to that youre not in the avant-garde" (1985, 71). We are left too with a sense of the price of any accommodation that we choose.

Turning now to Rothenberg, entire essays and books[17] might be devoted to his poetry, his activities as magazine editor, and especially his many groundbreaking (and ground-remaking) anthologies; I propose to investigate one facet of his contribution to an *oral* poetics, namely Rothenberg's work in "total translation." In considering translation in general, Rothenberg suggests, "To submit through translation is to begin to accept the 'truths' of an other's language. At the same time it's a way of growing wary of the lies in one's own, a point of vigilance that translators & poets should be particularly keyed to" (1981, 93–94). Particularly with Seneca and Navajo poetry, Rothenberg runs into the problem "that we, as translators & poets, had been taking a rich oral poetry & translating it to be read primarily for meaning, thus denuding it to say the least" (77). Especially with the Navajo Horse Songs, Rothenberg has to decide "how to handle those elements that weren't translatable literally. As with most Indian poetry, the voice carried many sounds that weren't, strictly speaking, 'words.' These tended to disappear or be attenuated in translation, as if they weren't really there. But they *were* there & were at least as important as the words themselves. In both Navajo and Seneca many songs consisted of nothing but those 'meaningless' vocables (not free 'scat' either but fixed sounds recurring from performance to performance)" (77). Rothenberg's solution, which he calls "total translation," is an immensely important activity that not only "opens up the canon" to Native American poetries, but involves a radical rethinking of the possible locations and natures of "meaning" in poetry: "Let me try, then, to respond to *all* the sounds I'm made aware of, to let that awareness touch off responses or events in the English. I don't want to set English words to Indian music, but to respond poem-for-poem in the attempt to work out a 'total' translation—not only of the words but of all sounds connected with the poem, including finally the music itself" (78).

By translating the sounds, and by giving the sounds of the poem a priority equal to that of thematized meaning, Rothenberg's total translations have the capacity to reshape our reading (and sounding) of poetry generally. Rather than evading those portions of the poem that cannot be recuperated in "meaningful" words, Rothenberg's sound-translations expand the realm of the "meaningful." As Charles Bernstein remarks in a slightly different context—Bernstein's more specific concern is with non-semantic or extralexical writing—

> the meaning is not absent or
> deferred but self-embodied as the poem
> in a way that is not transferable to another code or rhetoric. (1992, 18)

In fact, it is Rothenberg's successful encounter with the nontransferable elements that marks his work in total translation as a major poetic accomplishment: "It was the possibility of working with all that sound, finding my own way into it in English, that attracted me now—that & a quality in Mitchell's voice I found irresistible. It was, I think, that the music was so clearly within range of the language: it was song & it was poetry, & it seemed possible at least that the song issued from the poetry, was an extension of it or rose inevitably from the juncture of words & other vocal sounds" (1981, 86).

It is the overlapping space of poem, word, and song that resides in the meaningful-as-sound vocable of the Navajo Horse Songs that allows Rothenberg most fully to demonstrate the interconnectedness of so-called primitive (oral) poetries and twentieth-century experimental poetries (such as sound poems, performance poetry, Russian Zaum poetry, Dada, and others) and thus to confirm "the primitivity of avant-garde practice"

(Paul 1986, 132). In working out his method of total translation, Rothenberg decides to take a different strategy from David McAllester's literal transcription of the sounds in a Horse Song because "McAllester's more 'factual' approach—reproducing the vocables exactly—seemed wrong to me on one major count. In the Navajo the vocables give a very clear sense of continuity from the verbal material; i.e., the vowels in particular show a rhyming or assonantal relationship between the 'meaningless' & meaningful segments" (1981, 87).

The result is a poetry that, in the case of the beginning of "The Tenth Horse Song of Frank Mitchell," looks like this in Rothenberg's total translation:

> Go to her my son N wnn & go to her my son N wnn N wnnn N nnnn N gahn
> Go to her my son N wnn & go to her my son N wnn N wnnn N nnnn N gahn
> Because I was thnboyngnng raised ing the dawn NwnnN go to her my son N wnn
>   N wnn N nnnn N gahn
> & leafing from thuhuhuh house the bluestone home N gahn N wnn N go to her
>   my son N wnn N wnn N nnnn   N gahn
> & leafing from the (ruru) house the shining home NwnnnN go to her my son N
>   wnn N wnn N nnnn N gahn. (1968, 224)[18]

Rothenberg, in recounting his process of translation, says, "I decided to translate the vocables, & from that point was already playing with the possibility of translating other elements in the songs not usually handled by translation. It also seemed important to get as far away as I could from *writing*" (1981, 87).[19] Rothenberg sees his total translation process as "contributing & then obliterating my own level of meaning, while in another sense it was as if I was recapitulating the history of the vocables themselves, at least according to one of the standard explanations that sees them as remnants of archaic words that have been emptied of meaning: a process I could still sense elsewhere in the Horse Songs" (89).

Particularly as his poems and translations call into question our customary homage to the (merely) written word, Rothenberg "would like to desanctify & demystify the written word, because I think the danger of frozen thought, of authoritarian thought, has been closely tied in with it" (1981, 10). Such a position is very close to David Antin's preference for doing talk-performances rather than readings and for the ragged layout of his printed talk-poems:

> one of the reasons im talking rather than reading
> is that i dont want to carry any more weight than talk   that is
> this is as true or as important as it is and as it sounds   and
> its no truer and its not any heavier   if i put in paragraphs it
> wouldnt become truer or more important   it would look truer. (1976, 80)

For both Rothenberg and Antin, such antiessentialist thinking—which resists the notion of timeless masterpieces, enduring monistic truths, and authoritative/authoritarian modes of communication—marks a peculiar and important relationship to spiritual and religious dimensions of poetry. Of the two, Rothenberg is more commonly thought of as a poet of the sacred and of shamanistic practices. As Sherman Paul asserts, "What, after all, is the sacred? In a review of Eliade, Rothenberg says it is what we, the profane modern men and women of Eliade's account, experience 'through dreams and the unconscious'; it is a realm of 'human experience' poets may again open for us. This has been the burden of his work as poet and pedagogue, and what has been remarkable about it is that he has avoided the 'conflict between the culture of the interpreter and that of the creator' that Eliade resolved for himself by remaining primarily an interpreter" (1986, 122).

In the conclusion to his preface to *Technicians of the Sacred* (1985; the title is taken from Mircea Eliade), Rothenberg characterizes his own endeavors as an answer to "the question of how the concept & techniques of the 'sacred' can persist in the 'secular' world, not as nostalgia for the archaic past but (as Snyder writes) 'a vehicle to ease us into the future'" (1981, 189). However, Rothenberg's version of the sacred is no idealized space of pure goodness and light, but quite the opposite. In a long letter to Sherman Paul, Rothenberg clarifies the self-opposed nature of his relationship to the shamanic:

Thereafter, on the down side of the book [*A Seneca Journal*] . . . I would point out the references to Indian failure & culpability (the killing of the beavers in "Alpha & Omega," the killing of the harmless snake by Richard Johnny John, etc.); the occasional irritation with pretensions to new "religions"; the change from Turtle Island to Snake Island (a more ambiguous renaming of America than Gary Snyder's); &, most importantly, the refusal on my part to claim shamanship while keeping at some distance those who do, e.g. the prayer that ends "The Witness":
> the old people will dream
> ghosts will arise anew

> in phantom cities
> they will drive caravan across the land
> bare chested   gods
> of neither morning
> shaman   serpent in thy final kingdom   leave
> my house in peace. (Paul 1986, 178–79)

In his "A Poetics of the Sacred," included in this collection of essays, Rothenberg posits poetry "as a religion without assurances," and elaborates the paradoxical nature of such a religion: "The strange thing about it, for many of us, is that we so clearly recognize the origins of poetry in states of mind and in forms of behavior that we think of as religious in nature. And yet, speaking for myself at least and for many like me, our tendency has been to pull away from religion as such. It is a tension that I feel in whatever I've done as a poet" (1991, 2–3).

That tension, of a religion based very much on doubt, skepticism, and questioning—what Emily Dickinson called "that religion / That doubts as fervently as it believes" and described as "we both believe, and disbelieve a hundred times an Hour, which keeps Believing nimble"[20]—is most fully elaborated in the writings of Rothenberg and Antin that have to do with questions of their Jewish identity, an identity that, as one might expect, is based on refusal, questioning, and exile.[21] One way to think of such an identity (or faith) based on difference is to consider Charles Bernstein's interpretation of a remark by Kafka: "Franz Kafka once asked, 'What have I in common with the Jews, I don't know what I have in common with myself?' This can itself be understood as a Jewish attitude, but only if Jewishness is taken as multiplicitous and expressed indirectly" (1992, 7).[22]

Such a concept of self-opposition applies to Antin's version of the story of Abraham, Antin being drawn to "the way genesis poses abraham's sense of himself as jew against his fatherhood" (1989, 17), pitting these competing demands in a moment of choice. Though Rothenberg has edited a huge anthology called *A Jewish Book* (1978), he says, "In the end it isn't the idea of (so-called) 'Jewishness' that most concerns me—rather a specific set of language plays, feats of word magic & language-centeredness (in its most profound sense) that come to a visible point within the illusion of the ethnically specific" (1981, 143).[23]

For Rothenberg, the most important statement of his version of Jewishness occurs in his preface to *A Big Jewish Book:*

—a sense of exile both as cosmic principle (exile of God from God, etc.) & as the Jewish fate, experienced as the alienation of group individual, so that the myth (gnostic or orthodox) is never only symbol but history, experience, as well;

—from which there comes a distancing from nature & from God (infinite, ineffable), but countered in turn by a *poesis* older than the Jews, still based on namings, on an imaging of faces, bodies, powers, a working out of possibilities (but, principally, the female side of God-Shekinah—as Herself in exile) evaded by orthodoxy, now returning to astound us;

—or, projected into language, a sense (in Jabes's phrase) of being "exiled in the word"—a conflict, as I read it, with a text, a web of letters, which can capture, can force the mind toward abstract pattern or, conversely, toward the framing, raising, of an endless, truly Jewish "book of questions";

—&, finally, the Jews identified as mental rebels, who refuse consensus, thus become—even when bound to their own Law, or in the face of "holocaust," etc.— the model for the Great Refusal to the lie of Church & State.

And it's from such a model—however obscured by intervening degradations from *poesis*, impulse to conform, etc.—that I would understand Marina Tsvetayeva's dictum that "all poets are Jews." (1981, 122–23)

Sherman Paul sees in Rothenberg's investigation of Jewishness an activity that most clearly focuses and presents a universalized human perspective to Rothenberg's work:

Living in our time does not make it any easier to feel *placed*. For all of us. Because, as he knows, all of us, not only Jews, bear the burden of human history. Exile is not an experience or a theme peculiar to Jews—it is, for example, one of the things the Amer-indians and Jews of *Poland/1931,* those lost tribes, share. Rothenberg is fond of quoting Marina Tsvetayeva's remark, "All poets are Jews," because, as a non-Jewish poet, she learned that poets are not exempt from the kind of experience she associates with Jews. Yet such statements would have more truth if they were amended to apply to all of us. Because all of us—isn't this the burden of Rothenberg's work?—have in his large view of human history been exiled from the tribe to the state, from the primitive to the civilized, and are still wandering in search of the primitive (Stanley Diamond names the project), in search of the communality that will allow us to be fully human. (1986, 126–27)

Though there is commonality (and perhaps even communality) in the experience of exile (and in the hope of communal recovery), Antin's exploration of Jewish identity, in "Writing and Exile" (the talk-poem which he delivered at the *Tikkun* conference), focuses on the overlapping concepts of exile and refusal:

> you know i'm a dedicated atheist   when i hear jews say god i dont
> know who theyre talking about   i should say "what theyre talking
> about"   when you say "who" its even more shocking   the idea that jews
> can address an omnipotent an omniscient figure   an all powerful all
> knowing being localized with intention   and do this with reverence
> strikes me as preposterous but also offensive   so my experience
> of that sort of judaism   raunchy old men with earlocks who drank too
> much and read from books of prayer that when translated into english
> became more offensive than they sounded when you only had a vague
> notion of what they meant   this was my experience   from a few
> distant elderly relatives   and there were not too many of them
>   my family
> comes from a kind of left wing of the jewish tradition   the haskalah
> background   my grandfather was a hebrew scholar turned spinozan   and
> there was a family of marxists   chessplayers hustlers   the part
> of the family i liked   so to me jewishness was the sense of
> refusal   all these refusals. (1990, 50)

Antin's jewishness-as-refusal is a cornerstone of the cultural poetics I have been tracing in this essay. It is essential to the skeptical, questioning thinking that I have identified with Rothenberg and Antin. In "Writing and Exile" Antin says, "my sense of exile was then beginning with an examination of what i was exiled from   i was exiled from a kind of enthusiasm" (49). That exile is from virtually all forms of unreflected (and unreflective) enthusiasm—from poetry's dominant mode, from superficial philosophizing, from essentialist ethnic identifications, from "normative" expression, from writing as inherently superior to speech, from closure and conclusion instead of questioning, and from nationalistic patriotism. For Antin, it is a "kind of not understanding [that] was the beginning of my exile" (48). Crucially, such an exile includes a distance particularly from nationalistic enthusiasm, as seen in Antin's recollection of his dawning sense of distance from American World War II patriotism:

> i remember there was a children's costume contest in coney island
> where the costumes were supposed to be based on a theme and the first
> prize went to a six year old in commando clothing with a blackened

> face and twigs on his helmet with a rifle and bayonet called
> "dawn raid"
>   and this was a figure of a national allegory that
> celebrated innocent american violence   which was part of what i
> regard as the native experience   a construction of images for which
>   we have an unqualified enthusiasm because   they project a deeply
> satisfying sense of an "us" corresponding to a deeply threatening
> "them" whoever   they may happen to be   and in both of which we
> thoroughly believe. (49)

In enacting (with Rothenberg) a peculiarly intense, comic, and compassionate doubting faith, Antin, in rethinking the story of his ancestor Wolf Kitzes's interaction with the Baal Shem Tov, speaks the oddly affirmative position of exile, a refusal which is at once artistic, political, and ethical:

> and taking pity on his great teacher he answered once again in the
>   jewish tradition   "so what should i have said" and left it at
>   that   because there was nothing he should have said   because
> there is nothing you should say when youre addressed in this way   it
> is not an address fitting for an exiled human being at all   essentially
>   you must refuse this question because it is imbecilic   and my
>   ancestor was distinguished by rejecting this degrading delusion even
>   in the optimistic power of his love for the baal shem   because he
> he must have realized that exile is inherently written into the humanness
>   of the jewish tradition   which is the human tradition   and my
>   ancestor must have known this and martin buber would probably have
>   known this too if he had thought about it enough   if he had connected
>   it with all those situations that buber had to have thought about in
> his reading of jewish history   in his immigration to israel   where
> jews have become a nation and there is no exile   only a national
> experience and a community that creates an exile for everybody who
> is not part of that national experience and happens to be there   like
>   the arabs   or the jews who are not part of that national experience
> because they havent yet learned how to hate the arabs and dont want to
>   behave like a nation   which will behave like any nation
> or writers   who as writers cannot afford to be part of any nation. (52)

For Antin, and for Rothenberg, exile is a means of affirmation, providing a critical distance from faith-without-doubt, from a professionally sanctioned but noninnovative poesis, and from an enthusiastic but naively violent nationalism. Rothenberg concludes, "The only absolutes for poetry are diversity and change (and the freedom to pursue these); and the only purpose, over the long run, is to raise questions, to raise doubts, to put people into alternative, sometime uncomfortable situations, to raise questions but not necessarily answer them, or to jump ahead with other questions, to challenge the most widely held preconceptions in our culture" (1981, 223–24).

As I have been arguing implicitly throughout this essay, there is great cultural force and immensely important critical thinking in the poetic activities of Antin and Rothenberg. As Herbert Marcuse claims, "the critical function of art, its contribution to the struggle for liberation, resides in the aesthetic form" (1978, 8). And, as Marcuse explains, "it is not the business of art to portray the world as the possible object of domination" (36). The work of Antin and Rothenberg leads us into new and unsettling soundings and questionings; they do not offer us a mastered or masterable image of the world. It is that very lack of mastery, the contingency of thinking in the mouth, their *muthos*, that is generative of further thinking, singing, and making. Their cultural poetics and ongoing deed of poesis provide us with a pedagogy and presence of critical human importance.

Notes

1. For a more detailed discussion of the relationship between reading habits and characterizations of contemporary American poetry, see Lazer 1986.

2. See for example, Nelson 1989 and Perloff 1984, 1985, 1986, and 1990.

3. Of course such immediacy of the word need not be tied to the predominance of the oral qualities of poetry. The poetry of Steve McCaffery, Hannah Weiner, Susan Howe, Tina Darragh, John Byrum, Dick Higgins, and Stephen-Paul Martin is rich in examples of textual presence achieved by print-oriented strategies and by making adventurous use of the page as a unit of composition.

4. For a detailed discussion of the politics of form and its relationship to issues of self-representation, see Lazer 1990, 503–27.

5. For example, when Antin presented a talk-poem, "black warrior," at the University of Alabama in 1990, virtually no one from the English-department or creative-writing faculties would speak to him after the talk. Members of the art department, undergraduates, and other graduate students, however, were much less threatened by and receptive to Antin's performance.

6. Doty's description of mythography, though not intended as such, serves as an

excellent description of Antin's talk-poem "talking at the boundaries," particularly the talk's conclusion, where Antin focuses on the moral choices confronting a young marine.

7. My own interactions with David Antin over the past five or so years are consistent with his vision of a community of artists. His own layout of the talk-poems, which I think of as *phrasal*, has been crucial to my own writing practice. That method, as well as his remarks on collage, have led me to dedicate my book of poems *INTER(IR)RUPTIONS* (1992) to David Antin.

8. For a discussion of conventions and institutional politics of the poetry reading, see Lazer 1990b.

9. Such a declaration, it must be noted, applies as well to Antin's recomposition of his talk-poems for inclusion in book publications. That is, just as Antin's performances honor the present, so too does his act of transcription. Antin will revise, add, and delete as he honors a different present moment of poesis in the act of transcribing a previously presented talk-poem. In the tapes that Antin has made available to me, the most noteworthy difference is in the ending to "talking at the boundaries," where the marine's story on tape is much more rambling than the transcribed version.

10. As I had imagined before I had the chance to see Antin do a talk-poem live, Antin does engage in considerable preparation before a performance. The nature of that preparation seems to involve a meditative consideration of what particular narratives and questions engage Antin at the moment or period of performance, as well as some thought about which narratives and stories might be juxtaposed. Antin does not work from written notes.

11. For a more detailed consideration of these claims, see Lazer 1990b.

12. As a personal and pedagogical aside, which verifies Rothenberg's contentions, I recently began a graduate seminar in poetics (where our main objects of study were the writings of Thoreau and Dickinson) by presenting for discussion a Navajo coyote song that is transcribed simply as a set of transliterated sounds/syllables on page 8 of Rothenberg's *Technicians of the Sacred* (1985). I found especially illuminating the way in which this text immediately removed both my customary authority and the class's habitual modes of generating discussion. That is, the removal of the possibility of immediately directing a discussion to issues of theme and meaning led us in other directions, simultaneously exposing our usually unspoken presuppositions about what to do with poems and focusing our attention on ways in which sound itself (nearly apart from sense) communicates.

13. Such a description calls to mind Michael Oakeshott's and Kenneth Burke's independent elaborations of philosophy as a form of extended conversation.

14. It should, however, be noted that Antin does not engage in a flat idealization of orality's seeming immediacy over the seeming erasure of labor and immediacy in the book. The best discussion of the dialectical relationship between speech and writing that Antin works out of can be found in Sayre 1982.

15. I have intentionally devoted a good deal of my attention to relatively recent talk-

poems by Antin. I do so because in these talk-poems Antin's reflections on narrative as well as on issues of belief and exile (which I take up later in my essay) are most explicit. A number of these talk-poems (including "what it means to be avant-garde" and "the price") appear in *What It Means to Be Avant-Garde* (1993). I thank David Antin for making many of these talks-poems available to me and for discussing them with me.

16. Note that though earlier in "The Price" Antin had rather snidely dismissed the merits of French deconstruction, here he is engaged in a vernacular philosophizing both compatible with Derridean notions of *différance* and informed by such theorizing. I find it interesting that especially theoretically sophisticated academics who listen to Antin's talk-poems often fail to perceive that his humorous dismissal of theory masks his own vernacular and story-based participation in the same issues. When Antin presented "black warrior" at the University of Alabama (April 5, 1990), many theorists in the audience could not get past Antin's opening jabs at French deconstruction long enough to realize that his own thinking—and Antin is well read in linguistics, rhetoric, and philosophy, and has had close working relationships with French theorists such as Michel de Certeau, who was in residence for quite some time at the University of California at San Diego, where Antin teaches—participates in current theoretical issues but by means of a different vocabulary and methodology. Antin's is a thinking poesis which is open to "high" and "low" discourses, and it is a thinking poesis rich in anecdotal material. Thus Antin's work stands as a critique and an accusation of professionalized behavior in poetry, philosophy, and critical theory.

17. See, for example, "Founding: Jerome Rothenberg," Paul 1986, 71–183.

18. See also Rothenberg 1972 and Rothenberg's recordings of Songs X and XIII in *Alcheringa* 2 (1971).

19. Perhaps it is that supposed distance from writing that leads to a common criticism of Rothenberg's poetry generally and especially of the total translations: such poetry is not accessible for a reader who only has the printed page to consider. While I think there is a small element of truth to the complaint—obviously, access to Rothenberg reading/singing the poems *is* helpful—the implication that the poems are somehow "not successful" if they are not immediately accessible as written texts is a presupposition worth investigating. Such a presupposition depends on narrow assumptions about "reading," kinds of valued and professionalized forms of "meaning," and an implied version of mastery in reading. A Rothenberg total translation, even for a reader who has never heard Rothenberg sing the poem, offers an important and productive occasion for the reader to sound the poem (aloud!), to participate in the making of sounds, to learn about poetry's potentials and actualities by speaking/singing. Such pedagogy and experience is very much in keeping with the main title of this essay, "Thinking Made in the Mouth." It is not a form of thinking that appeals to readers bent on reading as a form of confirmation of presupposed certainties; instead, it is a thinking that confirms processes, sounding, and questioning.

20. Poem 1144, in *The Complete Poems of Emily Dickinson*, ed. Thomas H. Johnson

(Boston: Little, Brown, and Co., 1955), 512, and Letter 750, April 30, 1882, in *Emily Dickinson: Selected Letters*, ed. Thomas H. Johnson (Cambridge, Mass.: Harvard University Press, 1986).

21. Oddly enough, in 1990 at an international conference sponsored by *Tikkun*, the panel on contemporary Jewish poetry consisted of Antin, Rothenberg, and Marjorie Perloff, all of whom can be seen as Jews whose identities as Jews have very much to do with faith and doubt, exile, and an antiessentialist view of ethnicity. (Antin's talk-poem "Writing and Exile," performed at the conference, appears in *Tikkun* 5/5 (September/October 1990).

22. Bernstein's interpretation of Jewish identity applies equally well to Bernstein's own writing and to the work of a number of other similarly Jewish writers, including Rachel Blau DuPlessis, Edmond Jabes, Jacques Derrida, David Antin, myself, David Ignatow, Adrienne Rich, and others. It can be argued that such indirection of identity, especially in representing the divine, has certain affinities with orthodox Judaism (and prohibitions against direct images or names for the divine).

23. For a better sense of Rothenberg's complex Jewish refusals and identities, see Rothenberg 1978, and his two books of poetry, Rothenberg 1974 and 1989.

FAMILY PICTURES

Imaging America's Moral Landscape

IRENA S. M. MAKARUSHKA

The family is a natural image, right? Wrong: it is a culturally constructed ideal, probably the very ideal most socially developed. Although the way we are reared will inculcate this or that image, the range of the "natural" family is in fact astonishingly diverse: from extended, communal systems in which children are cared for by any available adult, to the new American suburban household with hubbie, wife, and 1.5 statistically significant children. It is unimaginable in some traditional cultures not to have an extended network of aunts and grandparents living in the same house; meanwhile, finding babysitters to replace such a network can preoccupy a working urban parent today. And gay and lesbian activists campaign for having among homosexual couples the same income tax deductions that are in place for heterosexual couples.

A sign of the changing nature of the family in America is that neoconservatives attack just about any opposing position in terms of its "antifamily" qualities. Instead of knuckling down to work out how best to support single-parent households or how to prepare children for the possibility (to a very large extent, probability) of divorce and relocation, conservative positions argue that the idealized heterosexual, long-married couple arrangement is somehow divine, and the answer to many of our social problems that seem only faintly related to marriage at all.

Makarushka points to a soft spot in this idealization, the fact that in a number of recent films (she looks primarily at Fatal Attraction *and* Crimes and Misdemeanors*), the ideal is sustained only at great cost to one or several persons who are experienced as threats to the primary bond. From a feminist perspective Makarushka critiques the ideal as a patriarchal construct that reinforces the culture's worship of male power. Directors Adrian Lyne and Woody Allen expose some of the nastier seams of the ideal, showing a mirror image that if taken seriously might lead us to reconfigure the moral landscape of our day.*

In *Amusing Ourselves to Death*, Neil Postman writes that "our metaphors create the content of our culture" (1985, 15). Postman's interpretation of the function and significance of metaphors invites a reexamination of *the family*, one of the most enduring metaphors of American culture. As an icon of all that is "right" and "good" about America, the metaphor of the family is inscribed with the dreams, ideals, and desires that constitute the content of American culture and determine the contours of its moral landscape. The "American family" represents the dominant culture's collective self-understanding. Its ideals are reflected on samplers that read "Home Sweet Home," in phrases such as "motherhood and apple pie," and in images of white picket fences protecting the American dream house.

At the end of the twentieth century, idealized images of "the family" are a powerful reminder of our resistance to confront the reality of family violence, incest, abuse, and abandonment. The box-office success of *Home Alone 1* and *2*, "comedies" that concern child abandonment and violence, for example, represents our collective denial of the prevalence of child abuse in America. Despite widespread evidence to the contrary, the American family is still imaged as a white, heterosexual, middle-class couple with two children. Single-parent households, single-sex couples, nonwhite, non-Western, and nontraditional families remain invisible. The Ozzie and Harriet model of the father-as-bread-winner and the mother-as-housewife still prevails. But these nostalgic images are more a wish of those in power than a reflection of the way things are, or for that matter, the way things were.

A great deal of concern has been voiced recently about the American family. The Republican convention in 1992 focused on traditional family values as the centerpiece of their national political agenda. They blamed the alleged decline in family values on the proliferation of cultural relativism, on women's rights movements, on the gay and lesbian coalition, and on affirmative action—collectively labeled by the Republicans as PC, the politically correct. Hillary Rodham Clinton represented the "bad" mother who chose to be a lawyer in addition to being a traditional wife and mother, whereas Barbara Bush and Marilyn Quayle were honored as "good" mothers who knew their place as mothers upholding the sanctity of the family.

The perception that the "American family" is under siege, that its structures are being challenged, that its very nature is being questioned, and that its future is in doubt, invites a number of questions. What is the nature of the ideal "American family"? What are its constitutive values? What are the underlying assumptions of those values? How is the ideal "American family" represented within contemporary culture? To move beyond lamenting the demise of the family, or hankering nostalgically for its return, it is necessary to inquire into the values inscribed in its iconic representation. Here I explore several representations of the "American family" and their underlying assumptions. I argue that the disparity between the ideal "American family" and ordinary experience is among the preoccupations of contemporary films such as Adrian Lyne's *Fatal Attraction* and Woody Allen's *Crimes and Misdemeanors*. Although *Fatal Attraction* and *Crimes and Misdemeanors* appear to have little in common, I suggest that both films reflect our culture's obsession with preserving the ideal of the "American family" at any cost. These films both represent an adulterous relationship that is resolved by murder. The proverbial "other woman" in each case is described as being out of control, and the adulterous husband is represented as a successful New York professional.

Lyne and Allen treat their subjects differently. Whereas Lyne creates a sensational formulaic thriller, Allen offers a morality play. The recent revelations of Allen's estrangement from his partner, Mia Farrow, and his relationship with her daughter, give the question of "family values" an ironic twist. Both Lyne and Allen raise a number of questions about the moral vision that is privileged in the metaphor of the "American family." Somewhat surprisingly, their conclusions are not dissimilar. Lyne and Allen interpret the American moral landscape even as they reconfigure its contours. Their readings of American culture as a text, and viewers' readings of their readings, constitute a deconstruction and a refiguration. I consider the processes of interpretation and reconfiguration to be religious insofar as they are engaged in the creation of meaning.

A similar view is expressed in the critical essays in *Breaking the Fall* by Robert Detweiler (1989, 30ff.), who addresses the possibility of reading fiction religiously. He suggests that postmodern and deconstructive attitudes toward texts invite a consideration of reading as a process that has religious implications. "Reading religiously" attempts to mediate between the privatizing impulse of the individual and the need to encourage community. I propose to take Detweiler's notion of reading religiously beyond the reading of fiction. His architechtonic of reading may also be applicable to the creative process per se. The creation of the text—whether the text is a novel or a visual representation such as a film or artwork, or whether it is a musical composition or even a scientific explanation—is always a process of interpretation. In short, an interpretative process engaged in the re-creation of the world as meaningful can be understood as religious. Hence Detweiler's notion of reading religiously can be extended to include the reading or interpretation of film. The director, as religious reader of culture, engages in an imaginative re-vision which in turn is "read" religiously by the viewer.

The interpretative strategy that characterizes my rereading of cultural values is feminist. I view feminism as a political movement committed to challenging the discriminatory practices of patriarchy (see French 1985, 442). Further, I consider the moral imperative of feminism as a call to overcome all oppressive practices, not only those against women but also those against men whose values conflict with the dominant patriarchal culture. Like other postmodern interpretative strategies, feminism engages in a rereading of traditional values in order to identify their underlying cultural attitudes. Moral values are neither neutral nor immutable "facts," but cultural constructs that describe and reinterpret human experience. Consequently the concept of moral obligation experienced as "ought," "should," or "must" becomes a question.

The move to a polyfocal understanding of moral values displaces the absolute claims of patriarchal value systems. Such a decentering of the moral imperative presumed in Western Christianity and culture also problematizes the relationship between individual and community values. Whether explicitly or implicitly, I argue, contemporary films reflect and engage a number of these issues. The problem of the "ought" with regard to "family values" is represented, deconstructed, and reconfigured by Adrian Lyne and Woody Allen. As they explore the underlying assumptions of America's moral landscape and the tensions between competing values, these directors focus our attention upon the complexity of human experience. With the "ought" problematized, the ambiguity of moral choice becomes more apparent.

Imaging the "Ought"

As the film *Fatal Attraction* ends, the camera stays focused on a photograph of Dan, Beth, and their young daughter, Ellen. The family picture reminds the viewer that the family is once more intact. With Alex's death, peace returns to the family and Dan's infidelity is forgiven. Similarly, *Crimes and Misdemeanors* ends with Judah and Miriam planning their daughter's wedding. They stand together framed by the doorway leading out of the room where Judah, on the pretext of suggesting a tragic plot for Clifford's next film, had just confessed his complicity in the murder of his lover, Delores. Absolution comes in his recommitment to his wife and family. Assuming that art—in this specific case, film—both imitates life and reflects a culture's values, what do these films reveal about the claim of the "American family" on the moral landscape? What do these family pictures—or better yet, families pictured—tell us about what (and how) the American family "ought" to be? How are we to read, interpret, and evaluate the moral landscape represented by Lyne and Allen?

Thinking about family pictures conjures up a riot of images, thoughts, and emotions. We recall the countless pictures of our childhood that predictably resurface at family gatherings (which in themselves become yet one more photo opportunity). As a visual history, family pictures narrate continuity and change, presence and absence. They also invite a degree of suspicion concerning the "truth" of the text, and raise in us a certain desire to reinterpret the family pictures in order to appropriate them as significant. As we struggle to recognize ourselves and others in those old family pictures, we may experience a sense of familiarity and strangeness. All too often, however, we find that there is a chasm between what the pictures tell us about what had been expected of us and what we have become. We grieve over disappointments we caused, and blame ourselves for failing to live up to the parental "ought." But how is this "ought" constituted? What values inform it? How does the "ought" function within the "American family"?

I suggest that the central structure of the "American family" is patriarchal. Patriarchy is "the manifestation of male dominance over women and children in the family and the extension of male dominance over women in society in general. It implies that men hold power in all important institutions of society and that women are deprived of access to such power" (Lerner 1986, 239). As the dominant political ideology, patriarchy defines the normative claims of the "American family" and determines our cultural values. The freedom to determine who one is and the nature of one's role within family and society is experienced under the conditions of patriarchy. The unilateral claim of the absolute authority of patriarchy legitimates the father's speaking for his wife and children. The "ought" is neither self-determined nor autonomously expressed. Rather, it is decreed by the privileged voice of the father. To live up to the "ought" is to be the little woman or daddy's little girl or good little boy. Given the internalization of the patriarchal "ought," obedience and subservience determine whether one is judged as good, successful, or accomplished. Patriarchy is oppressive and repressive with regard to women; insofar as patriarchy also defines what it means to be a man in this culture, it is also oppressive with regard to men.

The power of the law of the Father remains even "in the shadow of the death of God" (Taylor 1984, 239). The patriarchal order is a link between political and sexual economy. Monarchy and family have in common the idea of governance as domination by male power. After the death of the Father, this system of male domination becomes instantiated as utilitarian consumerism. Possession, which is perceived as a masculine drive, legitimates sexual and economic excesses that become self-destructive. Ultimately consumerism leads to self-consumption, a conclusion shared and developed by Christopher Lasch in *The Culture of Narcissism* (1978) and represented in such films as *Eating Raoul* and *The Cook, the Thief, His Wife, and Her Lover.*

The paradigm of the patriarchal family and the use of power as domination is normative in American culture, despite changes in social and family structures over the last century. Contemporary films represent variations on the theme of patriarchy, ranging from Lynch's experiment with the family as an expression of the grotesque in *Eraserhead* (it is a theme that Lynch also pursues in *Blue Velvet* and *Wild at Heart*), to the Coen brothers'

Raising Arizona, which parodies the American compulsion about family and children. Coppola, on the other hand, explores the structures that define "the crime family" in the *The Godfather* trilogy. More recently, Scorsese also took account of "the family" in *Goodfellas.*

Preserving the Patriarchal Ideal

Lyne's *Fatal Attraction* and Allen's *Crimes and Misdemeanors* represent the tension between the *ideal* of the American family and the actual experiences of family life. The central action of both films is hardly ordinary. Murder is not usually the last resort of our efforts to resolve moral dilemmas. Although they focus on extreme situations and violent behavior, both films explore ways in which the ideal of the American family is preserved in spite of violence. Lyne and Allen treat themes of love, pain, and worship described as the focal human concerns connecting private and public discourse, and inviting religious reading. Love, or the illusion of love, pain, and violence, is at the center of *Fatal Attraction* and *Crimes and Misdemeanors.* The relationship between individual actions and the values of community is at issue in each case. How are Dan and Judah to rectify their initial errors in judgment? What constitutes the right thing to do? Can two wrongs make a right?

Love and pain are treated in similar ways by Lyne and Allen, but not religious worship. Allen's concern with worship is more explicit insofar as his world is defined by the absence of God. Lyne's concern with worship is somewhat more oblique. He focuses on the moral implications of worship as idolatry, on perversion of the Protestant Principle, and on capitalist acquisitiveness as self-consumption. Lyne explores idolatry in the narcissism of the upwardly mobile, white, middle-class professionals for whom the sacred icons of money and power determine the morality of actions. Virtue becomes defined as an action that insures the continuity of a privileged life-style embodying the American dream of the white picket fence, the domesticated wife, and precocious children. In effect both *Fatal Attraction* and *Crimes and Misdemeanors* are concerned with what might constitute defensible behavior in relation to the ideals that configure the traditional moral landscape.

The plot of *Fatal Attraction* is simple and predictable. A happily married, upwardly mobile New York lawyer named Dan Gallagher has a weekend sexual encounter with a woman named Alex Forest, who works as an editor for a New York publisher. Dan and Alex have different interpretations of their encounter. She appears more intent on continuing their relationship than he does. She attempts suicide and engages in a variety of destructive behaviors that threaten Dan's harmonious family life. Finally, after destroying his Volvo station wagon, cooking his daughter Ellen's white rabbit, and trying to kill his wife, Beth, Alex is shot to death by Beth, and the family is saved. This simple story, however, is less simple than it appears on the surface. Lyne presents more than just a chilling thriller. He raises questions about the value that American society places on the family. In his representation the "American family" is fundamentally patriarchal with regard to the cultural construction of the role of women, and with regard to the social structure of the family in and of itself. However, he also subverts the patriarchal assumptions embedded within the traditional family by allowing the tears and inconsistencies inscribed in the ideal described earlier to surface.

The traditional view of the family defines the role of the husband/father as the provider and protector, and the wife/mother as the nurturer. In the patriarchal construction of the idea of woman, virginity, subservience, meekness, and obedience are counted among the privileged virtues that keep women in a subordinate and potentially less threatening position. Qualities that challenge patriarchal power are maligned (Detweiler 1989, xvi, 45–62). Women are denied the right to live as embodied and sexual beings who speak with the wisdom and authority of experience. Although women are expected to empower others, they are not permitted to have power.[1] The loss of power is orchestrated through the compartmentalization of women's experience into creator, thinker, mother, sexual being, begetter, bearer, and rearer of children, and so forth, as though the parts did not constitute a whole. Within this fundamentally polarizing scheme, women are catalogued according to opposing and mutually exclusive categories: either virgin or whore, either married or old maid; either a mother or barren; either passive and submissive or aggressive and shrewish; either silent or too outspoken. By breaking down women into parts, women become incapable of recognizing themselves in their wholeness as persons of many parts. Prevented from developing as fully integrated individuals, women suffer defeat at the hands of a repressive order.

In most films power is associated with the father, who provides the model for moral behavior and who is the hero in the face of danger. Prevailing by the superior authority of reason (over against the mother's emotional response), the father is perceived as the paragon of virtue upon whom the family depends in a time of crisis. The view that male reason is more effective than female emotionalism is evident in the high value that this culture places upon decisiveness and "getting results." Consequently the utilitarian model of ethics dominates: if it works it must be good; or the analogue of such a thesis, if it sells it must be good. In *Fatal Attraction*, however, the traditional patriarchal definition of virtue and heroism is decentered. Dan is not the hero. He does not save his family; rather, his wife, Beth, does.

Women Caught in Cultural Dualism

Lyne plays on the viewers' assumptions about family and the roles that men and women are expected to fulfill. Who writes the rules for adultery? Who decides what the response "ought" to be? What is the appropriate ladylike response of the proverbial "other woman"? How should a gentleman behave? In *Fatal Attraction* the situation in which Dan finds himself is far more complex than he could have anticipated. Alex is not just your ordinary femme fatale. She is a woman who is already other, as her androgynous name suggests. As a professional career woman—in this case, a professional editor—she is different from the image of the ideal of the virginal mother that American culture, given its Christian roots, defines as the proper model for emulation. Therefore Alex is the "other" woman in more ways than one. Bracketing for the time being the violence of Alex's response to rejection by Dan (a response that culturally is more often legitimated in male behavior than in female behavior), the subtext of the film becomes the story of Alex's attempt to create for herself a family which, as an unmarried professional woman, she is not expected to have. In effect, Alex acts to create that which Dan, through his infidelity, is in danger of destroying. The excessive value placed on a particular understanding of family life is played out in the violent behavior in which both Alex and Dan engage. Ironically, Lyne presents a situation in which the adulterous husband's behavior, in spite of its aberrant nature in relation to his wife and family, is perceived as "normal" by comparison to Alex's behavior. Their actions, however, can be read as a response to the cultural imperative to live the ideal of "American family" life. For Alex, this imperative is related to motherhood.[2]

The ideal version of the American family is associated with women who are defined by their reproductive capacities, not with career women. The American Woman "ought" to be the Betty Crocker type who is groomed to take care of her husband and children—she will be one who nurtures, not one who climbs the corporate ladder. Alex is antithetical to that ideal in a variety of ways. She is both the initiator and aggressor in her relationship with Dan. Her violent knife-wielding reactions are not ladylike. She is not subservient, or submissive, nor is she willing to be used and discarded. She insists that Dan take responsibility for his behavior and that he tell his wife about his infidelity. Alex's pregnancy raises the stakes. Culturally her impending motherhood legitimates her nature as woman. Women after all "ought" to be mothers. As a mother, she will fit the role she has been culturally assigned. However, Dan tells her that he is willing to pay for an abortion. His response would deny her the experience of motherhood. His attempt to do "the right thing" with regard to Alex is merely a pretext for protecting what he believes to be the sanctity of his family, which he has placed in jeopardy in the first place. His moral vision is blurred by his fear of exposure. He acts out of an instinct for self-preservation without regard for the broader issues concerning the breach of trust between him and his wife, and the implications of his behavior for the community.

Fatal Attraction has been read by feminist critics as yet one more example of the persistence of misogyny in late-twentieth-century male culture, which conceives of powerful women as destroyers of men, as castrating bitches.[3] Elements of misogyny are undoubtedly present in Lyne's representation of Alex as a woman who is defined by Dan's fear of her, or, perhaps of women in general. Nevertheless, I argue that the film not only represents misogyny but subverts its reductive interpretation of women by imaging women as complex individuals. More broadly, Lyne's representation of women within the framework of the family invites questions about the place of "the family" in American life.

Lyne images two aspects of the American moral landscape. On the one hand he portrays the culture's penchant for a dualistic understanding of moral behavior. On the other, he represents the illusory categories of patriarchy that veil the complexity of human experience. The cultural tendency to simplify morality into the good-guys/bad-guys model competes with the desire to live as though moral decisions could be avoided. In the film Alex is visually defined by black and white, suggesting that the immediate impulse for moral judgment will be determined by dualistic categories. She is dressed in either black or white. The interior of her apartment is white and is reached by a black elevator, off a black corridor in a black building that prophetically (or melodramatically) has a slaughterhouse on the street floor.

As in his other films, Lyne's use of black-and-white decor and costumes underscores the inadequacy of trying to understand the complexity of moral questions through a dualistic framework. Alex's violent behavior defies simple categories. Her violence can be read in several ways—a psychological reading is but one. The issue is not necessarily the justification of her behavior. Whether or not her behavior is justifiable, whether it is more or less violent *than* Dan's or Beth's seems to miss the point. Her behavior, one could argue, is imitative of male violence, which is culturally condoned when enacted by men against women but considered mad and criminal when enacted by women. National statistics on male violence against women support this claim, as do the criminal cases brought against women who resort to violence in order to protect themselves from abusive partners. Apparently in our culture women are meant to submit rather than to react violently.

Alex's violent behavior mirrors the violence of Dan's behavior. Her threat to his family is analogous to the threat that his choices pose to his own family, as well as to the family that Alex wants to create for herself. Alex's violence is not only destructive but self-destructive. In effect, Dan's willingness to deceive is also self-destructive behavior. He chooses to jeopardize all that he says he loves, all that he values as good and noble in his life. His behavior destroys the very trust that sustains his marriage. Infidelity and deception are morally violent and destructive choices. They are as self-destructive and suicidal as are Alex's violent and self-destructive actions. Dan destroys the trust of his wife and child when he chooses to gratify his male ego. His choice to deceive his wife creates the condition of Alex's siege. The image of the perfect "American family" is shattered. The illusion of perfection is vested only in Beth and Dan's new suburban house, which, in the end, is also besieged.

Alex's violence is a response to the events that Dan sets in motion when he chooses to spend the weekend with her. Within the narrative contours of the film, however, her violence reduced to her situation as a single career women. Being single places her automatically outside the realm of "normal" behavior. Therefore the moral of her story becomes: "See what happens when women don't marry, settle down, and have children?" In other words, see what happens when women don't do what they "ought" to do. The moral of Dan's story is somewhat different and less determined by what he "ought" or "ought not" to have done. Dan chooses to do what comes naturally. His sin is not infidelity but misjudgment. It is not that he did what he ought not to have done, but that he was careless in his choice of a weekend partner. The "blame" for the consequences is placed on Alex.

Lyne's representation of women is complex and ambiguous. Alex's violence brings to the surface male fears of castration and death. However, her actions also represent a rejection of the patriarchal model of feminine behavior. Beth also defies the culturally sanctified image of the good wife and mother. Lyne sees women as complex beings who subvert patriarchally defined roles. This is evident not only in *Fatal Attraction* but also in his two earlier films, *Flashdance* and *Nine and a Half Weeks*. He images women as determined individuals who take risks and act decisively. In some instances there is a gradual unfolding of power. In the case of Alex and Beth, power and decisiveness are experienced more immediately. Both Alex and Beth try to save what they consider meaningful in their lives. They react violently when they perceive that the well-being of their family (which for Alex is in the state of potentiality) is being threatened. When Dan finally confesses his affair, for instance, Beth does not hesitate—she throws him out. She takes marital fidelity seriously and acts accordingly. She acts as her own person, makes her own decision, and is willing to live with the consequences. By comparison, Dan is indecisive, almost fatally so. He consults with his friend and fellow lawyer about his liability in the matter of the pregnancy and (under the pretext of representing a client) consults with the police detective when Alex destroys his car. He deceives his wife not only by his adultery, but also by not telling her that they are in danger. He appears less anxious to protect his family than he is to protect his own good name. What, one may ask, makes this name good?

Lyne's images of the perfect suburban family life of wealthy upper-middle-class professionals are nostalgically shrouded in a literal mist. Lyne envelopes the perfect American dream houses in the perfect American suburbs in a haze that suggests an absence of a clear moral vision. Both the older generation, represented by Beth's parents, and Beth and Dan live in a moral fog, ignorant of the nature of moral choices. They live as though the Fall had never happened, and hence they try to recreate Eden in their Connecticut neighborhood. However their external civility is merely a thin veneer. Dan betrays his wife. When he feels that Alex has gone further than he thinks justified, he threatens to kill her. When Beth speaks to Alex after Dan confesses his affair, she threatens to kill Alex (and ultimately does so).

The viewer is relieved when Beth kills Alex. The triumph of the happy family is celebrated in the picture of Dan, Beth, and Ellen which fills the screen at the end of the film. The irony of Lyne's final image is significant. The cost of reconciliation, he suggests, is a human life. Violence becomes the only legitimate solution when things are allowed to get so out of hand. The preservation of the ideal of the American family, and the part that violence plays in that process, constitute a question that Lyne answers with an ironic visual image. After the Fall the moral landscape is marked by ambiguity. In *Crimes and Misdemeanors* Allen also explores the moral landscape after the Fall and comes to an equally ironic conclusion.

In God's Line of Vision

Near the end of *Crimes and Misdemeanors*, Judah and his wife Miriam dance at the wedding of Rabbi Ben's daughter. In this icon of family life, they appear happy and prosperous as they talk about family traditions and plan the wedding of their daughter, Susan. Again, the question is, What is the cost of preserving this icon? And once again the answer is murder. Judah doesn't pull the trigger. He pays someone to kill his lover, Delores, in order to prevent her from ruining his family life as well as his good name in the community. Judah (whose name sounds very much like Judas) is a successful ophthalmologist, a cultured man and a philanthropist. He can't afford exposure; he can't afford to be seen in a bad light. Judah's triumph after his complicity in the murder of Delores raises a number of fundamental moral questions. Restating the question that arises from contemplating the suffering of Job, Why do bad things happen to good people?, Allen asks, Why do good things happen to bad people? Why does Judah get away with murder and retain his good name? What kind of a world is it wherein the wicked prosper and the good suffer? Why does Ben, the wise and insightful rabbi, go blind? Why does Professor Levy, the philosopher of hope, love, and affirmation, commit suicide? Why does Halley fall in love with the slick womanizer Lester rather than with the intellectually and politically engaged Clifford (Allen's alter ego)? For director Woody Allen, these questions cannot be answered. At most they can be explored, narrated, discussed, filmed, argued, interpreted, and finally accepted as unanswerable.

The central action of Allen's film concerns Judah's twice-told tale. Judah both enacts the betrayal of his wife and his complicity in the murder of his mistress and, on the pretext of offering Clifford a new film plot, confesses to his crimes and misdemeanors. In Judah's story, Allen explores the relationship between private action and public morality. Under what conditions, he asks, would it be possible to justify the wickedness of an individual's actions? Do ends ever justify the means? Do individual actions ever stand outside of the moral order of the community? What is the relationship between private and public discourse? These questions are pursued on several levels and in the various subtexts that collectively form the film's core. In Judah's case, the absolute value he attributes to family life and a good name in the community allows him to justify the murder of Delores. By having her killed, he eliminates the threat to his public image and to his self-understanding as a good husband, a good father, and a good citizen. The guilt he experiences is temporary and assuaged by leaving the proverbial scene of the crime. He takes his family on vacation. When he returns, he discovers that the guilt is gone. His life proceeds with unparalleled success as though nothing had ever happened.

Allen is acutely aware that the human condition at the end of the twentieth century is determined by the absence of God (or as he would say, by God's underachievement). For Allen, Judah's restitution proves that God is not only an underachiever but myopic. Judah searches for a paradigm of a coherent and integrated moral worldview that reflects a harmonious relationship between lived experience and the cosmic or natural order of things. He looks at traditional religious values such as those lived by Rabbi Ben and at philosophical principles such as those espoused by Professor Levy. He looks at old movies that contrast to Lester's television comedies. Allen looks at women who live in the shadow of their husbands, like Judah's wife, Miriam; and at professional women like Halley, who is a lawyer and a television producer; or at Wendy, Clifford's wife, who is a professor of English literature. He looks at communities coming together to celebrate marriages and at couples whose marriages are in process of dissolving. Wherever he turns, human experience remains ambiguous. Allen concludes that the universe is indifferent. There is no evidence of a higher moral power concerned with justice. In the end Judah the ophthalmologist remains morally blind and escapes punishment, whereas Rabbi Ben's moral vision is rewarded by blindness.

Allen struggles with the possibility that what counts in an indifferent universe is the public image rather than virtue. Could it be that in the end only the surface matters? Judah becomes Allen's test case. He gets away with murder because he already has the respect of the community. After all, the police believe his version of his relationship with Delores. His public image is that of a moral man, an ophthalmologist, a husband, and a father. His family and his place in the community determine and define his worth as a person. He is judged by the community rather than by God. After he arranged to have Delores killed, Judah experiences guilt and remorse only as a momentary nostalgic return to the past. He revisits the past literally by going to visit his old neighborhood and his father's house. Images of his childhood and his family's traditional values surge to the forefront of his memory. He is reminded of his father's belief that God sees all and judges all. Such a view of morality assumes a coherence between private actions and the public sphere that he no longer experiences. As he had done in the past, Judah once again refuses to be judged in the sight of God.

Allen represents the American family through a number of complex images. Although he looks closely at New York's Jewish community, the problems of belief and unbelief, pain, suffering, and forgiveness are fundamentally human experiences that extend beyond the Hudson River. Judah's father and Rabbi Ben represent traditional Jewish family life as well as the belief that God sees everything and judges accordingly. Allen is persuaded that after Auschwitz the idea of God's justice is incomprehensible. Judah's aunt May, for example, rejects the God of the fathers and turns to a secular ideology in order to gain the ideal of a just community. Others, like Judah or Lester, or even Clifford, desire to maintain the ideal of the family without the traditional religious implications. Allen's assessment of the values that determine the moral order within the Jewish community is also a commentary on the fragmentation of the family in American society. He provides a catalogue of images of the various permutations on the themes of marriage and relationships. His characters are married, divorced, on the verge of divorce, married but involved with someone else, not married and pursuing the illusion of being in love, and so on and so forth. Although the women and men in Allen's films represent the societal changes that have altered the contours of America's moral landscape, they betray simultaneously a nostalgia for the way things were. Judah, for example, is torn between his father's traditional view of God as the all-seeing Judge and his own sense of standing outside of the line of God's vision. Although he rejects one aspect of tradition, he nevertheless sees the ideal family as patriarchal.

The patriarchal order determines Judah's perception of his place in the family. Allen looks at the relationship between public and private morality: What does it mean to value family life? How is this life constituted? Rejecting the authority vested in religious tradition, Judah sees himself as a sovereign patriarch and an arbiter of morality. He refuses his wife Miriam the right to her own voice, so that she functions as an extension of Judah, as one of his acquired possessions. Like a voiceless decorative object, Miriam's place within Judah's world is defined by him. He cannot tolerate her questions, her concern, or her censure. Her place should be that of the good little woman who nurtures her man and who carries his emotional burdens, yet who remains in the shadows without an identifiable self. Denying her the truth about his betrayal, he also denies her the opportunity to forgive him.

Whereas Miriam is obedient and subservient, Delores challenges Judah's authority. Insofar as Delores is not a part of his family, his patriarchal power is limited. Delores speaks in her own voice and accuses Judah of breaking his promises. He is unfaithful to his wife in taking a mistress, and to his mistress in refusing to leave his wife. By speaking for herself, Delores threatens Judah's absolute claim to power. She does not accept his interpretation of justice, and she suffers the consequences of such a position. Judah accuses her of being unreasonable, and of misconstruing his words. He refuses to take Delores seriously. Since Judah believes that the public image determines moral worth, he cannot see Delores as a person. She has no public identity and therefore no worth. Delores is not Jewish, not cultured, not a mother, not a professional, not even a voiceless wife. She is a nonperson in her film role as an anonymous, smiling air hostess, as an invisible mistress, and as a victim of a senseless crime. Hence when she threatens to expose his infidelity and his questionable handling of money entrusted to him by the hospital, she becomes expendable for a worthy cause: the preservation of his good name, his public image, and his vision of the ideal family.

The murder of Delores, from Judah's perspective, is an expedient way to arrest a potential rupture in his family life. Therefore, as he rationalizes in retelling his story to Clifford, the murder has a happy ending. Judah prospers and celebrates life with his family. Clifford is left nearly speechless contemplating the possibility that not every murderer suffers from guilt. Contrary to Judah's view that tragedy is an illusion and reality a rationalization and denial, Clifford insists that tragedy is the reality of taking responsibility for one's actions. To admit to the crime would make the perpetrator tragic. Judah's perspective echoes Lester's definition of comedy. Comedy, Lester tells Clifford, is tragedy plus time. Hence time becomes the great equalizer. In an indifferent universe, time is the only possible response to perplexing moral questions. When Judah experiences guilt and nearly confesses his complicity in murder, the time he spends with his family puts things into perspective. Tragedy becomes comedy. Judah's rationalization becomes a more powerful reality than justice in the eyes of God.

For Allen time may provide a momentary respite from guilt, but the transformation of tragedy to comedy is an illusion. Guilt is related to taking responsibility for choices and actions. Allen underscores the implicit irony of Lester's faith in time. The attempt to negate or overcome the tragic becomes an occasion to reintegrate the tragic into human experience. For Allen the ambiguity of human experience implies that comedy and tragedy are two sides of the same coin. The bond between comedy and tragedy is analogous to the connection between individual actions and communal values. Ultimately, the individual and the community speak a common language and live with the consequences of constructed values, alleged intentions, and idealized moral visions that translate into choices and actions such as the murder of Delores. Unpunished wickedness is not transformed into comedy but remains a part of human history that unfolds over time.

Conclusion

The picture of the American family that emerges from the films of Lyne and Allen is disquieting. Moral vision becomes myopia; image becomes more significant than substance; expedience becomes virtue. For Lyne, moral questions are terrifying. He creates images and situations to which the viewer responds with the same degree of raw emotion as is representative of his characters. In his films there is little time for intellectual engagement other than in retrospect. His critical perspective on the American way of life surfaces when the roller coaster ride is over and the viewer steps off onto firmer ground. If there is a moral to Lyne's story, it is framed within a worldview devoid of the traditional structures that once determined cultural values. Only nostalgia connects our world with the moral order of the past. Neither the "ought" nor the notion of a just God is an adequate deterrence to evil and wickedness. Lyne's universe is as indifferent as Allen's.

For Allen the absence of God becomes an opportunity. Allen steps in to fill the vacancy, and attempts to provide an anchor for the world that he experiences as spinning out of control, as hurtling through space with no direction or purpose. He reimagines the moral landscape as he creates filmic narratives. He writes, directs and acts and, at times, becomes the Greek chorus commenting on the nature of finitude, human frailty, and vulnerability, reminding the viewer of the broader communal or even universal implications of human behavior. Retelling the human story, animated by a sense of its mystery, Allen creates the conditions for seeing the world as meaningful. In an indifferent universe, one can only hope to retell the tale, and in the retelling to reconfigure the moral landscape.

Notes

1. For the classic medieval text on the dangers that women present to men, see Kramer and Sprenger 1971. Even more devastating than the misogynist text is the foreword written in the twentieth century. In his introduction Montague Summers concludes that "we must approach this great work—admirable in spite of its trifling blemishes—with open minds and grave intent. . . . The *Malleus Maleficarum* is one of the most pregnant and most interesting books I know in the library of its kind—a kind which, as it deals with eternal things, the eternal conflict between good and evil, must eternally capture the attention of all men who think, all who see, or are endeavoring to see, reality beyond the accidents of matter, time, and space" (xl).

2. Another film that represents the cultural construction of motherhood is *The Handmaid's Tale*, from the novel by Margaret Atwood. For an analysis of other films concerning motherhood, see Makarushka 1990.

3. Phyllis Palmer, "Men, Women, Sex, and Power," review of *Sexual Anarchy*, by Elaine Showalter, and *The New Woman and the Old Men: Love, Sex, and the Woman Question*, by Ruth Brandon, in *Washington Post Book Review*, October 28, 1990.

AN APOCALYPSE OF RACE AND GENDER

Body Violence and Forming Identity in Toni Morrison's Beloved

MARK LEDBETTER

Here we turn to another aspect of "the family," as in that famous photograph collection "The Family of Man," which now seems dated and simplistic, but not innocent: such a collection of various races and classes of people lumped together in a shapeless paeon to the human race appears today to cloak precisely the ethnic, racial, and regional differences that we identify increasingly as part of the crucial motivating spirit of humankind. We are not all the same, and rape does not have the same meaning in one community that it does in another. The rape of males does not carry the same emotional connotations that the rape of women does; brutalization of wives and of children has different sanctions; and so forth.

Ledbetter explores how Morrison's powerful novel is shaped uniquely by its mirroring of African-American slave experience. The very human body itself is configured by its submission to powerful white males; it is disfigured in Beloved, *striated and warped and destroyed to the extent that only Jewish and Christian concepts of apocalypse seem adequate to describe it. Yet the traditional apocalypse is not what Ledbetter finds in the apocalyptic suffering of souls and bodies in* Beloved; *he finds the traditional apocalyptic vision particularly male, even male-from-the-dominator-culture, and proposes that Morrison's African-American heroine reconfigures apocalyptic—as her body is dis/reconfigured—in terms of birth and rebirth, in terms not of ending terror and chaos, but in terms of living with them and through them, and in terms of remaining in charge of one's own soul and body even though to all outward appearances, one is but the tragic recipient of a slave culture.*

The heroine, Sethe, is a victor, within her own context: she "is making answers for her and for her children's problems within the context of the freedom afforded her." The chapter ends with the necessity of altering that context, which will happen only when the main cultural self-consciousness admits to hearing the painful cries and viewing the bodies deformed by "the silence"—heeding at last all those whose voices and images a prettifying culture of denial will seek to keep far from consciousness.

I have been raped
be-
cause I have been wrong the wrong sex the wrong age
the wrong skin the wrong nose the wrong hair the
wrong need the wrong dream the wrong geographic
the wrong sartorial I

I am not wrong: Wrong is not my name
My name is my own my own my own
and I can't tell you who the hell set things up like this
but I can tell you that from now on my resistance
my simple and daily and nightly self-determination
may very well cost you your life.

—June Jordan, "Poem About My People"

The relationship of gender and race to identity formation has an apocalyptic dimension in Toni Morrison's text *Beloved* (1987). Characters see and understand themselves and the world most profoundly when in the grip of terror. Using traditional, apocalyptic language, the restoration of self develops through a spiritual journey that involves violence and chaos which takes characters to the extreme of human endurance and, in turn, allows, even forces, self-discovery.

Yet I think that it is misguided to assume that *Beloved* is somehow attuned to a "traditional" understanding of apocalypse. I am convinced that it is not. While the language of *Beloved* is apocalyptic and while knowing about the world and self is born out of terror and crisis, any sense of restoration, as traditionally understood, is absent. Morrison's characters are fated to a "loneliness that roams." Her characters suggest that forming identity as a black female in a white male's world is to live in conflict with tradition, always to be "forming" identity.

Traditional apocalyptic literary modes, then, become complicated if not inverted. Morrison's characters at once live in violence and terror and cause violence and terror. Gender and race are the apocalypse. When a black woman lives true to her experiences, the world can only be startled and shaken by its encounter with her "otherness," that which is other than white and male. Thus, a woman's moment of knowing, in Morrison's *Beloved*, is a moment violently imposed on man's way of living. Crisis and violence, for which one accepts personal responsibility, are prelude to forming one's identity as woman in a male-dominated society. And the forming of racial identity is no less apocalyptic, in *Beloved*, as it too intrudes violently and chaotically onto a state of living and knowing other than itself.

This apocalyptic moment when black and woman impose themselves startlingly and profoundly on a world white and male can be insightfully explored by looking at body images in Morrison's text, *Beloved*. I agree with Julia Kristeva that in the human body is where "significance is inherent" (1982, 10). I want to look not only at body images but at body violence, in particular at the body disfigured, the body violated, and the body dismembered, as ways of understanding the apocalyptic moment of race and gender in Morrison's text. And I want to suggest that the painful willingness of black males and females to embrace violence done to their bodies, even to inflict violence on their own bodies, represents a profound "otherness" of black and woman so terrifying that the white and male body politic, seemingly whole and healthy, can do nothing but stand back frightened and overwhelmed by an experience that is to it alien and mysterious. And finally I wish to suggest that in this community of pain that is born of being black and/or woman, and *only* here, does healing of the broken and disfigured body begin.

Two brief but important asides, attempts at defining, if you will, to let the reader know how I am interpreting certain key issues. I am convinced that traditional understandings of apocalypse are male. It seems male, to me, to superimpose a story of meaning and order on a world chaotic and mean-ingless. Males love denouement; persons in power seek conclusion, con-clusions they define, as means of maintaining power. To put it theologically, the male apocalypse is eschatological, consumed with conquest and death.

But the apocalyptic that I am about to discuss in Morrison's *Beloved*—well, let me describe it according to a character in the novel, Sethe: "I was talking about time. It's so hard for me to believe in it" (35). "Nothing ever dies" (36). Apocalyptic, in woman's terms, is about birth, preparing for following generations, enduring.[1] Woman seems to know that life is not *simply* a loneliness that roams, but that life is *only* a loneliness that roams, and that we never have a moment that is complete, fully restored to some edenic quality. In this sense, Eve was wise to move us out of Eden.[2] So in *Beloved* the apocalyptic moment of race and gender, black and woman, is the birth of terror and chaos as ways of living rather than as ways of achieving a restoration of order and meaning, the white male's superim-posed story. Otherness, by its nature, frightens and causes disorder by the very nature of its difference.[3]

Beloved does not have a plot. A summary of the plot would suggest that the setting of the novel is an Ohio town, after the Civil War. Sethe, her daughter, Denver, and Baby Suggs, her mother-in-law, live in a house that is haunted by Beloved, Sethe's dead two-year-old daughter. While the ghost appears to leave when Paul D, Sethe's lover, moves in, she returns as a teenager, the age she would be had she not been killed by her mother, who sought to free her from the pain of slavery. Ostracized by her community because of the infanticide, Sethe nearly goes insane, only to be saved by the love of Paul D and a community of women who chase Beloved the ghost ("haint") from her life and bring Sethe back into their communion.

But I suggest that such a description is somewhat unfair to the novel because it imposes an order to the life of an enslaved people seeking self-identity, a neat, even romantic order. *Beloved* has no plot in the con-ventional sense but a series of plottings, stories within stories without respect for conventional time sequences of past, present, and future. In fact, the narrative has a profound disrespect for traditional time, a disrespect that is not surprising, since conventional understandings of time may be the most pernicious and certainly deadly of enslavers.

Beloved is a gathering of isolated stories, which need not refer to one another. Alone they lay claim to what it means to be black and/or woman in a white and male world. There is power in the isolation of the stories from traditional time sequences and narrative transitions. They point to the profound nature of each individual's struggle to gain a sense of self as victim. Yet the victims in these stories are not in isolation. Morrison tells stories with an eye to a larger story. These isolated stories do have some connection. They are connected by "rememory," Sethe's word, the rememory of things that never die—experiences of a people—the violence perpetrated on the body because of its race and its gender. And, perhaps more important, these isolated stories are connected by the "rememory" of the terror that revisits the perpetrators of violence, the body politic, when the victims, refusing to be victims any longer, do not simply endure the violence to body, but embrace it—an act that repulses their enslavers and binds the once-enslaved into a community of the damned and pained, now free and prepared for body healing.

We turn now to three types of stories from *Beloved*, stories that focus on the physical body and the violence done to the body. These stories are about the body disfigured, the body violated, and the body dismembered. Each story provides insight into a moment when black and woman, developing some new-found sense of identity within a community of the pained, release horror onto the world, a horror born of otherness.[4]

Body Disfigured

Sethe's mother, a woman she barely remembers, carries young Sethe behind the smokehouse one day, opens up the front of her dress, lifts her breast, and points to "a circle and a cross burnt right in the skin." She states, "'This is your ma'am. This,' and she pointed . . . 'if something happens to me and you can't tell me by my face, you can know me by this mark'" (61).

Tribal marking? Maybe. The presence of a cross suggests otherwise. Ownership? Probably, but we are never quite sure from the text. Either way, we have violence to the body, disfigurement. I think that the brand on Sethe's ma'am suggests that I, the slave owner, own you. Yet Sethe's mother interprets the brand differently. This mark, the imposed mark of ownership, becomes a welcomed mark of distinction, painful and necessary in a world of oppression, where little distinction exists, at least from the perspective of the enslaver. Taking a child from his or her parent or separating spouses from one another happened every day during slavery, and it was made possible by ignoring distinctions: these persons are not to be considered mothers, children, fathers, husbands, and wives. Such distinctions might very well suggest that these persons are human and like ourselves.

The world of slavery separated the black body-community from one another, often. Ma'am subverts the system by reinterpreting the indelible mark that causes her body disfigurement. The brand does not represent ownership by the white man but the bond between mother and child. The design itself represents the irony of Ma'am's relationship to the brand, with the cross representing the slave owners' use of Christianity to oppress their slaves and the circle representing the eternal nature of the relationship between mother and child. I am not suggesting that Ma'am is pleased to have the mark for identification purposes; rather I am suggesting that she takes the branding—an event over which she had no control—and uses the bodily disfigurement to her advantage by exercising freedom where there seemingly is none.

And Sethe has her mark; her body, too, is disfigured: a white man from the farm where she is a slave has whipped her back until the skin "buckled like a washboard." (We will discuss this additional body violation later.) Of course the punishment is severe, and her disfigured body is a horror in its own right. But the horror of her punishment is more profound to the white world when the reader realizes that Sethe had requested her disfigurement as a child: upon seeing her mother's mark, the circle and the cross, she exclaims, " 'But how will you know me? Mark me, too,' I said. 'Mark the mark on me, too' " (61). Such startling prescience from this black, girl-child who knows that she must bear the mark of body pain in order to be one with her community!

After her beating, Sethe decides to run away from the plantation. Pregnant, almost dead, she collapses in the woods during her journey to freedom over into Ohio. Lying in the bushes, she is discovered by a white girl who exclaims to Jesus after seeing her raw and bloody back and then does not speak for a while (79). The white world is reduced to silence by the terrifying portrait of body disfigurement. And of course the irony and terror is heightened for those of us in positions of authority, white and male, who remember that she has requested her mark—body disfigured—as a race and gender identity. And when the white girl gets her speech back, she utters the words, our words to "otherness": "Glad I ain't you" (79).

I am profoundly moved and shocked by the necessity of Sethe's markings when Paul D moves in with her shortly after she arrives in Ohio. About to make love with Sethe, he drops her dress off her shoulders and discovers the scars on her back. The disfigurement is in the shape of "a chokecherry tree" and is described as a "sculpture," the "decorative work of an iron-smith too passionate for display" (17). And we, who are not other, might very well be undone by Paul D's response: "And he would tolerate no peace until he had touched every ridge and leaf of it with his mouth" (17–18). This sculpted tree is the tree of life whose fruit (in this case, cherries) gives the knowledge of the gods to those who consume it, in this instance Paul D, and perhaps as well the knowledge that there are no gods to those whose disfigured bodies must bear the tree and its fruits. And such news is frightening to the body politic, a world where white men are the gods.[5]

A brief and final illustration of body disfigurement concerns the character Sixo, a slave who "didn't laugh at nothing" (191). Sixo, who is from the same farm as Sethe and Paul D, is captured during an attempted escape. As Sixo is rounded up, the foreman of the farm shouts that he wants him alive (225). Yet Sixo fights back, passionately, until he is subdued by greater numbers. All the time, Sixo is singing. Perhaps he is singing because he wishes to elevate the battle with the white men and his ob-viously eminent death to the level of ritual. Albert Raboteau observes that African singing had the power to raise any context to the level of ritual (1978, 36). Sixo sings, and he laughs. Perhaps Sixo is being satirical toward the whites. Such songs existed, says Eugene Genovese (1976, 199).

The whites decide to kill Sixo as an example, because he will be of little use on the farm now that he has become so disagreeable. But there is more. I think that they are undone, startled, by Sixo's response to his captivity and possible death—singing and laughing. So they burn him. And unex-pectedly Sixo continues to laugh, he who never laughs at anything. "His feet are cooking; the cloth of his trousers smokes. He laughs. Something is funny" (226).

Punishment? No! Freedom. Sixo laughs. Death is his only freedom and is welcomed. Yet Sixo knows more. His woman escapes because of his distraction, and she is pregnant. "Seven-O! Seven-O!" he shouts (226). The seventh day, creation begins—not ends. Remember black and woman's apocalypse is about birth. The white men are so shocked by Sixo's response, "They shoot him to shut him up. Have to," says Morrison (226). When Paul D describes the episode to Sethe, after she asks, "Did Sixo get away?" he does not say no, only that Sixo is dead: "He was woke. Woke and laughing" (228). Sixo's body disfigurement imposes his identity as a black man onto a white man's world, and reduces their world, not his, to ashes. He becomes worthless to them; he will not be sold, and he will no longer work the farm. Sixo has imposed chaos on their lives and at the same time begun the birthing of a new order, Seven-O.

Body Violated

Baby Suggs says that black persons are "flesh that weeps." "Yonder," she says, pointing to the enslavers, "Yonder they do not love your flesh. They despise it. They don't love your eyes; they'd just as soon pick em out. No more do they love the skin on your back. Yonder they flay it. And O my people they do not love your hands. Those they only use, tie, bind, chop off and leave empty. . . . *You* got to love it, *you*" (88).

Here ends the reading from the canon of slavery. I think that Baby Suggs leaves the pronoun *it* at the end indefinite by intention. Sure she means that they must love their eyes and hands; and I think that she means that they must love their bodies' violations. Perhaps I am too myopic to suggest that Baby Suggs is urging her brothers and sisters to seek *sparagmos* (the body ripped and torn), but I do not think it too narrow to suggest that body violation is the given through which her black community seeks and finds identity. Persons who are denied freedom find freedom within the context of the denial. Baby Suggs refuses to give total control to her oppressors.

Paul D owes his life to body violation. Down in Alfred, Georgia, Paul D is in a work camp. The black men live in doghouses; they cannot stand and can barely turn. Each day they are fitted with bits for their mouths. Like stock, they pull wagons. Each night, the bosses run a chain from dog shack to dog shack, restraining the men, the workers being obliged to pass the chain from house to house as they get ready for bed. The chains restrain and connect these men to one another and will provide them their freedom. During a mud slide, the shacks are covered, and as the men seek to escape suffocation, they find each other in the mud. They drag each other from the mud by the chains (forty-six in all), chained together and drowning, until they feel yanks on the chain much like each might feel when he chains up, but "the difference," says Morrison, "was the power of the chain" (110). And they are saved, the white man's purpose for the chain is defeated, and the violated black men go free. Escaping in the rain and the night, they discover a settlement of Native Americans, another group of "others," who set them free from their chains.

No longer is the irony of the situation sudden or deceptive but rather expected. The Cherokees who free them are isolated from their people; they are diseased bodies violated by scabs and sores. The Cherokees have immediate communion with these "other" bodies who are also violated, and hence they are not terrified by the black strangers—whom they call "buffalo men." Again race finds identity in its otherness from the body politic, in its communion with broken bodies.

Sethe is attacked, while still on the farm, by two white men. One holds her down while the other sucks/steals, she says, milk from her breasts. The men are rapists; they violate Sethe's body (I alluded to this story earlier). Sethe tells the farm boss about the violation, but her report results in no punishment for her violators; instead, she is whipped viciously.

I bring this episode back to our attention in order to suggest the "otherness" of being woman. While being black can impose a sadly undescribable terror of the white world, being woman possesses similar possibilities for man, black or white man. Halle, Sethe's husband, is in the loft of the barn, watching, as the men violate Sethe's body. Sethe is furious when she learns this, years later, from Paul D. "He saw them boys do that to me and let them keep on breathing air?" (69). Paul's defense is weak and characterized by a typical macho posturing: "A man ain't a goddamn ax. Chopping, hacking, busting every goddamn minute of the day. Things get to him. Things he can't chop down because they're inside" (69).

What "gets to" Halle is fear, though not your typical fear. I suggest that had the men been beating Sethe, maybe even forcing intercourse on her, Halle would have defended Sethe. Yet the men suck the milk from Sethe's breasts—implicating a tremendous mystery to the male, those moments of body woman, birth and nursing; the mystery can be so alien, terrorizing, that men become paralyzed at their manifestation. Sethe exclaims, "I thought he was dead." Indeed an appropriate metaphor, for she is giving life, perversely, to these white men with "mossy teeth" (70) and appetites, and she carries life in her womb and her breasts. Her husband, Halle, is dead to her experience.

The terror of seeing Sethe's body violated in this way and not coming to her rescue drives Halle crazy. "It broke him, Sethe," says Paul D (69). Halle now sits by the churn and smears butter on his face, his "rememory" of the milk stolen from Sethe. Yet the butter is not the milk; Halle is too late for the milk, a sad commentary on Halle's inability to know Sethe's violation. The emphasis here is gender: woman's body violated, man's inability to understand. The refusal to become one with the mystery of birth, to accept its overpowering otherness that is neither to be understood or explained, and certainly not renounced; "a man ain't a goddamn ax" will only encourage men to create and impose stories of avoidance. "Things get to him," which excuse and paralyze any possibility for man to know woman.

Morrison takes the epigram of her novel from the New Testament, Romans 9:25: "I will call them my people, which were not my people; and her beloved, which was not beloved." The final body-violation story to be mentioned here involves how Beloved, the daughter of Sethe, gets her name. It comes from the preacher's words spoken at the funeral, "Dearly Beloved." The naming is mentioned early in the novel in the episode wherein Sethe allows her body to be sexually violated in order to have the stonemason chisel the name Beloved into the headstone. She reflects on the encounter and the conversation with the mason: "The welcoming cool of unchiseled headstones; the one she selected to lean against on tiptoe, her knees wide open as any grave. Pink as a fingernail it was, and sprinkled with glittering chips. Ten minutes, he said. You got ten minutes I'll do it for free. Ten minutes for seven letters. With another ten could she have gotten 'Dearly' too?" (4–5). "Rutting among the headstones" (5), she decides the one word is enough, as the engraver takes her sexually, while in yet another violation his son looks on as his own sexual appetite appears for the first time.

Sethe's action does not represent a freely chosen barter. She must name the child, the child who was *not* beloved, the baby who has visited ghostly fury upon Sethe's home, "fury at having its throat cut"; she who was not beloved, receives a name. Again the moment is quickly, violently turned on its head. The language of the encounter clues the reader into its paradox. Sethe gives herself freely, "her knees opened wide open," and she is raped, for they are opened as wide "as any grave" (5).

People of power do not understand freedom in the context of an oppressive history. Indeed, my limited world's understanding of freedom would suggest that Sethe has a choice to refuse the engraver. But my body has no history of violation and/or deprivation. Sethe sees that she is free only to name her child, and she offers her body to be violated in order to do so. Perhaps even more unsettling is the willingness with which she embraces the violation—"her knees wide open as the grave, were longer than life, more alive, more pulsating than the baby blood that soaked her fingers like oil" (5).

Sethe is rebirthing her child Beloved by giving her her name, perhaps the most intimate of gifts, and in turn Sethe invites her Beloved, a ghost, into her home. Sethe gives her history a name, a history of slavery and death; she gives a specific name, and her act is important. Listen to Morrison's words: "Everybody knew what she was called, but nobody anywhere knew her name. Disremembered and unaccounted for, she cannot be lost because no one is looking for her and even if they were, how can they call her if they don't know her name?" (274). Sethe provides a name, one that will haunt her for the rest of her life, a name that will remind Sethe of what it means to be black and a woman in a white and male society. "I got a tree on my back and a haint in my house, and nothing in between but the daughter I am holding in my arms. No more running—from nothing" (15). Perhaps we are back now to my epigraph by June Jordan, "my simple and daily and nightly self-determination / may very well cost you your life." Sethe's confession of self-identity is an apocalyptic moment, and her self-assurance becomes white man's terror.

Body Dismembered

I am uncertain about the body violence that frightens me the most, and intentionally have not dealt with the *sparagmos* in Morrison's novel in any ascending or descending order of important elements. Nonetheless I find it interesting from a Freudian perspective that I come to body dismemberment last. Climactic? Anticlimactic? Indulge me one admission of complicity in the white man's world; I have been castrated by this novel; no, by an encounter with the "otherness" in it.

We come now to the part of the story wherein "the girl who waited to be loved and cry shame erupts into her separate parts, to make it easy for the chewing laughter to swallow her all away" (274). We've come to body dismemberment as the apocalyptic moment of gender and race identity in Morrison's *Beloved*, to the moment when Sethe murders (?, frees?) one daughter by decapitating her with a saw, and attempts to kill her three other children.

The chapter begins, "When the four horsemen came" (148), a heavy-handed allusion to Revelation, and an apt description of the war, famine, conquest, and death that white men have visited on the black community for well over two hundred years in this society. Four men have come to take Sethe and her children back to Sweet Home, the farm from which they have escaped. They arrive at an empty house and assume, because of the lack of activity, that they are too late. And they are; these white men are too late to take back into slavery a black woman who has discovered that she can pay the price for freedom.

Even the white men are aware that the clash of races can bring violence: "The very nigger," writes Morrison, "with his head hanging and a little jelly-jar smile on his face could all of a sudden roar, like a bull or some such, and commence to do disbelievable things" (148). But these white men are not prepared for the "disbelievable" things they are about to witness. They find Sethe and her children in a shed out back: four children, her version of the four horsemen of the Apocalypse, and gender balanced, namely two young boys; a young girl, Beloved; and the baby, Denver. The men start to the shed to visit their terror on Sethe and her family, only to encounter a terror more formidable than that which they bring themselves. Sethe has cut the throats of her two boys, decapitated another child, and is attempting to bash the head of the baby against the wall of the shed—perhaps an inverted reference to Psalm 137, where it is the heads of the children of Israel's enemy that are bashed.

Sethe is making answers for her and for her children's problems within the context of the freedom afforded her. But listen, for I do not do the text justice: "Inside, two boys bled in the sawdust and dirt at the feet of a nigger woman holding a bloodsoaked child to her chest with one hand and an infant by the heels in the other. She did not look at them; she simply swung the baby toward the wall planks, missed and tried to connect a second time" (149).

The men have nothing to claim now. Three times we hear from one of them, "What she go and do that for?" One of them thinks, "Hell, he'd been beaten a million times and he was white" (150). He has the answer. He has been beaten *but* he is white, not *and* he is white; rather, *but* he is white. His beating is one moment in the succession of time in which life gets better. But for Sethe, white man's time succeeds only in worsening her life and those of her children. One of the four horsemen, the schoolteacher, thinks to himself, "All testimony to the results of a little so-called freedom imposed on people who needed every care and guidance in the world to keep them from the cannibal life they preferred" (151). I am not surprised that Morrison puts such thoughts into the mind of a white male school-teacher—thoughts indicative and satirical of educators' exclusively myopic canons and of their abilities to distort truths and ideas for the sake of self-perpetuation.

Sethe's violence may very well be an act of freedom, but it represents her only choice if her children are not to grow up as slaves. The irony, if not a paradox, and indeed the narrative power of the moment, is that Sethe's act is one freely committed within a context that apparently allows no freedom whatsoever. Sethe has no choice but to sever the body from its enslavement to white men.

The sheriff, another of the four horsemen, as Morrison now takes on the legal system, wants to avoid the incident because it is so horrible. He remained cold and didn't want to touch a thing. Finally he utters to Sethe, "You've done enough to last you" (151). Enough, in that in a response to body violence visited upon her, she has visited body violence upon herself. What white men do not know, because they never had the experience, is that they cannot induce more violence upon the body of the oppressed than the oppressed are willing to inflict upon themselves for the sake of freedom. For the sake, in Toni Morrison's *Beloved*, of claiming an identity as black and woman in the white male society.

The voyeur, who gets his pleasure from body violence, must inflict the violence. Only then does he have control. And the self-infliction of body violence, in the presence of the voyeur, turns his head, takes his control away. The reversal of body violence in Morrison's *Beloved* and the willing-ness of black persons to receive, endure, and inflict violence to themselves achieve the uncanny result of stripping the white male of his power. While perhaps it does not empower the black community, it serves to create love, cohesion, and a sense of purpose in the community. As Stamp Paid explains about Sethe, "She ain't crazy. She love those children. She was trying to out-hurt the hurter" (234).

People who do the hurting find this hard to understand. And people who try truly to understand those who are hurt find that their worlds, once so neat and ordered, have become chaos. Yet for those who show empathy, the world of hurt and hurter merge, and the night visitations of angels and demons begin.

Concluding Comments: Body Silence

An ethic of reading and writing allows those persons silenced to be heard. Breaking out of silence requires tremendous sacrifice. I am not speaking of the pleasant silence, the late night, alone with one's self-indulgent reflections. I am speaking of the unnatural silence, an imposed silence because you are other: an other race, an other gender. This silence Tillie Olsen describes in *Silences* (1978) as "the unnatural thwarting of what struggles to come into being, but cannot."

Perhaps only *sparagmos*, the body torn, dismembered, disfigured, and violated, the *sparagmos* of the other, embraced by the other, will one day so horrify our normal and controlled existences that we become muted and the other is allowed to speak. The one ethic in this story of silence remains; those silenced must suffer great loss to be heard, even faintly.

Sadly, until those of us who hear the silenced are willing to suffer loss for their sakes, loss and not only terror, will a healing of body gender and body race begin. Even with such healing there remains much that is different between us, and each of us, even the most liberated, fears difference and otherness. And though a time may come when the silenced are no longer silent, even at this point, without a chosen, personal sacrifice of the powerful, I am afraid that *they* (the no longer silenced), my own frightened indefinite pronoun, will remain forever condemned to a "loneliness that roams."

Notes

1. For an extended discussion of these ideas, see Ruether 1990.

2. An excellent discussion of the role of Eve is found in Mieke Bal's essay "Sexuality, Sin, and Sorrow: The Emergence of Female Character (A Reading of Genesis 1–3)" in Suleiman 1985, 317–38.

3. I am aware that at this point in my essay I have become as ideological in terms of race and gender as those ideologies I so strongly oppose. Let me give some defense, meager though it may be, to my position. My own claim, in this case to a certain political, rhetorical strategy, is not a move toward the empowerment of an other gender or an other race. To me, it appears that power is the problem; therefore, to pass power around is only to perpetuate the problem. What I am suggesting is "chosen vulnerability," which may have powerful dimensions to it, but power is not its goal. And while

I do think that my reading and interpretation of these issues are responsible, I am by no means suggesting that they are right. Hence I am more than willing to remain silent in the fact of understandings and approaches other than my own, in particular those of persons of an other race and/or gender.

4. I wish to suggest here that "otherness" is horrible when it threatens existing and comfortable patterns of existence or, in political terms, existing, privileged power structures.

5. The most fascinating dimension of the Genesis story to me is that the serpent's promise comes true. In Genesis 3:5, the serpent says that if you eat of the fruit, "you will be like God." And in Genesis 3:22, God says, "See, the man has become like one of us." The human creature now knows good and evil. Indeed, Sethe and Paul D have gained knowledge from the tree on Sethe's back.

THE FUNCTIONS OF IMAGES AND THE IMAGINATION IN MORAL AND ETHICAL REFLECTION

DAVID H. FISHER

Care for language surrounds every essay in this volume. Here we learn about the care for language in ethics and moral philosophy. Fisher contrasts the use of visual images and narratives in the two recent positions pro- and antiabortion. Values can be imaged through figures long familiar in sacred or patriotic stories, so that a modern politician may be treated as a "second Washington"; or the figures are directly pictorial, and advertisements portray models of personal beauty and happiness that they want to be associated with the product they sell.

Fisher notes that "the values that matter most to individuals and cultures are figured before they are thought," but much of the modern climate mitigates against the direct influence of figures, as part of the secularization that has left much of the culture ignorant with respect to morality (the beliefs upon which actions are judged right or wrong) and ethics (the explication and justification of such beliefs). Persons concerned to influence the moral climate need to pay more attention to the ethical bases, and to develop a more sophisicated iconography, or study of figures, and how they originate.

The analysts and poets of other chapters are joined here by the ethicist in emphasizing the importance of the picturing of moral values, especially given the short-range focus of postmodernist culture, with its impatience with traditions or history and its ready acceptance of the quick changes of attention typified by channel surfing across cable television channels. Influential images are rooted within cultural traditions—hence the awkward joins when the contemporary American physicist becomes enamored of Buddhist traditions—even when they are not explicitly at the forefront of attention, or when they are presented in a postmodernist visual mélange like that which greets the purchaser of any slick popular magazine today.

The deepest thing in our nature is this *Binnenleben* . . . this dumb region of the heart in which we dwell alone with our willingness and unwillingness, our faith and fears.

—William James, *The Will to Believe*

From the perspective of concerned, educated readers and listeners, contemporary arguments over moral issues often seem interminable and incapable of resolution other than by imposed resolutions that satisfy only one side of the debate. Matters sometimes appear otherwise from the standpoint of philosophical ethics. For example, one of the most difficult of public moral debates, the abortion debate, is over as far as many ethicists are concerned. While there are still professional philosophers on both "sides" of the debate—"prochoice" and "prolife" or "liberal" and "conservative"—there are few philosophical ethicists willing to argue about what the moral issues are, or about the proper conceptual tools needed to define them. These issues include the moral status of the fetus from conception to birth; whether there are natural or cultural moral criteria for personhood; the relative weight of respect for equal liberty or equal life as social-cultural values; the characteristics of victimhood and what unique rights or standards of judgment victimhood confers; and the relationship between technology and human values.

At the same time, from the standpoint of another public discourse, that shaped through newspapers, national magazines, television, mass mailings, and protest actions, the debate has only begun, but the terms of this debate are visual rather than verbal. Visual images of aborted, dismembered fetuses (or about-to-be aborted fetuses, as in the film *Silent Scream*) play a significant role for those advocating a prolife position. In contrast, narratives—stories of impoverished, minor victims impregnated through rape or incest and tragically unable to find means to end their pain—play a significant role for those who adopt a prochoice posture. In each case debate is fueled and continued by the agency not of ideas but of conflicting figures, namely visual or verbal representations of scenes of moral conflict. Such representations are not merely means with the aid of which partisan advocates seek to communicate their causes to an inattentive public. They are themselves the indispensable sources of moral reflection. Attending to the figures now prevalent in this as well as other contemporary moral issues, rather than focusing on second- or third-order conceptual abstractions used by ethicists or social scientists, reveals the way moral reflection proceeds.

Modern Ethics and the War Against Images

The values that matter most to individuals and cultures are figured before they are thought. The figures through which values are carried take any of several forms. In cultures that combine a strong linear sense of history with verbal forms of expression, values are often imagined through narratives, as in the stories told by ancient Israelites about patriarchal wanderings, an exodus from Egypt, or the conquest of Canaan. In cultures where images play a significant role in daily life, values are often represented and shaped in pictorial form. Hence statues of the Buddha's serenity after enlightenment represent ideals of contentment and harmony throughout China and Japan, while the Marlboro Man represents aspects of mainstream American culture's valuation of masculine individualism and freedom. Finally, in highly literate cultures for which history has become problematic, values are often carried in figures of speech. The metaphor of "enlightenment" for a period of European cultural history is one of the most easily recognized of such figures.

Unfortunately for those who value the exploration of linkages between sources of practical reflection and critical analysis of possible outcomes under the aegis of principles, there is a prejudice among moral philosophers against figure, a prejudice evident in the familiar distinction between *morality* and *ethics*. In normative philosophical ethics, *morality* typically refers to the actual set of beliefs held by persons and/or communities concerning right and wrong action or ideals of human life. Morality is often said to be the proper focus for social-scientific descriptive study, while normative *ethics* refers to the philosophical discipline that seeks a rational, universal form for, and/or justification of, such moral beliefs. The justification hierarchy usually moves from rules (such as those against killing), to abstract principles (such as the principle of respect for persons as ends in themselves), and finally to normative theories (such as Kant's version of deontology). These theories are ultimately seen as "grounded" in abstract concepts of the right or the good.

A primary reason for the movement away from figures of value entertained by popular imagination to conceptual systems can be found in the cultural-historical context from which modern ethics first was developed as a philosophical discipline. The attempt to ground or justify everyday morality on a secular, rational basis came about in response to complex social/cultural changes in Western society that had eroded traditional Judeo-Christian religious sanctions for morality. The aim then was to develop a secular basis for moral identity (both for the identity of persons as moral agents and for the identity of a universal moral community) within which persons as moral agents might flourish, achieve the good, and receive respect. From the perspective of modern philosophy, it was thought that the statement of clear foundational principles, rather than reflection on narratives or images, would lead to success against the forces of relativism.

The role of figure in morality was suspect both because of the previous role of images as icons of religious faith, and because of the passional basis for human attachment to images—after all, modern ethics was determined to be both dispassionate and secular. The bias against figures can be seen in the paucity of examples in works of classical modern ethics, and it remains a bias today even in such seemingly "practical" subdisciplines as applied ethics. Examples, including the case studies that fill contemporary textbooks on applied ethics, are not chosen for their literary or aesthetic or figural qualities. Instead, examples either are selected for their "authenticity" as chronicles of "real" events containing moral dilemmas, or, when manufactured, are created as disposable, heuristic devices intended to illustrate theoretical points. Case studies usually involve "thin" narratives populated by transparent characters confronting well-defined action dilemmas that will not distract students from the theoretical point under discussion. Truth, from the "moral point of view" defined by modern ethics,[1] is to be determined by analysis of the conflict between abstract principles, not by reflective response to the particulars of a case.

This aniconic or iconoclastic bent of modern ethics, with its emphasis on abstract universal reason rather than figures that depict, engage, and develop particular moral passions, particular moral relationships, and/or particular moral communities as a basis for morality, has been under recent critical scrutiny in the work of Carol Gilligan, Martha Nussbaum, Annette Baier, and others interested in exploring connections between gender-linked perceptions of a shared or communal self and moral philosophy[2]—a different but parallel critical perspective that likewise challenges the atomistic moral individualism and imageless abstraction of modern ethics. It has been offered in narrative versions of an ethic embedded in traditions supported in different ways by "communitarians" like Charles Taylor or Michael Walzer, or by antiliberals like Alasdair MacIntyre and Michael Sandel.[3] What is being rediscovered by these and other voices in moral theory is some of the important roles played by the imagination in responding to phenomena *as* moral phenomena.

The remaining sections of these remarks explore the imaginal dimension of moral response by distinguishing between the roles played by figures in two reflective processes: moral reflection and ethical reflection. Having made this distinction, the essay then discusses some technological/cultural factors that have made it increasingly difficult for paradigmatic figures to function in moral reflection. This difficulty suggests that those concerned about an adequate basis for contemporary morality or for a coherent moral community need to engage in ethical reflection rather than in moral reflection moved by the demand to resolve specific dilemmas. A final section returns to the question of abortion in order to illustrate some of the demands implied by the extended discussion of moral and ethical reflection.

The Role of Images in Moral and Ethical Reflection

In *Iconology* W. J. T. Mitchell notes that "the image is not simply a particular kind of sign but a fundamental principle of what Michel Foucault would call 'the order of things.' The image is the general notion, ramified in various similitudes . . . that holds the world together with 'figures of knowledge'" (1986, 11). What Mitchell claims for the epistemological role of images or figures is true as well in ethics. In responding to perceived phenomena, imagined figures initiate a reflective process that ends in action. In moral reflection, figures present in memory when the process begins serve as the background, motivating force that moves reflection from initial perception of phenomena *as* requiring moral attention through subsequent stages of analysis, judgment, and decision.

A situation narrated by a colleague illustrates how this process occurs. A young man educated in an interracial context during high school was accepted by a highly competitive college. Having formed the figure of a learning environment that included members of minority and majority racial groups—that is, a story about how good it had been to develop friends from more than one cultural background, combined with a visual image of a class including more than one racial group—he was suddenly confronted with an environment in which there were few if any non-Caucasians. At first he simply missed what had been "normal," describing the situation as "weird." Later, as he reflected on it, he began to analyze, to compare the reasons that his parents had chosen an interracial context for his earlier education with the reasons that had led the college not to include more members of minority groups; he concluded that some form of action was appropriate to resolve the perceived lack. The initial contrast between reality as perceived and the image of reality as it ought to be motivated reflection.

Images can also serve as the final rather than the motivating cause of reflection in a different process. In ethical reflection, images of a special kind—sublime images—are the sought-for culmination rather than the initiating factor in imaginative movement from moral paralysis to aesthetic/moral acts of representation. Struggles to express what they had witnessed on the part of poets like Rupert Brooke, who experienced the horrors of trench warfare firsthand during World War I, or by artists like Pablo Picasso when confronted with narrative and visual evidence of the Holocaust, illustrate the difficulties involved in ethical reflection as a process. The distinction between two forms of reflection is the difference between reflection motivated by images already at hand toward decision and action, on the one hand, and reflection motivated by an absence of images to engage in a search for images, on the other.

In moral reflection, agents are responding to perceived contrasts between figures of circumstances and ideal figures of what ought (or ought not) to be the case, the latter usually derived from an inherited moral tradition or traditions. In such reflection, the perceptual image of circumstances is the "figure" and the ideal image—of what should or should not be the case—is the "ground." It is the initial contrast that is relatively clear in this case, while the end of the process, including judgment as to how the contrast should be evaluated, or the degree of pressure it places on the agent for action, remains to be clarified.

By contrast, in ethical reflection agents are moved by some overwhelming experience (personal or collective), such as that of mass death, individual loss, or intense suffering, to respond to a complex situation that seems to demand moral attention but that also resists being thematized—in the perceptual sense—into any single, coherent contrasting figure. Because of the complexity and/or extent of the phenomena confronting the agent, there are no readily available contrast images available from a moral tradition against which to "see" what is already problematic. Thus in ethical reflection, as opposed to moral reflection, the process moves toward the formation of an "adequate" image in response to initial ambiguity, rather than from a contrast of images toward action.[4] The continuing search among American artists—painters, filmmakers, poets, musicians and others—for an adequate narrative, trope, or visual representation of the Vietnam War is but one example of the ongoing process of ethical reflection within a contemporary cultural community. Moral reflection achieves closure in action; ethical reflection achieves closure through a figure or figures.

All-Consuming Images: The Disappearance of Tradition in Technological Culture

Figures—visual or verbal—are able to serve as backgrounds for moral reflection or as the product of ethical reflection for a number of reasons, such as their individual aesthetic qualities or their ability to be effectively recalled or to evoke rapid response. However a more compelling reason for the pervasive authority of figures in moral and ethical reflection is their embedded place within moral traditions.[5]

Reflective figures functioning as moral paradigms assume the existence of moral traditions and emerge from them—and viable traditions, as traditions, are taken for granted and seen as self-evident. As Jean-François Lyotard notes concerning the knowing conveyed by narrative figures, "narrative knowledge does not give priority to the question of its own legitimation and . . . it certifies itself in the pragmatics of its own transmission without having recourse to argumentation and proof" (1984, 27).

Traditions are complex processes, products of culture formation and preservation carried out over time through cultural institutions. At the base of traditional processes of "world making" is the development and preservation of primary, paradigmatic figures—"metanarratives" in Lyotard's sense —that can be reiterated across time. It is the reiteration of such paradigms across time that provides tacit legitimacy for the "overbeliefs" of the tradition in question. In addition to the sheer force acquired through reiteration, those who accept or "indwell" traditions in Michael Polanyi's sense often believe as well in the unique power of traditional images to "appresent" realities otherwise beyond representation.[6]

"Appresented" realities are not literally present to vision; they are believed to be on "the other side" of the visible, adhering to it as the obverse side of a visible surface adheres to the side that can be seen. Traditions survive *as* traditions in part because their adherents do not question this power of presiding figures to function as vehicles for the appresentation of hidden realities. It is this believed capacity of images to bring into presence that which hides itself as well as their power to bring that which cannot be imagined into the realm of the imaginable that gives traditions a large measure of their "aura" of authenticity and power. One problem confronting the search for figures of the moral imagination in contemporary society is the effect of modernization on the ability to make use of figure in any foundational sense.

In the literature on modernization, beginning with Max Weber's metaphor of an "iron cage" as a figure for secularization and extending through Jürgen Habermas's recent debate with postmodernists over rationality as the basis for ethics,[7] much has been made of modernity as the inevitable rationalization of reality. This process, involving radical suspicion of all foundational myths or "metanarratives," is said by many to have foreclosed the possibility of *any* image's functioning "symbolically" (see Adams 1983), let alone paradigmatically. Those today who defend, for example, the Neoplatonic tradition of "depth symbols" "participating" in the realities they represent or appresent, such as contemporary followers of Carl Jung in psychology, are likely to be dismissed by rational modernists as well as by suspicious postmodernists as being flawed romantics who are naive about the nature of language and/or the mystifications of ideology.

Such arguments over the limiting character of modernity are worth pursuing. But in the effort to analyze the cognitive structures supporting modern, premodern, or postmodern *épistèmes* (systems of thought), those who debate them often ignore the background of popular cultural life from which such structures emerge. In an increasingly visual popular culture the expansion of visual technologies has both enhanced and limited contemporary possibilities for imaginal life. Perhaps it has not been so much a "hermeneutic of suspicion" against ideologies that has led to the evacuation of value discourse from contemporary popular culture as it has been the prolonged effects of multiplied images, seen in two representative technological/cultural developments—namely, photography (and its dissemination via photomechanical reproduction) and television—that have rendered images as reflective paradigms problematic.

The development of mechanical reproduction (lithography, photographic copies) inevitably weakens tradition by destroying the unique aura surrounding visual originals as icons. The same process challenges the "place" of narrative originals as classics maintained by the custodians of tradition, at once multiplying and decontextualizing original stories in a variety of contexts. The dissemination of televised images has accelerated the decontextualizing process begun by photography, ending in the substitution of images for material goods as objects of desire.

The loss of a transcendent "aura" surrounding image paradigms in an "age of mechanical reproduction" was first noted by Walter Benjamin in "The Work of Art in the Age of Mechanical Reproduction" (1969, 217–52). Benjamin saw that with the development of photography and lithographic printing, an "original" graphic image could no longer be a mysterious, unique entity surrounded by an "aura," but was now the original *of* a reproduction: "Even the most perfect reproduction of a work of art is lacking in one element: its presence in time and space, its unique existence at the place where it happens to be. . . . The presence of the original is the prerequisite to the concept of authenticity. . . . The authenticity of a thing is the essence of all that is transmissible from its beginning. . . . that which withers in the age of mechanical reproduction is the aura of the work of art. . . . the technique of reproduction detaches the reproduced object from the domain of tradition" (211).

The loss of "authenticity" in Benjamin's sense means a loss of power of an image to appresent the invisible through its unique qualities when detached from the support of tradition. The same point applies equally to the appresentational power of a visual image or to the power of the gestalt of a verbal narrative (the contrasting pattern displayed in structural relationships between compositional elements in a story, or in temporal relationships between its beginning, middle, and end). What gives the image power, in either case, is its unique status as an appresentational window onto the invisible, and this is lost when it can be readily "copied" and placed in a multiplicity of contexts.[8] As reframed against differing backgrounds, the "same" image can even be applied over against its original context. Just as custodians of unique visual objects tend to resist their reproduction, so those who preserve and transmit sacred or founding narratives resist their displacement by alternative versions.

Since Benjamin wrote his essay more than fifty years ago, graphic images have become progressively detached from a representative or appresentational function—from roles as signifiers of signifieds—to become themselves objects of consumption, as Stuart Ewen argues in *All Consuming Images* (1988). In a cultural climate characterized by the loss of credible tradition, coupled with growing popular desire for the creation of appearance as style (rather than for the reality signified by style), the relationship between signified and signifier has become increasingly confused, and the ability of a signifier to indicate anything—other than itself as a possible object for "consumption"—becomes problematic. Youths who kill other youths for popular jackets or athletic footwear see only themselves as images and do not see their victims as persons.

Ethical Reflection in Contemporary Culture

One can respond to the absence of effective, paradigmatic images for moral reflection in late modern or postmodern popular culture in a variety of ways. Antiliberal communitarians such as Alasdair MacIntyre call for a return to shared "realistic" or mimetic traditions of narrative representation as sustaining fictions for currently eclipsed value traditions. The problem with this, as MacIntyre recognizes, is that an essential aspect of a "working" or nonproblematic tradition *as* a tradition is its tacit acceptance. Once any tradition and its claims have become subject to extensive, self-conscious argumentation, it can no longer function *as* a tradition.

An alternative approach to the popular cultural context of all-consuming images is to begin by accepting the emptying of value images from cultural space as a given, implying thereby the need for sustained ethical reflection rather than attacks on widespread cultural indications of "emotivism," "relativism," or "subjectivism." The experience that begins ethical reflection is an awareness of phenomena that demand moral attention, coupled with deprivation of effective images to cope with what one senses. Ethical reflection begins with an experience of circumstances demanding moral attention that exceed the representational ability of one's moral imagination. Overwhelming indeterminacy, and the accompanying mixture of pleasure and horror occasioned by initial perception of such circumstances, serve at once as "ground" and "unground" for the "tremoring" process of ethical reflection that ensues.

Indeterminacy is the "ground" of ethical reflection in the sense that it is the troubling absence of any focused, initial figure for what has been experienced that initiates the process of ethical reflection in the first place; it is "where" response begins. Indeterminacy is also an "unground" in the sense that there is no available background, paradigmatic image against which to contrast what is perceived as demanding moral reflection. Through ethical reflection the mind seeks to produce "sublime images" for phenomena that "present" themselves as essentially unrepresentable.

A successfully "sublime" figure, when formed at the end of this reflective back-and-forth process, captures the "tremoring" back-and-forth movement of consciousness itself in confrontation with that which exceeds its grasp. Just as Jackson Pollock and other abstract expressionist artists sought to make physical movements of the artist "present" in the "static" final painting, so the sublime figures produced by ethical reflection make apparent the process by which they were produced. A sublime figure also thematizes the abyss against which the "tremoring" movement takes place: the figure "stands in place" of phenomena that both demand and yet resist representation. A "boundless" image[9] is consciousness's way of indicating that there are phenomena that both demand and resist the closure of representation. Yet in spite of the pressures that occasion it, there is considerable resistance to ethical reflection on the part of most individuals and in most societies. The resistance is based on a powerful desire for closure.

Refiguring Abortion: Seeking An End to Blindness

How would ethical consideration of the abortion debate proceed from the perspective outlined here? At the minimum, it would begin by trying to discover—in a nonadversarial, nondismissive, nonreductive quest—just what ranges of fears and hopes motivate individuals and groups to figure abortion as they do now. It may be true, for example, that visual representations will be more likely for persons nurtured by an allegorical or symbolic sense of natural phenomena as indications of transcendent reality. It may also be true that narrative representation will be more likely for those whose primary experience has been one of marginalization and a corresponding lack of access to shared social or cultural symbols. But inquiry into the multiple sources of tales told to the dark or images projected into darkness needs to go further than this binary opposition implies. In the end, there is a need to allow the juxtaposition of visualization and narrative to work their way through one's moral imagination to the point at which a figure adequate to the deeper fears that fund this cultural issue can emerge. It would be presumptuous, in the context of these largely expository remarks, to attempt to propose such a figure: no adequate background given out of which it could appear exists. But such a figure is needed as the end of ethical reflection if the impasse over abortion is to be resolved through other than brute political or legal muscle.

If human response to moral phenomena necessarily moves from or toward figures, from or toward that "dumb region of the heart" evoked by William James in the epigraph to this chapter, this does not mean that it is unhelpful to continue critical, conceptual debate among philosophical ethicists on broad moral issues, such as the issue of abortion. It simply means that we cannot expect the kind of closure achieved by such abstract deliberations to be satisfactory, beyond the limited circle of ethicists, given the lack of a coherent cultural background out of which figures function in moral reflection. The arguments produced by philosophers will remain unconvincing when they are not anchored in figures of the moral imagination; but this is not (mainly) the fault of philosophers.

Even were philosophers to become less hostile toward figure as a basis for moral or ethical reflection, what Paul Tillich once remarked of symbols remains apt for figure in general: "Symbols cannot be produced intentionally. . . . They grow out of the individual or collective unconscious and cannot function without being accepted by the unconscious dimension of our being" (1957, 43). In a highly visualized culture such as ours, in which commercial and political manipulation of images and the substitution of images for desired goods have weakened the ability of persons to live in the moral spaces established by images, it may be the case that waiting, learning to experience what it means to be empty and in the dark without images, is the beginning of moral wisdom. That is at least where ethical reflection begins.

Notes

1. For a classical modern statement of this position on ethics, see Baier 1958.

2. For a representative collection of such perspectives, see Kittay and Meyers 1987. For a specific response to the classical modern-ethical emphasis on principles and public rationality, see "The Discernment of Perception: An Aristotelian Conception of Private and Public Rationality," in Nussbaum 1990, 54–105.

3. The debate between advocates of communitarianism and universalism in ethics is outlined by the various authors collected in Rasmussen 1990. For a different perspective on current issues in moral theory, see Clarke and Simpson 1989.

4. The position developed in these remarks on roles played by images in moral and ethical reflection builds on Jacques Lacan's notions of the role played by chains of images in the unconscious as a "symbolic order" structured like a language. For Lacan, in the words of one recent interpreter, "image, sound, effect, and sensory response combine to form individuality as an identificatory composite—or representational entity. . . . the role which Lacan assigns to the image is so central to the formation of the mind that without it there would be no human identity, no perceptual basis to which to apply language" (Ragland-Sullivan 1986, 22, 143). From a Lacanian perspective, any visual perception of spatiotemporal objects is always the surface of an inexhaustible depth of associations leading to the perceiver to reconfigure the thing seen into an overdetermined "object" in the psychoanalytic sense.

5. The role played by tradition in ethics has emerged as a central problem thanks to Alasdair MacIntyre's account of practices and traditions in morality in *After Virtue* (1984) and *Three Rival Versions of Moral Enquiry* (1990). For discussion of the sociology of tradition, see Shils 1981.

6. On the notion of legitimacy of paradigm, see Habermas 1973; see also Paul Ricoeur's discussion (1986) of Max Weber on tradition.

Polanyi writes that "scientific value must be justified as part of a human culture extending over the arts, laws, and religions of man, all contrived likewise by the use of language. For this great articulate edifice of passionate thought has been reared by the force of the passions to which its erection offered creative scope, and its lasting fabric continues to foster and gratify those same passions. Young men and women brought up in this culture accept it by pouring their minds into its fabric, and to live the emotions which it teaches them to feel. They transmit these emotions to succeeding generations, on whose responding fervor the edifice relies for its continued existence" (1964, 173–74).

"Appresentation" is a concept defined by Alfred Schutz in "Phenomenology and the Social Sciences" (Schutz 1970, 1:125): "By [appresentation] an actual experience refers back to another experience which is not given in actuality and will not be actualized. In other words the appresented does not attain an actual presence. For instance, by looking at the obverse of an object the reverse is appresented."

Maurice Merleau-Ponty notes the co-operative character of the appresented invisible: "What is proper to the visible is, as we said, to be the surface of an inexhaustible depth:

that is what makes it able to be open to visions other than our own. In being realized, they therefore bring out the limits of factual vision, they betray the solipsist illusion that consists in thinking that every going beyond is a surpassing accomplished by oneself" (1968, 143). Learning to see against the background of a viable, appresenting tradition is what renders the solipsist illusion impossible.

7. See Benhabib and Dallmayr 1990 and Bernstein 1985 for different accounts of this debate.

8. Berger 1972 illustrates the democratic reframing of originals in a call for collage juxtapositions of reproduced images on personalized "billboards."

9. See Kristeva 1982 for a psychoanalytic approach to the genesis and formation of boundless sublime images within the "semiotic *chora.*"

10

SILENT MYTHS SINGING IN THE BLOOD

The Sites of Production and Consumption of Myths in a "Mythless" Society

WILLIAM G. DOTY

The contemporary attenuation of community has been a recurrent theme in this volume. Here the editor argues the importance of the communal context of our languages and our mythic stories and ritual actions; we are probably no less mythical than earlier generations, although we like to tell the story as if we were. Something of a materialistic reading of myths-in-societies, the essay leads to the hortatory recommendation to engage seriously in the creative image and language work that is the poets', the writers', the story-tellers', the artists' burdensome yet simultaneously joyful task. Taking our images of cultural values with utmost seriousness, we cannot avoid the necessary historical probing and theoretical analysis of how images are derived and how they function to seed ethical behaviors. Mythography ought to be "a discipline that teaches empowerment to citizenship as we now so self-consciously regard the interfaces between the past and the present."[1]

Myth is the hidden part of every story, the buried part, the region that is still unexplored because there are yet no words to enable us to get there. Myth is nourished by silence as well as by words. A silent myth makes its presence felt in secular narrative and everyday words; it is a language vacuum that draws words up into its vortex and bestows a form on fable.

—Italo Calvino, *The Uses of Literature*

Modern people do not always consciously have the myth we have told in mind, but then people never constantly sit around recounting their myth. That is reserved for festal occasions. But even when a myth is not being told it sings in your blood.

—Stephen Crites, *The Modernist Myth Exposed*

In terms of what we might call the economics of mythic communication, the most expensive moments in our society may well be those devoted to persuading us to spend money: commercials for a recent Super Bowl football game were billed at $800,000 per thirty-second spot. At that rate my university lectures would generate $24 million a week or $384 million a semester! Yet we all know there are communications and there are communications, and somehow what transpires in the humanities does not count as much as what touches the purse strings that many advertisers loosen by their lies and half-representations.

In this essay I highlight aspects of the functioning of mythological images and stories in our culture in terms of some of our driving marketing metaphors. Even though academic discussions often ignore the political, commercial, mercantile sectors of our society, we ought to be attentive to them as they express cultural values. For instance, I am sure that a list of the one thousand highest-paid individuals in the country would include no single poet, musician, philosopher, theorist, painter, writer, theologian, historian, linguist, geographer, classicist, sociologist, psychologist, mathematician, critic, or—to be truly humble—teacher of humanities in a state university. Such a picture of our cultural values might suggest that we've no regard for the production and consumption of myths, since myths concern most of the professions I've named, but I'll argue that mythic images and stories are very much part of everyday experience, even if embedded *un*self-consciously in our communications systems. We are familiar with references to our time as "the age of communication," but today even communication is so important not primarily because our *com-munications* media have something in *common* to pass along in the *com-*

*mun*ity, but because communication is treated as merely another transitory *commo*dity in the selling and buying and storing of information.

Within such a context we ought to take very seriously indeed the various rhetorics and literary types of communications, such as myths and related materials, as well as the sites of their production and consumption—where they originate, who is responsible for creating them, who for their interpretation, and which agencies train us to interpret and appreciate myths and symbols. And of course other factors ought to be engaged, such as how to identify the traces of myth in a postmodern society that celebrates its own "mythlessness" because it considers itself truly "scientific"—a claim that societies have made ever since the earliest myths were reappropriated by later generations. Whenever the euhemeristic reteller argues that the terms of a myth can only mean "such and such," the stipulated meaning has been considered *post*mythical (on positive and negative uses of myth, and euhemerism, see Doty 1986, 4–9). Perhaps we will eventually recognize that human civilizations *as such* are mythic when they claim that a particular belief bypasses the limited materiality of historicity and taps directly into a transcendental superstratum of pure reason, that is, when they treat their ideas as being timelessly valid, their own deities as utterly omniscient, although simultaneously nonmaterial and transcendent (obviously the lack of logical coherence here indicates that a mythic rather than a scientific basis determines the ways cultures regard themselves).

The recent philosophical movement known as deconstruction has stressed the lack of self-consciousness about such claims during the period when the West developed the consequences of the Enlightenment perspective, or when, during the last few decades, the chimeric securities of the statistical or laboratory proofs of the social or natural sciences gained authority. A formulation in Jacques Derrida's famous essay "La mythologie blanc" conveniently summarizes the deconstructionist call to intellectual self-awareness about our assumptions that our "scientific" society is so noble or "postmythical": "Metaphysics," Derrida writes, is "the white mythology which reassembles and reflects the culture of the West [in which] the white man takes his own mythology, Indo-European mythology, his own *logos* . . . for the universal form of that [which] he must still wish to call Reason" (1982, 213). We have assumed that our own limited historical experience ought to determine universal human values expressed in myths, but deconstructive challenges to traditional Western standards from the perspectives of non-Western, Third World, or minority cultures call us to heed our positions of social and economic privilege and to expand our standard canons to include literature by women as well as that of previously marginalized peoples.

After looking at the question of mythic origins, I'll explore ways in which I think we are today just as mythically inclined as any culture. I will discuss as cultural dominants both the myth of mythlessness and the myth of progress, two of the American frames that determine how we react to myths in the fields of philosophy and political science. Later I turn to the analysis of the tracks or imprints of myths in societies, and to reflections on the relationship of myth to the literary imagination and to ideology. I look at the role of myths and religions as providing the coherences of meaning that pull the disparate elements of society into some sort of cultural integrity. I conclude with the admonition to learn to appreciate what is truly creative about mythic or poetic languages (in the widest sense, including film, fiction, music, the arts, even critical analysis), since in those languages a healthy economics of the human spirit challenges the merely mercantile values touted during our socially conservative era.

Myths of Origin/s and the Originary

Although there are many different types of myth, and within a given society each type may have its distinctive social context, twentieth-century myth analysis is influenced heavily by the insight that myth-using peoples especially privilege stories about the times and occasions of origins or first occasions, which are not treated as only the first in a series so much as normative, always effective, "originary." The mythographer Mircea Eliade illustrated repeatedly the priority of creation or origin myths, cosmogonic accounts, while he stressed the concomitant role of religious ritual: it is the means by which the powerful, holistic times of the origins are made available as sources of power in the present. Overcoming the distance of history, the ritual celebrant temporarily annuls time in order to enter into the creative or re-creative primal times when everything was (and is, on a mythical plane) potent and entire.

The conformative power of the primordial accompanies the celebrant who leaves the ritual time and space marked, perhaps, with a bit of palm-leaf ash on the forehead on Ash Wednesday, or a vividly painted penis sheath modeled on those of the alcheringa (the Australian "dream-time," the mythic plane of existence from which this historical plane is derived). In many sites where myths are heeded fully, the turn to the past funds the contemporary finding-of-meaning: because on this night the Holy One, Blessed Be He, brought *us* out of Egypt, every Seder connects our past with who we are today; for Christians, "on the night on which Jesus was betrayed" and instituted the Eucharist becomes not two thousand years ago, but a second ago. Hence in an important sense we *are* who our ancestors *were*; our roots are not just lying discarded back there somewhere, but continue to bring up contemporary nourishment for our souls. Hence Bronislaw Malinowski's famous appellation "charter" as the defining function of many myths: he saw them (and today we would add rituals as well) as serving societies both as founding documents and as justifications for the present-day structure of things.

And of course etiological myths everywhere refer back to the beginning epiphanies of important sites, or to the originary first occurrences of traditions and objects. Hellenistic handbooks contained compilations of the "first finders" of various cultural artifacts and practices, while the diagnostic physician today will not think of beginning medical treatment until the precise etiology of the disease is determined. There is even a legend about the origins of Superman's ultra-high-tech powers derived from kryptonite, a modern use of story reflecting the same insights that attend the anamnesis performed by the twentieth-century psychoanalyst or the demand that a doctoral dissertation begin with a *Forschungsbericht* (literature survey) recounting the history of the problem to be solved.

Finally we may mention the ducked heads whenever someone refers in our culture to the book of Bereshith/Genesis—a nod that actually cloaks, in my experience of teaching Tanakh/Old Testament, an almost total ignorance of the formation or scope of that literature. This much-recited book, which collects writings about Israel's *earliest* periods, has been the object of more commentaries in the rabbinical and Christian traditions than any other book. However biblical and nonbiblical writings from the *postexilic* period of Israel's experience were immeasurably more influential upon the formation of the actual religious beliefs of primitive Christian Judaism, even though few Christians today pay them much heed—and we can recognize in this instance some of the cultural bias I wish to identify and highlight. Although these late-biblical and apocryphal writings shaped the Judaism out of which Christianity actually originated, in some important sense they *weren't early enough*—that is to say, originary in the causative rather than the temporal sense—and so the materials of Genesis and Exodus that are ironically contemporaneous with these other postexilic materials, yet *refer* to Israel's *beginnings*, repeatedly dominate the network of symbols instead. The Hellenistic flowering of Jewish and Christian apocalyptic eschatology did reflect the contemporary materials, but the apocalyptic perspective was quickly repressed within both normative Judaism and patristic, antignostic (and antifeminist!) Christianity.

In such a situation of ignoring the actual historical situation, the religious historian or myth critic can speak only of willful blindness to the historical contexts, yet it is a blindness that attends many aspects of religious histories. Only within the last couple of decades, for example, have Christian biblical scholars given up the search for *Urtexte* (passages earlier than the gospels in which they appear) or "the living oral words of Jesus" because redaction criticism and contemporary critical theory finally abolished the presumed primacy of the earliest, which was also considered normative, originary. We realize now that any redaction is itself originary or determinative within its own specific context, and whatever might be tracked "back" at all would already be another redaction, another interpretative transmission, so that "back to Jesus" can only mean something like "back to the anti-miracle-worker Jesus of Mark," or Matthew's Jesus the dynasty founder, or Luke's oddly Roman Jesus.

Likewise it has taken blockbuster works like Elaine Pagels's *The Gnostic Gospels* (1979) to shatter the illusion of completeness in the canonical accounts of Jesus traditions, even though in my own teaching (and many textbooks today) the apocryphal Gospel of Thomas has equal ranking with the canonical gospels as an important historical source. Joseph Campbell's recent references to the apocryphal gospels caused hardly a Christian eyebrow to raise, although I find that few audiences have any sense of the historical situations of these materials within the history of patristic canon formation. Surely the ongoing religious commitment ought to include a dedication to rethinking and reconceiving the past in the light of contemporary knowledge, yet there are no hotbeds of contemporary biblical scholarship among the congregations I know anything about, if indeed parishioners have even been made aware that such criticism is extremely active and productive. Applied to scriptural myths, originary status can mean that they remain frozen in their original chronologies, hence effectively unavailable for reappropriation. One might point, for instance, to the widespread ignorance of the many feminist reinterpretations of those passages in Bereshith that have seemed only masculocentrist all these centuries but are now being appropriated anew in nonsexist, nonpatriarchal retellings.

The Holistic Yoke of Myth

Generally across our culture, in a motorized time ruled by Henry Ford's message that "history is bunk," there is still a superficial regard for scriptures, for the past, tradition, and hoary antiquity, so that Ralph Lauren can successfully package "the country look" to sell everything from underthings for the boudoir to napkins for the breakfast nook. We give lip service to the past mostly as a sort of rhetorical substitute for our ignorance of it. Our immediate experience is cast in terms of today and tomorrow, and woe betide the analyst who observes how we *contemporary* people might be said still to be functioning nonscientifically, to be operating out of (presumably old-fashioned) mythic frames. Indeed, the dichotomy between the past and the present, with the assumption that only the present really matters, determines important contrasts between the presumed American norms and all other worldviews. "We" are nonmythic, up-to-date, but "they"— you can insert any appropriate cipher, such as primitives, Native Americans, Europeans, Iraqis, or Auburn University football players—are myth-worshiping robots, illogical innocents retarded by the dead hand of the past, and of course, and perhaps worst, as we used to say about Soviet Russians, not yet free-market capitalists!

Yet it is clear that the term *mythic* names an element of all culture that can never be ignored: it is one of the fundamental elements by which "civilization" adds the communal sharing of the city (*civis*; compare "civic duty") to the individual experience of living in the world, even when that world in its postmodernist dimensions lacks the cohesiveness and elegance of earlier ideals. I'll not argue here about technical distinctions between mythic and legendary, or mythic and religious. But I will suggest that myth-ed stories are the linguistic funds from which social discourse is always drawn, the "language vacuum that draws words up into its vortex and bestows a form," as Calvino puts it. Mythical examples orient aspirations; their underlying monotheisms or polytheisms arrange the players on both the human and the divine playing fields and determine that one or another species dominates all others, as in the mythical gardens of Genesis, or coexists amicably with others, in the sorts of healthy utopian fantasies that we often find in speculative fiction.

Myths geographize the natural contours of creation; they organize perceptions as they seed civilization's worldview and the ethos that differentiates "my kind" from "the others." Mythology is the superordinate system that gives coherence and meaning to all the rest (Liszka 1989, 14); mythic narratives provide the coherence of life-as-lived, the ideal models that make ideology seem natural, "our way of life" as opposed to any other. At the junctures where coherence is struck dumb by tragedy, or the individual feels isolated and alone, myths centrifugate identities and significances that societies choose to enforce and celebrate. "Myths give focus and meaning to otherwise discriminate interest," as Stephen Daniel puts it (1990, 8): they articulate what a culture means by success and the healthy personality, or by failure and misanthropy.

Above all, myths link meanings, they form holistic *yogas* that connect; hence their epistemological rule—synthesis, linking, holding together—is opposed to that of science, the very name of which is derived from the Latin *scire*, "to know," cognate at Proto Indo European levels with the Greek *skhizein*, "to divide or separate" (cognates: schizo-, scission). Ernst Cassirer noted that myth brings things together by finding substantial similarities between them, rather than by subsuming different things under general rules (Krois 1987, 138); we might say that it collates horizontally rather than dividing vertically.

But of course the mythic is one thing when studied in the classroom, when we study the great mythical plots of the coherences called world religions, and quite another when one tries to determine just how seriously the filmmakers Stephen Spielberg and George Lucas mean it when they attribute cinematic inspiration to Joseph Campbell's *The Hero with a Thousand Faces* (1956). Philip Cousineau cites the film critic Michael Ventura's observation that "no book has come close to influencing contemporary movies as pervasively" (1990, 175), and I would wager that no other single volume has so informed academic criticism of literature and the arts. Then we have Northrop Frye's analytic structured around the four great seasonal tropes that he finds in all of world literature; the various Jungian analyses initiated by Maud Bodkin's *Archetypal Patterns in Poetry* (1934); or various treatments of specific themes in literature such as the quest, the Orphic voice, or figures such as Oedipus or Theseus. Once beyond the influence of the ritual-dominant school, analysts since the 1950s have charted and tracked mythic emplotments everywhere, not just in ritually based "religious" material.

The Performances of Quotidian Myth: A Transformative Seedbed

But instead of showing how mythological literary criticism has worked, as I've already done (1986, chap. 6), I work here on a more everyday plane. Our daily encounter with myth is less that of discerning the Christ figure in Faulkner's "The Bear," or even mythic aspects of the self-conscious prayer, or the ideological substrate of the mumbled Pledge of Allegiance, than it is that of the indirect allusion, the ingenuous emplotment of a short story or novel, or the thematic distancing of the artist, such as Robert Mapplethorpe's much-reproduced self-portrait with the skeletal skull on his walking cane: in each case we are describing ways in which the mythological story or image adds significance to the real-life everyday, ways in which a culture's Enframing leads it to give priorities to one or another aesthetic or ethical ideal.

Of course any mythic subtype is experienced variously as people occupy different stages of life or as they are within or outside a religious community, or as one works as creator or analyst of a "mythic" work of art (see my discussion of Levels of Operational Vitality, 1986, 49–51). Curiously, I seldom find great narrative or expository power in the most explicit mythical retellings such as Cesare Pavese's *Dialogues with Leucó* (1989), Jascha Kessler's *Classical Illusions* (1985), or John Barth's *Chimera* (1978). On the other hand the sorts of indirect revisionings in Kafka or Borges sound the mythological dynamics by exposing the logical or alogical seams of mythical stories and plots: ah yes, what if Odysseus *had* remained forever in Kirke's arms? What if Prometheus had been powerful enough to resist Zeus? (I think of the sexually supercharged hero of Alfred Jarry's *The Supermale* [1977]: after eighty-two instances of sexual intercourse in a twenty-four-hour period, he is hooked up to a twelve-thousand-volt electric dynamo. *Still* more powerful than the machine, he actually reverses the flow of electricity so that *he* drives *it*—but that ultra-Promethean effort causes his death.)

Mostly we have theorized a great gulf between the concretizing art-work and the abstractionist fields of mathematics, the sciences, and even the denaturalized-language movements of modern analytical philosophy. Hence it is especially striking that a contemporary philosopher, Stephen Daniel, in a work entitled *Myth and Modern Philosophy* (1990), speaks once again of the primacy of myth in philosophical realms, after so many centuries in which philosophical critics of the religiomythic proclaimed the *independence* of logos from myth if not indeed the overcoming of the latter by the former.

Following influential nineteenth-century German scholarship, authors of most history-of-philosophy books situate the beginnings of philosophy precisely at the point of myth's decadence. But we now recognize that such a distinction ignores the evidence of the early linguistic identity of logos and mythos (see Detienne 1986 and Adkins 1990), and it suggests that a modern Kantian or Hegelian dialectic has been transposed back into pre-history inappropriately. Recently Frank E. Reynolds and David Tracey (1990) have published papers from a University of Chicago Divinity School project organized explicitly to question the traditional opposition between logos and mythos within the fields of the philosophy of religion and com-parative religions.

Nonetheless the distinction between myth and logic is still accepted gen-erally, and many philosophers are irritated by the suggestion that, as contemporary philosophers such as Richard Rorty intimate, there are artis-tic or creative or mythic aspects in philosophical discourse today. Many professionals in my field have had something like the experience I had a few years ago when joining a faculty meeting to confront the issue of "cre-ationism" that was plaguing southern school systems (almost a decade later that plague has abated only slightly): a senior professor of philosophy was volubly upset when I suggested that there might be "mythic" aspects to scientific work in the state university. "I refuse to believe that we're like those primitives!" he stormed.

So when Stephen Daniel now considers it necessary to understand the role of myth *in* philosophy if we are to understand contemporary philo-sophical issues (1990, xi), I am most interested. And when Daniel goes on to speak of "the performance of meaning in mythic language," sounding much like writers on metaphor from the first half of this century, I am both surprised and delighted. Daniel suggests that myth does not just give objective information *about* something, but literally brings it into speech

(3–5), a position similar to the neo-Heideggerian positions of what was known in the 1960s and 1970s as the New Hermeneutic; instead of previous attempts to demonstrate permanently fixed theses by means of falsification principles, Daniel argues that in philosophical discourse "each performance is the immediate source of meaning" (9). Likewise Lynda Sexson argued recently [1990] that myth brings a particular *kind* of knowledge to speech, although I worry about that approach, since it sounds like the Kantian sequestering of the emotive-aesthetic that left that human faculty homeless within the technical-economic frames of the modern world, a world wherein the empirical, the participative, is devalued in the ruling, artificial, masculinist fantasy of objectivity. Part of the problem is that once a few types of myths are identified, "myth" is taken to refer only to stories of long ago or from somewhere else, and we fail to recognize the genuinely mythical aspects of recent, even postmodernist, societies.

Daniel emphasizes that we need not restrict our attempts to locate the metaphor-creative to the initial, primordial, cosmogonic, or originary, since *each myth-performance is itself a creative acting out, its discourse a bringing-to-speech*. Myths, Daniel suggests (5), display not how meaning once happened, but how it happens *now*. Myths frame the "grammar of the story" that allows for embeddings of meanings, and it is the awareness that the world is being importantly staged in myth that leads to our conservatism toward how a myth ought to be repeated (hence canons and scriptures and textbooks and religious seminaries). Of course Plato must exclude the poet/myth-maker from the normalized polis, because such a figure will always be reappropriating the traditional materials in unheard-of attacks on the commonplace. To read scriptures or to tell myths is always to call the present into question because it suggests that the contemporary is only one limited source of knowledge and meaning.

Myths represent crystallizations of revered societal meanings, but any single myth remains "a seedbed of symbolic forms" (Pavese 1989, vii), and symbols are gestures toward whole vibrating networks of intertextual significations: they are not merely algebraic integers in the premodern poet's allegorical toolkit. Myths are not passive objects, but *transformative*: "a properly mythic expression . . . opens the possibility that the relational or ontological character of the world might be changed" (Daniel 1990, 6). Myths and their interpretations can be *revolutionary*, then, and we see just why the official interpretations of religious or political myths entrench themselves so firmly, delimiting both the sorts of myths that can be told and how any given myth may be interpreted. In the progress of any war—of bullets and bombs, or of political or theological concepts—it becomes increasingly difficult to determine the incoming information: Is it propaganda from our side, or theirs? A reflection of the "real world" or a specious attempt to develop our adherence to a particular political interpretation?

Myth as Lie and as Science

One consequence of the growing postmodernist recognition that socially regulative standards and mythic scenarios are components of our socially constructed (but often hidden) value systems is that much of our society regards myths even more negatively than other creative literature. Indeed, James Hillman (1990, 225) observes that myths are regarded pejoratively in all sectors of our society except the academic! And Paula Gunn Allen notes how traditional American dictionary definitions of myth repetitiously refer the concept to a fictitious world that is contrasted rhetorically with the supposedly "real" world of scientific experience (alleged *vs.* factual, religious *vs.* natural, and others). No wonder "*myth* is synonymous with *lie*" for many people; "moreover it implies ignorance or a malicious intent to defraud" (Allen 1986, 102–3). Part of the reason for such mistrust derives from the claims made by positivists to recover the past, or the natural world, directly and abstractly. But the observer's impact on the observed is now acknowledged across the sciences, and new postpositivist models are widespread. Perhaps we may soon relinquish the inherent triumphalism that Allen observes underlying the metamyth of science that "imputes factualness to certain assumptions that form the basis of western perceptions without acknowledging that it does." (In chapter 1 I pointed to the role of other assumptions that have constituted the Enframing of modernist culture and contributed substantially to the series of exclusions of those occupying roles defined as inferior by the dominant culture.)

Contemporary epistemology across the disciplines now stresses the controlling if not stultifying role of research paradigms and/or the personal motivations of the researcher or the political influence contributed by an institution's needs to receive governmental research grants. Seldom before has our culture been so aware of the *extra*scientific factors that powerfully influence research aims, procedures, and results. Various metacriticisms have disclosed to us how rarely we are fully aware of the political values driving research programs, and James Hillman notes how our confidence wanes as we learn to recognize the arbitrary frames and perspectives that have determined our findings. It is first when we've developed a distance from a myth that we see it *as* an informing perspective—"a living myth is not recognized as myth until we step out of the certitude it affords" (Hillman 1990, 242). Many of the contributors to this volume clarify the myths that have remained unidentified or unemphasized as mythic in postmodernist American contexts: family values (Makarushka), political positions (Kochhar-Lindgren), a particular style of poeticizing that often excludes recent experimental developments (Lazer), racial/class/gender presuppositions (Ledbetter), the "artistic" nature of the soul's lifework (Noel), and the priority of certain graphic figures over others in ethics (Fisher).

But while it is always difficult to see one's own myths in operation, it seems especially so in today's certainty that "the latest is the best." As Edward Whitmont notes, "the modern myth is no longer sung by bards [but] has to be pieced together from the jottings of news commentators and editorial writers" (1982, 150). When in our own late-capitalist economy we consider ideas and aesthetic values as nonmaterial and hence less important than a Super Bowl advertisement or a Mack truck, we are expressing a mythic substrate that few of us ever question until our children make career decisions. Then we realize that poet or novelist offspring may not be very well situated to finance the declining days of their older parents, or that sometimes one must indeed make real sacrifices to the muses (who do not, the cynic in me observes, usually drive Cadillacs or BMWs) if a noncommercial career is what one's inner self requires.

The mythic substrate underlying the clique-talk of the mass media itself bears ideological values, bears them so effectively precisely because they come to seem "natural" or "historicized," as Roland Barthes emphasized repeatedly (1972): even the food recipes in the weekend newspaper supplement encode "necessities" such as the latest microwave oven or food processor. Like Barthes, Robert Jewett and John Lawrence, in *The American Monomyth*, identify as a common feature of myth its penchant "not to reveal its presence to those it enthralls" (1989, 94). Particularly in the contemporary West, these authors suggest, we are enthralled by "the myth of mythlessness" that portrays that society as having transcended myth ultimately.

Analyzing the TV series *Star Trek*, Jewett and Lawrence point out how the myth of mythlessness is trafficked across the galaxy: every episode

assumes "that meaning is purely of this world, any threshold to mysterious, transcendent reality firmly denied" (11). A similar construct is the
euhemeristic explanation, such as von Daniken's *Chariot of the Gods*
(1968), that figures treated by ancient cultures as transcendental gods actually must have been space travelers from another planetary system, or de
Santillana and von Dechend's claim (1969) that myth is misunderstood
science or astrology. Lynda Sexson's refurbishing of the sacred *vs.* secular
dichotomy that I reviewed in chapter 1, however, might lead in a different
direction, toward a concept of the sacred aspects of life that need not be
comprehended as antithetical to scientific reasoning, but as its complement.

Jewett and Lawrence point out (20) that behind *Star Trek* a consistent
pseudoempiricism portrays the very "scientific" assumptions themselves as
functioning mythically. They point out how the controlling power of intellectual paradigms and models is doubly reinforced when it is not self-
conscious. Often its rule is experienced first when someone attempts to
achieve new knowledge not encompassed by the paradigm, as many truly
creative scientists have learned to their professional dismay: often break-
through ideas and data have been excluded strictly from the standard disciplinary journals and societies, so that their proponents have had to develop
their own subdisciplines before their work is accepted. Or the power of the
scientific myth becomes manifest at the points where commercial persuasion is exerted most extensively—as in advertising, where everything from
deodorants and detergents to over-the-counter medicines is presented
attractively by a good-looking male "scientist" or "physician," wearing
dark-rimmed glasses and a white lab coat.

Just using the term "the scientific myth" may seem to represent a confusion of that mythos-logos distinction that we looked at earlier, but it is
useful to characterize the way scientific values have themselves become as
ahistorical and transcendent as religious values were earlier. Anthropologist
Henry A. Selby, contributing to a symposium on Myth and Reason, noted
that while he had trouble with the use of *myth* by literary specialists, in
contrast to categories a field-worker ethnologist like himself would use,
"science" actually *functions* for contemporary society the way myths of
traditional societies do: "Listeners and tellers pay rapt attention to science.
They take it seriously and believe it applies to them in their lives, is
timeless, and encodes profound truths about the human condition" (Selby
1973, 161; see also Toulmin 1970). In his remarkable statement, Selby
continues his comparison by observing that

science is an elaborate ideology based in unprovable axioms about the world—and so is myth. Science involves the classification of discrete categories of events and invents categorical distinctions for its own purposes; so does myth. Science involves the elaboration of very formal systems, the invention of languages that relate classes of events, and so does myth. The distinction between myth and science lies in the way these things are done. Science is more highly constrained than myth. A scientist rests his case on the assertion that there exists a high probability that relationships which he obtains ideologically will have empirical correspondences in the real world. A myth makes no such claims; in fact myths constantly play with relationships (like the "mad scientist") and speculate about things that were, but are no more, things that cannot be, and things that never were, but are. There *is* reason in myth, just as there is reason in science. It is not the same reasoning, but nevertheless it is reason.

Selby notes that many television viewers abroad refused to accept the U.S. moon landing as something actually happening. To them it could only be a myth in the sense of a fraud or a manipulation; but on the other hand, "we smiled, because we believed in the moon landing. It was a reality to us, and we shared in Walter Cronkite's tearful awe at the mystery of the knowledge and technology that made it possible. Cronkite was creating modern myth before our eyes," whereas for viewers elsewhere, accustomed to nationalistic self-aggrandizement through false televisual image-making, only ideology was being displayed, and there really could be no living human beings on the surface of the moon itself.

The Ideological and the Commercial

Such an example helps to disclose how easily politically motivated scenarios are thought to replace verifiable events, but it is always easier to sight political-ideological perspectives in a culture other than one's own, where the traces of ideologies are almost always hidden or assimilated to nationalist ideals. Once the ideological system is fully operative, just about everything imaginable can be coded in its terms; I have in mind particularly a news item filed by the Associated Press (Rochester [New York] *Democrat and Chronicle*, 25 June 1990, 6A) accompanying a photograph of an Iranian family mourning its relatives who had been killed in an earthquake in Manjil:

> An anti-American newspaper in Iran said yesterday [that] the United States is partly to blame for the death of tens of thousands of people in last week's earthquake.
>
> The "criminal role of America in Iran's past became evident once again in the recent earthquake," the *Jomhuri Islami* said.

The anti-American newspaper stops short of suggesting that America *caused* the earthquake, but it blames the country for "plundering Iran's oil and other resources," an act that evidently prevented Iran from pursuing urban development projects and other renovations that might have reduced earthquake damages. The United States's role in this natural disaster is then conflated with its role in international politics:

> "If the United States has real humanitarian objectives and intends to help the Iranian nation, it should do only one thing, stop hatching plots," the newspaper said.
>
> It called on Iranians to reject relief offers by the United States.

And ideology is especially evident when a society brags about its accomplishments, as in an official account of Chinese climbers reaching the summit of the highest mountain in the world in 1960: "Summing up our conquest of Everest, we must in the first place attribute our victory to the leadership of the Communist Party and the unrivalled superiority of the socialist system of our country" (Bernbaum 1990, 41; Bernbaum cites parallels from ancient times when the emperor would climb T'ai Sahn, the most important peak in China, in order to perform sacrifices that would witness to the success of particular dynasties).

Today the ideological is often hidden in the commercial, as I noted in looking through a recent catalogue of art books from an American university press. There the categories of the field reflect very clear professional boundaries that are itemized partly by geographical distinctions, and partly by cultural: European Art and American Art rate five and six pages of offerings respectively, followed by Crafts and Textiles with three. But then suddenly "American" reappears: *Native* American Art books are listed on three pages, and the catalogue then includes four pages on a combination of Asian, African, and *Latin* American Art books. Such hidden ideological notions often make another culture (even on one's own continent) seem inferior or less influential. That they are part of commerce becomes obvious when laissez-faire capitalism ships out its piecework to nationals of other countries who can be devalued as human beings by paying them less than a quarter of what an American worker would be paid: only a strong ideological myth featuring American supremacy could support such a situation—which is justified subsequently by the economic system so that it seems "natural." Some of Kochhar-Lindgren's experiences in contemporary Europe in chapter 2 illustrate some of the ways such designations are increasingly called into question along with concepts such as communism or democracy.

Developing Mythological Muscles

Learning to recognize the ideological substrate is part of the sort of intellectual muscle building that the liberal arts portion of a collegiate education ought to foster. We have yet to look more closely at how the hermeneutical biceps learn to flex around the concept of myth. I have trouble, for instance, with Selby's remarks: I would not say that Walter Cronkite was "creating . . . myth" but that his awe and excitement about the moon landing indicated that we were assuredly in the presence of a mythic epiphany, a numinous site where there was an acute awareness of extraordinary reality even if not numinous in terms of a revelation of personal deity, as usually conceived in Western religion. It is important to recognize sites of sensitivity to and self-awareness of myths in the culture, as we develop contemporary mythographic skills appropriate to our postmodern self-consciousness, which is primarily nontheistic and must include the pop star Madonna along with Our Lady.

While Jewett and Lawrence call for a "technomythic critical theory" to train us to see through and behind all cultural products, I would highlight first the practice of all the various hermeneutics of deceit that give us important perspectival handles on such products of civilizations: I mean the *Marxian-materialist* critique that discloses the power relations and vested economic interests lodged even in the supposedly transcendental realms of the arts, education, and religion; *Freudian* interpretive theory, calling to our conscious attention that both individual and cultural materials reflect deeply rooted unconscious psychological drives we'd prefer to forget about; and *linguistic* analysis, which shows us repeatedly the relativity of values—they exist not absolutely in some atemporal essence-chamber, but within networks of moral and historical choices that lead one generation to shout fervently about the beauty of shedding American blood for the sake of the world, and the next to burn their draft-registration cards. Two other hermeneutics of deceit are the *feminist*, which has disclosed the implicit masculocentrist biases of our scientistic and hierarchal "objectivity" and hence requires new epistemologies as well as nonsexist ethics; and the *rhetorical*, which enables us to recover a notion of the constructedness of social discourse that is parallel to what art history and iconography clarify for visual representations.

These various interpretive perspectives disclose to us the sites of production and consumption of myth as they direct attention to the specific historical and socioeconomic bases of our common assumptions, our ideologies, and our modern allergies to something like internationalism, for instance. It is not at all accidental that we trust statistics and popular-opinion polls—but we should be aware that our populist rhetorics now reverses millennia of belief in eternal laws and divine interventions into history that were considered to have occurred entirely independently of human belief or will. A cartoon in the *Utne Reader* captured the irony of our situation: she reads him a newspaper account stating that 90 percent of people no longer believe that statistical surveys matter! It is difficult to sustain trust in statistical sampling of whatever sort when even the U.S. census is administered so politically and ineptly that it has to be corrected by statistical guesswork.

However we design mythographic skills, I emphasize the importance of ongoing education in the realms of the symbolic and the iconographic. Although our culture is quick to learn the latest mathematical or business calculus, we become impatient when confronted by the long process of gaining an education in the subtle symbolic and allusive elements of cultural history. But knowing such culture-factual elements means knowing the tools by means of which the *prima materia* is now reshaped in particular realizations, the repeated archetypal shapes that are the ways particular oikotypes (or ectypes, or epichoric, local manifestations) structure meaning and significance. We have to admit that there is some wisdom in those awful repressive suggestions about a minimum cultural literacy, but one hopes that fundamental educational competence can be conveyed as well as literacy in our symbolic heritages, and alongside the linguistic-structuralist knowledge of how combinations of canonical knowings are regulated and shaped rhetorically by professional schools of education and boards of professional or disciplinary examiners. Such knowledges are what make us aware of just what is truly new and creative, and what merely second-rate and derivatively repetitious. It is *not*—advertisers appealing to our snobbish self-centeredness to the contrary—just a matter of some sort of innate "taste." And it is still important to be able to speak of a good or bad work of art, so long as one stipulates the historical and social perspectives from which the work is being valued. The eye and ear can be trained quite as successfully as those bulging pectorals produced by the latest and most expensive muscle-building equipment, but school systems always cut back on education in the arts before they ever eliminate a staff position on the phys-ed staff (one of the reasons many persons today have never been exposed to serious classical music; they are often delighted to discover its formal discipline, structure, and adventurousness).

Tracking Myths in Societies

To say that one lives within the myth of the state, the myth of macho masculinity or Debbie Sorority, of the postmodern, of the welfare state, of reincarnation, of the papacy, of science, of mathematics, of the team sport of Ultimate Frisbee, or the myth of the overhead cam: to say that one lives within any one of those myths is to mean something different from saying that one lives within any of the others. But in this case the term *myth* can become so diffuse that we must constantly redefine it. Indeed, now there is a whole industry devoted to criticizing Joseph Campbell's lax and contradictory uses of the term, and major literary figures puzzle through just what myth means in structural and linguistic terms as it infuses whole bodies of literature—I think especially of Italo Calvino's sensitive reflections on the superstructural, even mechanistic, armatures of myths behind literary expression (1986), or of Eric Gould's *Mythical Intentions in Modern Literature* (1981), with its emphasis upon "mythicity" instead of upon thematic chronicles of myth-in-literature.[2]

But few would quarrel with my suggestion that there are myths and then there are myths, in the multiple senses that there are myths that function as overarching worldview determinants, myths and value judgments and data-rich conclusions that determine the national budget; and there are myths in terms of the ways our multistoried lives refract Aphrodites and Madonnas, and Paul Bunyans and Mercurys, and George Washingtons and—perhaps even—Ronald Reagans and Norman Schwartzkopfs and Arnold Schwarzeneggers. Different types of myths, and different types of realizations or appropriation. One must recognize the particular situational context in which a myth, mythic fragment, theme, or image appears in any given instance, since the generic constraints of the context may have considerable influence upon the meaning/s.

Pulling together the several references here to the nature and manifestation of myth, the various ways myth means or signifies may fill a typology like the following:

1. *Overarching cultural frames* that determine perspectives, perceptions, and worldviews (such as the evolutionary-progress model of the industrialized West; unconscious gender modeling; projected role choices and aspirations; or the relating of nature to technology).

2. Passing *references* to mythic figures, elements, themes, traditional mythic metaphors; for example: "just as Herakles develops a new Greek technology in diverting a river to clean out the shit-filled stables, so the Californian research and development companies are . . ."

3. *Language* used unself-consciously *that* yet *lodes a mythic background*—words like *edenic, narcissistic, empyrean* (see Asimov 1961), or used self-consciously in the traditional myth-in-literature patterns (for a bibliography of the many studies, see Doty 1986 and Bodkin 1934).

4. Fabula or *plot* (as for instance Campbell's monomyth of the hero [1956], or the plot types catalogued by Frye—see Liszka 1989, 129). Here the tendency seems always to develop an algebra, such as Vladimir Propp's list of functions in Russian folktales or the formulas devised by Claude Lévi-Strauss for the mythical armature of the Americas.

5. *Rhetorical structures:* for instance "the city set on a hill," or the Western Frontier studied by specialists in American Literature and more recently in critical rhetorics (see for example Rushing 1986; Homans 1977 is excellent on showing the bare bones of the relevant psychological and rhetorical images in the classical cowboy movies).

6. *Archetypal* patterns *vs. local manifestations:* the trail of reactions to repeated historical situations faced by many different people, rather than innate psychic preconditioning and structure; "recurrent pattern" or "type," a ratio of regularly manifested relations that Hillman (1990, 240) refers to as the invariant relationship between things in the same ecological field. I find it instructive to return repeatedly to Lauter's archetypal approach to cultural analysis (1984) that works deductively from a database of

a thousand woman artists, rather than inductively from the abstracted predefinition of a timeless archetype.

7. *Ideal constructs:* the use of mythicized images for later reappropriation. For example: "The myth of the Reformation is that the Scriptures provide, in the midst of a corrupt society and a decadent Church, a model one can use to reform both society and the Church" (de Certeau 1984, 144).

8. *Mythoclastic attitude:* explicitly distancing oneself from a practice or belief: for example, a Marxist writing an exposé entitled "The Myth of Free-Market Capitalism," or explicitly refuting a mythic perspective that is otherwise taken very seriously.

9. *Falsely held belief,* epidemic false beliefs, called *pseudodoxia epidemica* in the seventeenth century (Wetzels 1973, 160), but now indicated by the pejorative use of the term *ideology,* as when speaking of the Nazi misappropriation of Teutonic nature mythology, or in racial and cultural stereotyping. Terry Eagleton's books on aspects of ideology remind us repeatedly that like myth, ideology is what we consider other people to possess (see 1991, 4, 50), and Michel Foucault's sociohistorical analyses have articulated how seldom participants within an ideological "discourse" are aware of their complicity with it.

10. *Deracinated or desacralized mythic relic:* when "belief withdraws from a myth and leaves it almost intact, but without any role, transformed into a document" (de Certeau 1984, 181). Perhaps this is not so much a "type" as a way in which myths are regarded on a later social trajectory. I'd place here many of the biblical stories, such as those reflecting millennia-old scientific and medical views that are only laughable in any literal sense today, although they may still provide sustaining stories for various believers. It is always important to recognize that a relic may be simultaneously revered and rejected or ignored by close neighbors in a particular population.[3]

Ethical Interpretation/s and the Canon/s

We have seen repeatedly in the essays in this book the importance of hermeneutical or interpretive perspectives and ideologies. In addition to a wide range of ways in which we understand ideology or myth to be present in societies, and the levels of viability according to which one credits or denies significance to any particular mythic element, we must recognize further the importance of myth *selection, transmission* and canonization, *interpretation*, and *signification*. Myths are not transmitted because they are ephemeral; they are transmitted because they are considered extremely important, and hence we must ask what leads to the demise of an effective myth or why previously weak myths become powerful once again—as for instance when Peter Homans (1977) explores why it was that in the 1950s movie Westerns that had been associated previously with adolescent escapist fantasies such as the dime novel came to dominate the American entertainment media. How mythic patterns surface, and whether in only a tiny portion of the population or as major cultural mythos, is largely the result of the *paramythological* interpretation or signifying—hermeneutical guidelines established to restrict the independence of the myths—that always forms the canonical context of the transmission, its ideological limits.

Perhaps especially in a postmodern society such as ours that is marked by a stern self-conscious ironic detachment, the interpretive determination of the meaning becomes even more important than the material itself. Faced with an nation infuriated that President Reagan would honor the Nazi cemetery at Bittberg, Germany, the governmental censors insisted that network TV camera tripods be stationed in such a manner that no reference to the historical nature of the site would be evident. Only a few years later, President Bush's administration put similar caps on the public's right to information: "Weeks before the [Persian Gulf] war started, clear-cut plans were made for supervising press movement and reporting, thus determining the kind of coverage and the channels through which information, especially TV images, would flow" (Goethals 1991, 10; cf. Rushing 1986 on Reagan's suppression of negative reactions to his Star Wars project by many scientists).

We are surrounded today by mythic resources—the low-cost paperback revolution sometimes seems to be the twentieth-century cultural equivalent of the printing press, and now there are the videodisk and hypertext resources—and what comes to matter is not the *availability* of stories but the selection of the few that become especially operational, one's effective canon within the (literary or mythic or scriptural) canons. The issue grows crucial when a culture like ours becomes extremely diverse and disjointed: I've long given up on finding texts (even cinematic or televisual resources) shared by all my students, coming as they do from all the schools and divisions of a contemporary culturally diverse university. Perhaps the most one can hope for now is a similarity of approach, a growing-together in our manners of reference, as we shuffle through a raft of sources and the several paramythological methods for interpreting them. When occasionally today something like "critical theory" appears, a number of individuals are able to speak the same language across the academic continental divides. More usually we experience academic disciplines as dividing us from each other, so that unless one studies or teaches in several parts of the university, one can locate few dialogue partners except for the purposes of negotiating unintegrated general education ("core" curriculum) courses or divisional graduation requirements.

Clearly there are valuational, ethical aspects to the choice of texts in curricular issues, as well as in their interpretation; only if the textbook canons of the public schools remain as open as possible will we assure that important cultural voices are not excluded merely because they are gay or nonwhite or from another cultural heritage. Nor can we ignore the political and ideological aspects of transmission and interpretation, since always the sorts of myths and perspectives to which we have been referring convey cultural values, even if in condensed, transvalued, displaced, or distorted versions. Liszka notes that myths "provide a set of lenses which focus, invert, distort, obscure, and distance the culture of which the myth is part" (1989, 14–15). For example Lynda Sexson points out (1990, 79) that we dare no longer follow the ahistoricizing paths that the popularizer Joseph Campbell takes when he retells myths in a manner that ignores the value systems of their historical and social contexts, or as I have observed previously, when his own predilection for Kundalini Yoga leads him to incorrect characterizations about the repressive qualities of Western monotheisms. We may no longer fantasize that the old stories Campbell retells are lacking political baggage. Likewise we must recognize that there are ideostories such as those about Mother Earth (138, 142) that can have negative, shadow sides as well as positive: the Earth can be thought of as a totally forgiving creature who will always be there for us to harvest, and it will recover automatically from being raped repeatedly. I am impressed when the author of a comprehensive textbook in psychology of religion begins and ends his massive volume remarking that "*how* a person is religious and what the ramifications of such a faith may be" (Wulff 1991, 638) is more important than any particular doctrines, as our civilization faces the "unprecedented crisis" (1) of the worldwide ecological nightmare that we will confront within only a few years.

Looking Ahead: Mythic Pictures of the Future

If mythical references to Mother Earth draw after them whole attitudes toward the planet, there are also weighty values lurking in the simplest forms of folk diction. Frequently I urge people to read an analytical essay by the folklorist Alan Dundes that was originally published in 1969, "Thinking Ahead: A Folkloristic Reflection of the Future Orientation in American Worldview" (1980, 69–85). The essay is one of those gems whose case is built gradually and solidly and in the terms of the claims it makes, namely that Americans are uniquely oriented toward the future and against the past. Using a series of dichotomies listed by Dundes, I can summarize much of what I am developing; in each case the second term surfaces throughout our public language as the favored term: past/future; before/after; backward/forward; behind/ahead; beginning/end; old/new; tradition/original (72; I have not documented each occasion here and in the next paragraph, where I rely on Dundes's analysis).

Americans are end-oriented, anticipating the future, savoring the new and essentially repudiating the past, looking forward to the next generation rather than asking about the achievements of the previous: all in all "the best is yet to come" and "there's a better day acomin'." Prediction is all-important, and even fiction has a special category of futuristic speculative or "science" fiction (a category, by the way, whose volumes account for the largest number of book sales in America). One hopes future research will bear out the present analysis, but as you might guess I'd have to conclude here, Only Time Will Tell!

Such a mythical future orientation is fostered in America by residual Calvinism as well as by social Darwinism. In his 1988 Memorial Lecture at the Society for Values in Higher Education, "The Modernist Myth Exposed," Stephen Crites analyzes the way the Euro-American view of progressive development of the social order functions in our culture as an implicit *religious* conviction. Crites notes that a powerful myth serves many different and even contradictory purposes (1990, 6), even when the culture is playing at metamyth or the myth-of-mythlessness discussed above, in which case, instead of being a major harmonic, "it sings in your blood" (7). He continues: "The modernist myth may not precisely *sing* in the blood, but it murmurs there, tacitly shaping the imagination."

In fact it is an important part of the modernist myth to be tacit or ironic and antimythical, to lodge all ultimacy within purely human competencies (as I have suggested above and Crites addresses, 9). It is part of our usual modern argument against the mythic dimensions of society as such, part of the approach that supports the turn away from the primitive, the under-developed, to emphasize what seems to be our mythlessness. We now recognize that such an approach has left hidden the many political assump-tions that have led the United States to its outrageous Manifest-Destinying across the hemispheres, a policy that has led to worldwide chaos in many of our lives and those of the nations we have felt obliged to make more like us. A mythic worldview oriented toward the future and against the past drives a culture already impatient with yesterday's products, and suggests that even more of the planet must be transformed according to our own model of consumption and destruction: if you need to know about the correlation of low beef prices and the destruction of the South American rainforest ecologies, you may be physically situated in the twentieth century, but your values stem from the expansionist images of the nineteenth.

Throughout this essay I have urged greater self-awareness, more thor-ough acknowledgment of the ideological-political bases of our application and use of mythic materials. We live in postmodernist, not modernist times, and the dwelling place of irony needs to be resettled by explicitness today, especially as we face the issue of survival in the twenty-first century. Crites suggests helpfully in this regard that "myths are projective, not primarily retrojective. The energy of the myth comes from its vision of the future, for which the myth prepares us by giving us a past appropriate to it and a story line strong enough to join the two" (1990, 12). We need desperately to tell the right stories that sustain life in order to replace our terrifying technologies of waste and destruction so that our vision of the future may be imaged and narrated strongly enough to overcome the pri-vatistic greed into which most of Western capitalism has fallen. We are about to enter a period in which myth will be cited against myth, future projections against others, and poetic explorations of alternate futures simply must become a spiritual athletics we all exercize if we are to salvage the wreck that modernist politics bequeathed us.

The Opening Up of Mythic Poesis

In my critique of aspects of our contemporary worldview, I have stressed various dysfunctional features; in this section I argue for the functional role of the poet, both as writer and as reader, as a role of mythic re-creation, which means returning to the theme of cosmogony engaged earlier. Poesis—the Greek term "making" *(poiēsis)* which is generally used nowadays to refer to the whole process of fictive creativity—is the process of finding meaning for the contemporary world by the process of metaphoring. Metaphoric poesis is the construction of new meanings from out of the meanings already available, so that it is often reconstructive or corrective. Poesis is a regulative yoga, that is, an ordering-yoking of the fragments of our lives, a speaking-together of our selves in ways that give us courage and hope. Of course I do not mean to restrict poesis to the professional poet or writer—rather, my drift throughout this essay has been toward a postmodernist posture that treats the ordinary, daily centers of life as being just as significant as the rarefied marginal discourses of the officially recognized "poet" or "artist." The "writer" stands in for us all insofar as s/he is representative of the late-twentieth-century person, quilting together cultural values in postmodernist America that only begin to articulate the lineaments of the twenty-first century.

What is such a "writer" for, if not to link together our aspirations and our sorrows, our ecstasy and our tragedy into patterns that transcend the merely personal? In the process the writer reestablishes and refounds the language from the disconnected bits that have become only randomly chaotic: hence the process of writing or interpreting is a creative process of ordering analogous to the cosmogonic feats of the primordial times, and it becomes difficult to avoid the "religious" quality of writing or myth making as such: as we saw in chapter 1, *religare* (from which English *religion* most likely is derived) also means etymologically tying things into a *ligature* or bundle of meanings.

Perhaps that is why so many creation myths feature creation by the divine word, thought, dream, laughter, or fantasy: what one learns from such myths is not the status of particular sets of deities but how to function as a creator, how to speak into coherence those bits of language mud, those discarded shards of metaphor, that can only be combined at *this* time and place. That task is uniquely one's own, and simultaneously a function of the language and cultural worldview at any given moment. Contradictory valences, to be sure, but I think of Claude Lévi-Strauss speaking about his vast mythemic analysis as having been merely an occasion, a site for myth to pass through; or of the interpretations by which Roland Barthes, Michel Foucault, and others have made us reconsider entirely what we mean by an "author." Certainly it is no longer anything like the Romantic notion of individual passion and enthusiastic creation "out of nothing" emphasized since the Romantics' version of the "creative" artist/poet whose primary contribution lay in going against the mainstream in devising challenges to the status quo and whose *difference* rather than typicality was most emphasized.[4] Oddness rather than typicality: we continue to talk about the poet/artist as the ideal role in Western culture although even children know that any other professional person will be paid infinitely more in annual income. Yet nonetheless the poet-interpreter-writer remains valued in terms of selecting and emphasizing the cultural values that are stitched together into meaningful wholes. Poets and religionists find ways of correlating individualities and wholes; they integrate and interphase singular events, images, and significances within the encompassing perspectival frameworks (Enframings) that any one generation or culture defines as "human." Daniel notes that "it is the functioning of the metaphoric expression within the larger myth that determines meaningfulness" (1990, 11). We ennarrate significances by revoicing mythemes whose significance derives from their situations in the cultural myth as a whole, either by telling them on in new guises or by the equally poetic work of interpretation and criticism, a work that need not overwhelm a text so much as it can bring its living depths back to view in a later context.

What poetic languages do that makes them parallel in function to creation myths is *to open up*, to make available for participation ways of experience in the world that are, first of all, uniquely one's own, and yet secondly reflect the psychic and notional parameters of any given culture's moment on the historical stage. Obviously the metaphoring artist must find ways of sharing her or his images: the images cannot be too odd or no one understands them because they spring from outside the frames of received meaning. And she or he must find ways of managing publication or sales ("consumption") even when only certain dominant styles are replicated endlessly. The problem is easily sighted in cinema, where the small-budget movie may be the only venue available to directors whose image making deviates even slightly from the establishment pictures of the megabuck studios.

Hank Lazer (1988, 1990a) points out a further problem: many theoreticians and critics who complain about the banality of contemporary poetry, the lack of true creativity, are either quite ignorant of the many new directions in poetry such as the "language poets," or are beholden to the small numbers of genres of poetry that dominate schools and writing workshops. Hence the system regulates the types and range of poetry that get published in the important presses and journals, and revisionist poetry newsletters, cassettes, and anthologies have created an American poetry underground (see for instance the publication *Poetry USA* or the many 'zines, wildly printed small journals and chapbooks often available only by subscription).

Here then we come back to the threat of the poet already evident to Sokrates' society: the poet/writer threatens to unleash some of the primordial powers of language that have been shunted aside when metaphors became fossilized dictionary language. If myth brings coherence, order, and pragmatic-artistic *technē* to the chaos elements, the threat is always that by undoing or revising the myth, one might release those world-shaping elements once more. As certain fictions are sacralized and canonized as sacred myths, they are worshiped for having brought coherence, order, a sort of protective technology that shunts aside the elemental electrical potency of the chaos elements. Reacting against new appropriations and interpretations, the conservative will always suggest that there can be only *one* appropriate type of literature, *one* authorized sort of painting, *one* type of photography, *one* school of classical music—and the list grows on and on as the raw powers of the originative chaos get solidified and desacralized in restrictive blue-serge-suit hierarchies, poet laureates, and appointments to endowed chairs.

The Wounds of Our Narcissism

But mythologically speaking, to reject reappropriation and revision, to strive for unending sameness, is to strive like Narkissos, the figure whose flower was a synonym for narcotics, for death. Richard Underwood (1965) points out that coming to recognize that change and not sameness rules existence is perhaps the *fourth* great narcissistic wound that the modern world has had to face. Traditionally, as Freud sketched them, the first wound was that caused by Copernicus, when we discovered that we weren't the center for much of anything except a pallid second-rate dead reflective moon, that indeed (as we've learned subsequently) there are galaxies upon galaxies out there and within us, and that any moment of stasis or motion is fully relative to the whole shebang.

The second narcissistic wound was that of Darwin, when we learned that our precious self-confidence that human beings were ranked at the top of the orders of being ignored a very long period of evolutionary development that may well continue beyond the human species. Unfortunately the traditional religious interpretation of Genesis 1:28b—"Be fruitful and multiply, and fill the earth and subdue it; and have dominion over the fish of the sea and over the birds of the air and over every living thing that moves upon the earth" (NRSV)—has left us raping and dirtying and destroying the very earth we might want to dominate.

The third narcissistic hurt derives from Freud's own teaching, namely the recognition that the noblest products of culture are but excrescences of unresolved childhood sexual traumata and other psychic neuroses; that no matter how hard, with all moral rectitude, we will to do anything at all, we are less masters of our own minds than tools of instincts incredibly older than our own limited being. Both Freud and Karl Marx taught us always to be suspicious of *surfaces*, which frequently distort the underlying realities, the latent causes beneath the manifest images or acts. Even if neither strict Freudian nor orthodox Marxist schools are widely influential today, this suspiciousness of the apparently obvious has affected every interpretive approach now in vogue.

Underwood suggests that a fourth narcissistic wound is that of Hermes, that of the double sight and multiple vision of the fictions by which we connect or yoke together the meanings that sustain us and so keep us from shooting ourselves (see also Doty 1990c). It is the hermetic insight that nuclear power can also mean atomic death, that devoting our own economy to self-aggrandizement and bigger and better American cars means at the same time destroying the standard of living in other parts of the international economy. The hermetic hermeneutics drives home how preaching constantly and simultaneously against sexual pleasure, abortion, and birth-control education can leave a state such as my own with an infancy death rate higher than that of many so-called Third World nations, although the arguments are couched in the obfuscating rhetoric of the "right to life" (anti-women's-freedom) movement. One wishes for more attentive readers of Margaret Atwood's chilling novel *The Handmaid's Tale* (1985), but at least Makarushka and Fisher in this volume provide some of the necessary double-sighting that trains one to see the ethical importance of the *images* (family values or pro/antiabortion scenarios) that are never merely "aesthetic" in the sense of nonmaterial, free-floating, or values-free.

The hermetic wound is also the wounding of the progress model driven by self-help ego psychology, by the specious moralism of the "Just say no!" variety, by all the modernist projects that elevate the individual at the expense of the commonwealth—it should surprise no one that fewer than a third of American voters cast congressional ballots, when we've no notion any longer of how a congress might develop policies cooperatively instead of merely providing a showplace for competing individual careerists, each of whom has become a master of the individualism campaigns that claims she or he is "different" from any other competitor! Instead of being a role model for the rest of the world, we've become the depressive example of how a society can lose a sense of *Mitmenschlichkeit* (basing society upon shared humane values) to the extent of becoming too absorbed in spending money to recognize that our proportional income has become less, not more, equivalent across the population. The get-rich-quick dream is still present—but it is never for the improvement of the living conditions of the masses, only for the solitary entrepreneur whose ego feeds off dominating others. The ego, however, is a fragile instrument in contrast to the soul of a culture. The isolate individual has about as much sense of history as your neighbor's zucchini plants. What happens to me, to you, to others, has significance not as individual seizures of power but as collectively, archetypally, significant across the span of human history.

Why has there been such an interest in Joseph Campbell's interviews and lectures? At least one reason is that the materials to which Campbell pointed repeatedly (if not always Campbell's own proindividualistic stance) are materials of the world psyche. They send one back not just to one's own mother, but to Cosmic Mother; not just to the entrepreneur's cleverness but to the notion of Cosmic Fate; not just to the issue of private masturbation but to the *hieros gamos*, the Sacred Marriage, which celebrates the union of truly transcendent principles. Our tellings of these mythic figures and images will have to be our own transformations and modifications, but the important storehouse of traditional imagery is still the long-range repository of cultural significance that we ignore only at the risk of being tyrannized by the superficialities of the merely contemporary or popular.

Matthew Fox's report on the revisioning and reenacting of the Stations of the Cross devotional that was originally devised by Francis of Assisi in the thirteenth century describes a fresh re-creation for our own time. The Findhorn ritual Fox discusses reflected long-familiar religious behavior and

symbolism—most Catholic schools, hospitals, or churches set aside a meditation area wherein the Stations are represented by niches or wall plaques.
Yet the content was entirely new, the symbolic referents inescapably contemporary (Chernobyl, AIDS, battered wives, and so on). Such rituals
indicate responsible use of traditional religious images to interpret contemporary pictures of cultural values.

Polysemic Remythologizing

Finding our way through? Connecting the mythic past time with the
existential contemporary? Another place I would search for examples would
be South American literature: so much of the "magical realism" of recent
fictionists has opened our eyes to the depth dimensions of *wonder*—Can
anyone remain untouched by the cloud of butterflies hovering around the
old patriarch in Gabriel García Márquez's *One Hundred Years of Solitude*
(1970)? Butterflies are the Greek visualizations of the psyche or soul, and
sometimes on funeral vases they are led by Hermes, the guide of souls
between the worlds of the living and the dead. In Márquez the butterflies
indicate symbolically that there's still a lot of life left in the terminal years
and wisdom of our elders where much of the society finds only emptiness
and death.

I'd use the example yet further to suggest that the butterflies are not
there casually or "decoratively" the way people often dismiss fantasy and
science fiction tropes. Márquez has reiconified, remythologized, an ancient
figure that is allowed in his fiction to recreate even for our so-sophisticated
audiences a moment of epiphany. The symbol had effectively died: Márquez revivifies it, and that's one task of the creative writer generally, bring-
ing the gods back to meaningful reemplacements in our stories—as Guy
Davenport put it, "we must learn to question what gods have come to dwell
among us in the internal combustion engine, the cash register, and the
computer" (1981, 24).

Throughout this concluding essay I have been reiconifying and asking
about resacralizing. When a culture has moved as rapidly as ours has, there
must be periods of recollection and rediscovery. For us that means in
particular reconnection with the feminine, with the tangible and the material, with that which is not abstractly regulatable, but insists upon the

necessity of working out an ethics fully responsive to each situation. I've kept diverting attention away from a simple answer to this or that, but instead have piled up layers upon layers in what seems to me to be precisely the mythological idiom, since myths, like old-fashioned attics, do not simplify but complexify—Bernard Sergent reminds us that "the essence of mythology is of course to use polysemous signs, meaningful on more than one level" (1986, 89). Mythic symbols point to momentary clearings of narrative coherence, but only within the framework of the narrative requirement of human existence that makes us learn our own stories, makes us learn why we often reject others' too soon, makes us sensitive to the cosmogonic moments in the newspaper no less than in the poetry chapbooks.

Of course Bill Moyers's highly edited mass-media presentations of figures such as Joseph Campbell will appeal to audiences bored to tears with simplistic explanations they know seldom reveal the full truth. Of course Campbell will be listened to when he speaks to significant images and issues usually trivialized or ignored—as when he points out that mythic figures do not all have orthodontically perfect smiles but that some possess terrifying visages that can blind one in an instant. I wish he had acknowledged more frequently the shadow sides of many of the mythological images and themes he discussed (on the shadow see Rushing and Frentz 1989 and Frentz and Rushing 1990), and made clearer just how one might bridge today the gaps between the individual and the corporate. Furthermore, Campbell himself seemed monotheistic in returning over and over again to a select group of myths in ways that left me cold. But for many persons today Campbell's materials open the many polytheistic doors of the mythic worlds. And he made it clear that it takes dedicated labor of the heart and mind to operate within a mythically rich culture; it takes concentration and repetition and studious attention to the past that now gestures toward us as promise, not merely as constraint. And in this case I'll sing a more complimentary ode for Joe, since Campbell's own religious meditation, he mentioned several times, was studying and underlining books! His famous "Follow your bliss" message, he stipulated (cited in Doty 1990b) meant the sort of study one gets in a college liberal-arts curriculum. Never a trivializer, Campbell insisted on publishing the cultural representations and images alongside the myths and his own analyses. His language is thick and rich, and the concepts and images he discusses complex and textured.

Singing Together Our Own Landscapes

However ours is a generation dominated by full-page advertisements on which maybe one or two words stand out over the picture of a box of cigarettes: BUY! or SWITCH! or NEW! A recent advertisement for men's cologne, in a women's clothing magazine, consisted solely of the torso of a young man, nude from just above the penis to the chin, and a single word—the name of the cologne.[5] Can we expect iconographic or mythic sophistication from audiences trained to respond to such stripped-down postmodernist images? Or to "sound bites" of politicians carefully staged to last no more than twenty seconds? Or to the trivializing of cultural values and struggles in something as insipid and shallow as USA Today?

Contemporary analysis looks at the construction of meaning in social contexts in ways that were perhaps not possible before: we see the multiple determinings and overdeterminings, the gradual attribution and removal of ideological significance. But that analysis needs to be supplemented by pushing people away from the USA Today shucks toward more complex media of the mind; training eyes to appreciate the intricate and powerful moves of the modern dance troupe or the complex photographs and paintings at the contemporary art museum; clarifying social constructions of meanings and the careful manipulations by politics and advertising, so that we see the multiple determinings and overdeterminations, the gradual attribution of and then removal of signification in each political campaign, so that people vote on the basis of hair styles and skin tone rather than on the person's demonstrated competence or the social significance of the party platform.

Mythography cannot remain merely a tool for the objective viewing of things such as myths "over there" somewhere. It is a discipline that teaches empowerment to citizenship as we now so self-consciously regard the interfaces between the past and the present. I do not preach a return to simplistic values of the "mythical past," when "men were men and women knew their place." Nor do I advocate a retreat into a pre-mass-comm world of parchment or lead pencils (I'd be lost without my three computers!), or a triumphal progression into a chrome-and-vanadium heaven where someone else does all the cooking, and it's wonderful.

I do claim that poesis is the proper mode in which to carry forward the necessary soul work of a culture that has achieved so much, only frequently to retreat from any sustained, in-depth nurturing of its historic mythic values and roots. Poesis, either as creative writing/reading or as creative analysis, is a sort of singing, one of the ways that myth, in Crites's phrase, "sings in your blood." In many cultures music and the word never separate. We hear touching stories about the Australian native peoples who continue to sing the myths of their geography, lest all traces of the landscape vanish. I conclude with the admonition that we shepherd and care for the long-term myths of our souls' geographies, lest they—and with them our most important and intimate landscapes—vanish for ever.

Notes

1. An earlier version of this essay was given as the annual lecture for the Athens State College Myth and Metaphor Conference, April 1991. Another portion was presented at the Myth and Literature seminar at Emory's Graduate Institute for the Liberal Arts, to whose instructor, Robert Detweiler, I'd like to dedicate this essay as a token of appreciation and esteem. One segment I did at Athens as a workshop is being developed as an ancillary essay on appreciating and anticipating new modes of the heroine and hero (Doty n.d.).

2. Some of my own emphases in looking at what mythic materials do in cultural semiotics will be found in Doty 1990a; in Doty 1991 I survey a raft of recent mythographic analyses, including those that are now shaping a revision of archetypal analysis.

3. John Thompson, in his "methodological framework of depth hermeneutics" (1990, 21), attempts to link structural features, symbolic forms, and sociohistorical conditions as ideologies operate to legitimate, dissimulate, unify, fragment, or reify various aspects of societies (60–67).

4. Wright Morris credits Ezra Pound with being "the first to give the thrust of doctrine to the American instinct to *make it new*" ("About Making It New," 1975, 79), yet Morris immediately notes that already Alexis de Tocqueville (in *Democracy in America*, 1835) had recognized the American abhorrence of obsolescence. Morris wisely cautions the contemporary writer against seeking newness for the sake of novelty itself: "The periodic resurgence of the avant garde attests to the vitality of the imagination, but the deliberate pursuit of what is new proves to be a limiting performance, anticipating its own early obsolescence. If the talent is adequate, and the age provokes it, something new will appear as a matter of course; if not, the effort to make it new will result in little more than novelties [in the pejorative sense]" (81).

5. In a volume of essays on the male body, I will treat such issues in "Baring the Flesh: Some Aspects of Contemporary Masculine Iconography."

RENEWING RITUALS

The Stations of the Cross Retold

MATTHEW FOX

A recent film, Wiping the Tears of Seven Generations *(1990), demonstrates how a wisdom person's vision led the Sioux of the seventh generation after the massacre at Wounded Knee to ritualize the needed healing of the nation. The ritual was enacted five times, in the bitter cold South Dakota winter weather, a large group retracing a route on horseback over two weeks each year; the fifth was the ritually significant one, the one that ended the mourning for the dead, and each day was dedicated to healing some aspect of the Sioux nation: children, old people, the ill, prisoners, spirits. The ceremony sought to prepare the present younger generation to revive older traditional ways, especially important since knowledge of three of the seven sacred rituals has now been lost.*

Seldom does one have such a sense of successful ritual—of spiritually successful ritual—even though Sioux social and religious customs will be foreign to many Americans. Just after noting how powerful the film was to the members of my Native American Religions class, a second account of a ritual reshaping came to my attention, Father Fox's straightforward ac-

count of a contemporary revision of the old Catholic devotion called the Stations of the Cross. It appeared in the journal Creation Spirituality *along with photographs not reproduced here.*

Made-up rituals, or contemporanizings of ancient ritual forms, often seem awkward; ritual language is above all language smoothed out through hundreds of repetitions until the "flow" is just right. But I could imagine anyone, of whatever religious persuasion, feeling confronted by this version of the old familiar meditation on the Stations. I could imagine such a person substituting the sufferings of his own generation or subculture for each of the stops on the processional way. I want to imagine that this essay and the others in this volume provide just such mirroring as the seventh station here: a reflection of our own worst violences. And that such reflections lead to a new concentration on the pictures of moral values and ethical behaviors that determine our future actions.

In the spirit-filled lands of Findhorn retreat center in northern Scotland amidst the windswept hills of a cold Good Friday afternoon in April 1991, about 250 persons gathered to do prayer in an ancient format. The form we chose was that of the Stations of the Cross. But we did them differently, not concentrating so much in a literal fashion on the fourteen stations that traditional piety has applied to Jesus' carrying of the cross but rather reinventing this form of prayer in light of a theology of the cosmic Christ, that is to say, as the suffering of the Earth and her creatures represent the new efforts to crucify Divinity in our midst.

The "we" who gathered included myself and the retreat co-leader Joanna Macy who is a Buddhist, though the daughter of several generations of Calvinist preachers; and persons who had come to the retreat during Holy Week dedicated to undergoing the Pascal Mystery of the Life, Death, and Resurrection of Mother Earth. Among these persons were Swedes and Americans, Canadians and Germans, Scots and English, Irish, French and Dutch. All religious persuasions were represented: Protestant, Anglican and Roman Catholic, Jewish persons, New Age persons and persons wounded by their church upbringing ("Recovering Christians" I call them).

We divided the group into fourteen "home groups," and each of these groups determined for itself what area of suffering in the world it felt called to represent in the ritual. Groups made placards, gathered chants, created banners, and collected musical instruments for the processions.

Around noon the procession began with everyone gathered together to hear a brief reading of the Gospel story of Jesus' journey to Golgotha as we gathered outdoors around a rock. Drums rolled and a somber mood filled the air as we processed to the first station where Joanna Macy and her husband, Francis led us in a mourning ritual around the facts of Chernobyl: the leukemia of the children, the contamination of the soil and food, "Chernobyl AIDS," lack of housing for evacuees—these somber facts were all attested to. In response to this litany of pain the large group was instructed to sing a Russian "Kyrie Eleison"—"Lord have mercy." Joanna and Francis Macy brought real passion to this station, particularly because they have spent considerable time in the Soviet Union communicating with citizens from that country who have visited the United States. Immediately following this Easter Retreat they were headed for Chernobyl itself.

On the way to the next station the procession continued with a somber drum beat and the ongoing chant of the Russian "Kyrie Eleison." The second station commemorated the crucifixion of the air. This was enacted by a circle of people praying who first breathed deeply together and then began choking on the air they were inhaling. The dying of forests and the choking of our children was invoked along with laments and chants about "Breathe on your people, breath of Gaia."

The third station commemorated persons afflicted with AIDS. There persons were invited to call out the names of people they knew who had died of AIDS. The litany was powerful and extended, and it seemed to include persons from every country represented at the retreat. The children of Rumania and Africa were also invoked and the millions of others who were nameless to us. We were reminded of the Immune Deficiency that the Earth itself is going through in our time with the mining of the Earth, the testing of nuclear weapons in the Earth, the destruction of the ozone layer. Appropriately the words of the Gospel were invoked: "As long as you do it to the least of these you do it to me." Somberly, with drum beating, we moved along the road and through a grove of trees to the next station, which commemorated the Sacred Web of Creation. All were asked to kiss silently the web of Creation, which had been woven of yarn.

The fifth station was named "Oppression." There a litany of nine oppressions was called out, including Racism, Homophobia, Anti-Semitism, Classism, Ageism, Sexism, Ableism, Sizeism, Speciesism. We were invited to enter into this pain "not through the lens of guilt but the lens of truth" and to realize the interconnectedness of how one act of oppression links to the others. We were reminded that none of us was born racist, for example, but rather curious about each other. We were asked to break into pairs and to name a lie about another person or group that we had somehow been taught during our lifetime. Our partner was instructed to say, "This is a lie," and together each person released this lie to the universe.

The cold and wind were getting more bitter as we made our way over the hills to station number six. There we were invited to approach a stick with a mirror on it, with a chant ringing in our ears: "Behold the crucified, behold the crucifier"—a chilly reminder of how we ought to resist projecting our own violence onto others. A ceasing of the objectifying of violence.

The eighth station centered on Abuse. Women in recovery from abuse led us in this prayer, announcing that "a force that tried to separate us from Creation and our deepest selves" and that temporarily committed soul-murder would no longer hold sway over them. Mention was made of physical, sexual, emotional abuse that had "harvested shame." No mention was made of religious abuse which, I feel, is equally in need of being addressed in today's world. Amidst a chant about sadness and crying and screaming came the pledge to "thrown down the shackles of shame." Some of the leaders had their faces painted for a skit depicting a mother abusing her child with questions like, "Why can't you be like everybody else?" and the child asking "just love me."

At the ninth station we were reminded of the crucifying of the Earth, air, water, and fire. Passing an Earth ball around, each person was asked to make a promise in praying over it of their commitment to its healing. Wailing and real grief were expressed at this station, as at so many others. A Gospel text was read and it carried immense weight in the present context: "Daughters of Jerusalem, do not weep for me. Weep for yourselves and your children." Other creatures, each a Cosmic Christ, spoke out with a similar message. The whale exclaimed: "Weep not for me but for your children and your children's children, for I cannot give you my gifts if the poisoned ocean destroys me."

The theme of the tenth station was "What We Are Afraid of." Each leader spoke to something that made them afraid: "I fear being separated from all I love," said one. "I fear that we are not going to make it as a species," said another.

At the eleventh station a skit on the topic of waste was performed in the sand dunes. Following a party the group threw its trash all around. There was coughing, tripping, and falling into the junk that piled up. A Tibetan horn played sonorously along the horizon of the sand dunes. There was a lightness but also a deadly seriousness to the story that was told and the mood that was evoked.

At the twelfth station we meditated on "Disconnections" before a large map of the Earth which commemorated forests, the children, humanity, and other species losing their connections with one another. A chant was sung: "I am Gaia; I am scared."

The thirteenth station was named "the Crucifixion of the Feminine." The killing of women during the "Burning Times" was named and we realized that we did not know the women's names. People broke into a discomforting wailing. An older woman who was dressed like a wise sage spoke: "Earth speaks to us and tells us to go into the void, the darkness, and find who we are before it is too late."

The fourteenth and last station took place on a sand dune within sight of the North Sea. The wind was howling, and the air was cold; I and others were wearying of all the processing and praying and entering into the passion of the Cosmic Christ—a procession that had been going on for almost three hours. But our attention was reawakened by a torturous sound: A man dressed in a hooded outfit was beating the ground itself with a large fir branch, scourging the Earth. He addressed us and told us he destroys what he does not understand. The whipping brought back memories of Jesus' being scourged at the pillar. Other persons spoke out: "I am a lizard. My home is in the rainforest—where is my home?" Another spoke: "I am a fish. Where is my home, since the lakes have died of acid rain?" "I am an unborn child. Is there a home for me?" The theme of Homelessness took on a more poignant and even cosmic dimension.

Then the participants took a map of the Earth, nailed its four corners to a cross, and erected the cross on the top of the sand dune as the wind howled through us. With the nailing to the cross, as the pounding echoed along the beach, the morphic field—the memory of Jesus crucified—awakened. Participants wailed—even those who had never heard of this medieval prayer (the Stations of the Cross) imbibed the message. The wailing was spontaneous. The keening was real. Silence followed. We walked back defeated and tired to our living quarters a mile from this sight. Later I learned that the group that led this last station was itself so moved by what they had reenacted there that they all stayed at the foot of the cross for half an hour in silence, unable or unwilling to move.

Clearly the Spirit was at work in this Good Friday retelling of the Stations of the Cross. A deeply prayerful attitude permeated the world. There was a discomfort to it—as there was to the original march to Golgotha after all. There was genuine creativity that emerged from each group's taking responsibility for its Station. There was no rehearsal, for it was not a production. It was prayer. There was complete participation of body, soul, spirit on the part of all participants. The outdoor march and the cold wind demanded the body's attention, and with it the heart's ample participation. There was a naming of real pain in our lives and that of our times and our societies. And there was an invitation to simple chants by way of portable musical instruments like drums and whistles. It was a time for children— serious and grieving children, but children nonetheless. Francis of Assisi, whom history credits with having invented the Stations of the Cross, would have been at home with our prayer. Indeed, I'm sure he was there. A lot of spirits of our ancestors were there.

Why not develop your own version of the Stations of the Cross on Good Friday in your community, borrowing some of the ideas from this story? The Cosmic Christ deserves to be represented in our churches. If we commemorate only the historical Jesus we probably risk sentimentalism, which is a certain way to destroy the message that Jesus taught. With the issues of homelessness and rape of the land, joblessness and lack of health care, greed and fundamentalist fear, youth in despair and addictions in abundance, a politics of trivia and resentment, there is no lack of Stations that deserve to be named and prayed in our own land at this time.

LOOKING BEYOND THE PICTURE FRAME

Living a Reservation Culture
Remythologizing and Transforming the Images of Our Time

LYNDA SEXSON

As I noted in chapter 1, Sexson's materials here come from the end of her book of more than a decade ago, yet they seemed most appropriate here (as the book itself seems relevant enough to appear in reprint, 1992). These remarks reflect many themes of this volume, such as the place of traditions, a phrase such as "behind our ethics are images," or the importance of narratives, and above all the importance of the contemporary imagination. Instead of merely complaining about how much the postmodernist world has lost, by comparison with a fantasized past history that was doubtless much rougher and crueler than anyone wants to remember, Sexson invites us to remythologize. Remythologizing, recovering the sacred seams that bind together experiences, the interpretive threads that enable us to celebrate the finding of meaning in the midst of chaos—these, Sexson suggests, are a form of virtual creation, language creating, image creating, that founds universes.

Visiting some friends on the Northern Cheyenne reservation, I watched the woman's beautiful brown arms, adorned in turquoise and silver, making order in the form of a stack of fried bread, while the man entertained us, honoring his guests with his eloquence. Insects followed the children, invading and swarming patterns that mocked chaos. Up near the ceiling, hidden behind other things crowding a narrow shelf, the man removed a small photograph. It was bent, much handled, very precious, a picture of himself and a woman dressed up in "authentic" Plains Indians costumes as they appeared on a movie set. Such heirloom clothing had mostly disappeared from the reservation, sold to outside collectors; and to see themselves as "Indians" required makeup and play. In some sense we are all captives of a reservation culture, our heirlooms lost, our only claim consumerism.

The means that we have available to make ourselves and mark that making are as varied as making bread, telling stories, saving something on a high shelf. To mislay or discard all "pictures" of ourselves is to be, not without mere heirlooms, but without religion—the connecting, authenticating principle of human existence. However, intentionally to turn away from or to deface familiar images of ourselves is a creative and even a religious act. Marking out is still marking; a time of disruption, or of iconoclasm, is a time of transformation. On that high shelf, or in a box, behind the clutter, is a picture; what will we be able to see in it, reinterpreting and reimagining those old visions?

Behind our ethics are images; preceding ethical consciousness is metaphorical consciousness; behind the laws are the stories. Behind the law: "When a stranger sojourns with you in your land, you shall not do him wrong. The stranger who sojourns with you shall be to you as the native among you, and you shall love him as yourself" is the image: "for you were strangers in the land of Egypt." The Hebrew concern for the stranger is bound up in the Hebrews' "photograph" of themselves as wanderers. Unless we look behind our ethical premises to the images that are their foundations, we cannot develop within our ethical realm, or within its foundation, poetic consciousness.

Having forgotten or rejected the traditional texts, we must fabricate, make up our sacred stories as we go along. If the traditional story of the Fall now reverberates with dualism and its sexist and anti-ecological subcategories, and yet our personal memories keep insinuating the same old images even though we have neglected the old story, what shall we do?

Medieval travelers tried, by means of geography, theology, and imagination, to find their way back to Paradise. The contemporary imagination no longer seeks that prelapsarian womb; if we make the journey to Paradise, we want to look over its walls and glimpse the Garden after the Fall:

Is the Garden overrun with weeds?

Does God himself tend the Garden now that the expulsion of his farmer leaves it to tangle and leaves it to run back to chaos?

Is the Angel who guards the Gates of the jungle-it-has-become snatching an overhanging, overripe pear or pomegranate, wiping the juice on his sleeve, and searing the surroundings with his glance, looking for interlopers? If we cannot quite see what has become of Paradise, we can see that the surrounding land is all barren from the intensity of the piercing, searching gaze in the Angel's history of watch.

Now and then God wishes to walk up and down in the Garden in the cool of the evening, as in the Good Old Days, reminiscing about the youth of eternity, feeling the little Serpents slide out of his pathway.

God trips on tangled vines and gnarled, exposed roots, almost Falling himself. The undulations of the Serpents wave the tassles of seeded grass like flags of truce.

He steps with his bare feet into rotted fruit on the Garden floor and dissipates once more into the air, memory unfulfilled, queasy again at his creation.

The Angel looks at the shimmering spaces where God no longer appears, smiles, and queries, "What has God rot?"

There is another Punishment.

God sends the Angel falling in a curving arc; and God himself guards the Gates. The Angel, banished from the doorway to Eden, is plunged to deeper passages and portals.

Now how will anyone walk in the Garden? The little Serpents massage their bellies on the wrinkled pits and slip through the slime of the fruit spilled by the Tree.

God looks at the fallen fruit and muses, "It's a little spoiled, a little overrun, but still Winter hasn't dared to creep in under my gaze. Perhaps it's salvageable."

And the ideas of salvation and winter, rebirth and dying, again sneaked through the Gates of Eden through the mind of God.

Deep in the Garden, though, the little Serpents were pointing the directions with quicksilver tongues, grazing the magenta-tipped, brown-spotted leaves, making loopy hollows under the earth, spaces in the shapes of their wingless, legless bodies.

Looking toward a long night, they sang to one another, "Once God imagines something, it manages to sneak in past him."

Another little Snake said, "Winter and salvation for Eden, imagined in one divine breath."

"How," another asked slyly, "when we slip back out of hibernations, will we be able to tell whether we are in the Garden or out of it?"

A long, old Serpent, dripping out of a Tree from above, suggested, "But the fruit had been rotting already."

And the little Serpents all curved round and asked, "Who could have thought it?"

God turned his gaze from the Garden toward the desert. "I want to remember how it was that I imagined the Fall when I meant, I think, to make Eden never Winter."

Another little Serpent said, "If God has begun to watch the Gates himself, he's imagining someone trying to get through. They'll get through the same way. He's already let them past by thinking it possible, or necessary to prevent."

"What shall we do to welcome their arrival?" smiled the Serpents to God.

The new arrivals in the Fallen Eden will make myths to account for History, the myth of demythologizing. They will laugh and know, too, that they will die. They will do no more, perhaps, than all of us do, caught in those moments that transcend themselves precisely because they make no more than their ephemeral, transitory claim.

My wedding dress was satin, sewn with seed pearls on the bodice, with tapered sleeves, with yards of skirt. While I was away studying the Comedies, my mother had made it to fit me precisely from her perfect memory of my body still curled inside her. She made only one error on the dress: she pricked her finger with the needle and a minuscule drop of blood stained the waist. No one would see it. My mother was peculiarly pleased, and she said to me over and over, "Oh well, no one will see it—and," laughing lightly, "it's got my life blood on it."

My mother was not aware of the fairy-tale motif the Grimms gathered nearly two centuries ago, of the mother who sent her daughter off on a journey. To seal her safety, the mother gave her daughter the only amulet available to her: she pricked her finger and stained a pure white hand-kerchief with three drops of her own red blood. Even if we do not recall the stories, we will make them.

Through remythologizing, or entering the imaginal, one transforms time and space. They are not lost, denied, or distorted; but they become qualities rather than quantities. Whatever it is that we do or undo, think or forget, we are participating in the creation of the universe. In making ourselves we make the universe.

REFERENCES

Adams, Hazard. 1983. *Philosophy of the Literary Symbolic*. Tallahassee: Florida State University Press.

Adkins, Arthur W. H. 1990. "Myth, Philosophy, and Religion in Ancient Greece." In Reynolds and Tracy 1990, 95–130.

Alberti, Leon Battista. 1966. *On Painting*. Translated by John R. Spencer. New Haven, Conn.: Yale University Press.

Allen, Paula Gunn. 1986. "Something Sacred Going On Out There: Myth and Vision in American Indian Literature." In *The Sacred Hoop: Recovering the Feminine in American Indian Traditions*, 102–17. Boston: Beacon.

Althusser, Louis. 1984. *Essays on Ideology*. London: Verso Editions.

Altwegg, Jürg, ed. 1988. *Die Heidegger Kontroverse*. Frankfurt am Main: Athenäeum.

Antin, David. 1972. "Modernism and Postmodernism: Approaching the Present in American Poetry." *Boundary 2* 1/1:98–133.

———. 1976. *Talking at the Boundaries*. New York: New Directions.

———. 1984. *Tuning*. New York: New Directions.

———. 1985. "what it means to be avant-garde." *Formations* 2/2:53–71.

———. 1989. "The Price." *Representations* 28:14–33.

———. 1990. "Writing and Exile." *Tikkun* 5/5:47–52.

———. 1993. *What It Means to Be Avant-Garde*. New York: New Directions.

Aronowitz, Stanley, and Henry A. Giroux. 1991. *Postmodern Education: Politics, Culture, and Social Criticism.* Minneapolis: University of Minnesota Press.

Ash, Timothy Garton. 1990. "The Revolution of the Magic Lantern." *New York Review of Books*, January 18, 42–51.

Asimov, Isaac. 1961. *Words from the Myths.* New York: New American Library.

Atwater, Margaret. 1985. *The Handmaid's Tale.* New York: Fawcett Crest.

Baier, Kurt. 1958. *The Moral Point of View.* Ithaca, N.Y.: Cornell University Press.

Bal, Mieke, and Norman Bryson. 1991. "Semiotics and Art History." *Art Bulletin* 73/2:174–208.

Barnaby, Karin, and Pellegrino D'Acierno, eds. 1990. *C. G. Jung and the Humanities: Toward a Hermeneutics of Culture.* Princeton, N.J.: Princeton University Press.

Barth, John. 1978. *Chimera.* New York: Rand.

Barthes, Roland. 1972. *Mythologies.* Translated by Annette Lavers. New York: Hill and Wang.

Belenky, Mary Field, Blythe McVicker Clinchy, Nancy Rule Goldberger, and Jill Mattuck Tarule. 1986. *Women's Ways of Knowing: Development of Self, Voice, and Mind.* New York: Basic.

Bell, Catherine. 1992. *Ritual Theory, Ritual Practice.* New York: Oxford University Press.

Benhabib, Seyla, and Fred Dallmayr, eds. 1990. *The Communicative Ethics Controversy.* Cambridge, Mass.: MIT Press.

Benjamin, Walter. 1969. *Illuminations.* Translated by Harry Zohn, edited by Hannah Arendt. New York: Schocken.

Benveniste, Emile. 1971. *Problems in General Linguistics.* Translated by Mary Elizabeth Meek. Coral Gables, Fla.: University of Miami Press.

Berger, John. 1972. *Ways of Seeing.* New York: Viking.

Bernbaum, Edwin. 1990. *Sacred Mountains of the World.* San Francisco: Sierra Club.

Bernstein, Charles. 1992. *A Poetics.* Cambridge, Mass.: Harvard University Press.

Bernstein, Jay M. 1987. "Aesthetic Alienation: Heidegger, Adorno, and Truth at the End of Art." In Fekete 1987, 86–119.

Bernstein, Richard J., ed. 1985. *Habermas and Modernity.* Cambridge, Mass.: MIT Press.

Bodkin, Maud. 1934. *Archetypal Patterns in Poetry: Psychological Studies of Imagination.* London: Oxford University Press.

Bryson, Norman. 1983. *Vision and Painting: The Logic of the Gaze.* New Haven, Conn.: Yale University Press.

Burtt, Edwin A. 1954. *The Metaphysical Foundations of Modern Physical Science.* Garden City, N.Y.: Doubleday.

Calvino, Italo. 1986. *The Uses of Literature: Essays.* Translated by Patrick Creagh. San Diego: Harcourt Brace Jovanovich.

Campbell, Joseph. 1956. *The Hero with a Thousand Faces.* 2d ed. Princeton, N.J.: Princeton University Press.

Cassirer, Ernst. 1963. *The Individual and the Cosmos in Renaissance Philosophy.* Translated by Mario Domandi. Philadelphia: University of Pennsylvania Press.

Clarke, Stanley G., and Evan Simpson, eds. 1989. *Anti-Theory in Ethics and Moral Conservatism.* Albany: State University of New York Press.

Connor, Steven. 1989. *Postmodernist Culture: An Introduction to Theories of the Contemporary.* New York: Blackwell.

———. 1992. *Theory and Cultural Value.* Cambridge, England: Blackwell.

Cousineau, Phil, ed. 1990. *The Hero's Journey: Joseph Campbell on His Life and World.* New York: HarperCollins.

Crites, Stephen. 1990. *The Modernist Myth Exposed.* The Seventh Annual Memorial Lecture of the Society for Value in Higher Education, August 9, 1988. Pamphlet preprint from forthcoming issue of *Soundings: An Interdisciplinary Journal.*

Daniel, Stephen H. 1990. *Myth and Modern Philosophy.* Philadelphia: Temple University Press.

Daniken, Erich von. 1968. *Chariots of the Gods? Unsolved Mysteries of the Past.* Translated by Michael Heron. New York: Putnam.

Davenport, Guy. 1981. *The Geography of the Imagination: Forty Essays.* San Francisco: North Point.

de Certeau, Michel. 1984. *The Practice of Everyday Life.* Translated by Steven Rendall. Berkeley and Los Angeles: University of California Press.

Derrida, Jacques. 1982 (1971). "White Mythology: Metaphor in the Text of Philosophy." In *Margins of Philosophy,* translated by Alan Bass, 207–71. Chicago: University of Chicago Press.

de Santillana, Giorgio, and Hertha von Dechend. 1969. *Hamlet's Mill: An Essay on Myth and the Frame of Time.* Boston: Gambit.

Descartes, René. 1971. *Philosophical Writings.* Translated and edited by Elizabeth Anscombe and Peter Thomas Geach. Indianapolis: Bobbs-Merrill.

Detienne, Marcel. 1986. *The Creation of Mythology.* Translated by Margaret Cook. Chicago: University of Chicago Press.

Detweiler, Robert. 1989. *Breaking the Fall: Religious Readings of Contemporary Fiction.* San Francisco: HarperCollins.

Doty, William G. 1986. *Mythography: The Study of Myths and Rituals.* Tuscaloosa: University of Alabama Press.

———. 1990a. "Writing the Blurred Genres of Postmodern Ethnography." *Annals of Scholarship: Studies of the Humanities and Social Sciences* 6/2 and 6/3:267–87.

———. 1990b. "Dancing to the Music of the Spheres: The Religion in Joseph Campbell's 'Non-Religious' Mythography." In Noel 1990, 185–89.

———. 1990c. "Contextual Fictions That Bridge Our Worlds: 'A whole new poetry.'" *Journal of Literature and Theology: An Interdisciplinary Journal of Theory and Criticism* 4/1:104–29.

———. 1991. "Myth, the Archetype of All Other Fable: A Review of Recent Literature." *Soundings: An Interdisciplinary Journal* 74/1–2:240–70.

————. N.d. "From the Traditional Monomythic Hero to the Contemporary Poly-mythic Hero/ine." In Bernard Scott and John L. White, eds. Robert W. Funk Festschrift volume, *Foundations and Facets Forum.*

Downing, Christine. 1992. *Women's Mysteries: Toward a Poetics of Gender.* New York: Crossroad.

Dundes, Alan. 1980. *Interpreting Folklore.* Bloomington: Indiana University Press.

Eagleton, Terry. 1990. *The Ideology of the Aesthetic.* Cambridge, Mass.: Blackwell.

————. 1991. *Ideology: An Introduction.* New York: Verso.

Edgerton, Samuel Y., Jr. 1975. *The Renaissance Rediscovery of Linear Perspective.* New York: Basic.

Ewen, Stuart. 1988. *All Consuming Images: The Politics of Style in Contemporary Culture.* New York: Basic.

Farias, Victor. 1991. *Heidegger and Nazism.* Philadelphia: Temple University Press.

Fekete, John, ed. 1987. *Life After Postmodernism: Essays on Value and Culture.* CultureTexts. New York: St. Martin's.

————. 1990. "Literary/Cultural Theory, Value, and Postmodernity." In Kreiswirth and Cheetham 1990, 171–90.

Flax, Jane. 1987. "Postmodernism and Gender Relations in Feminist Theory." *Signs: Journal of Women in Culture and Society* 12/4:621–43.

Fox, Matthew. 1990. *Creation Spirituality: Liberating Gifts for the Peoples of the Earth.* San Francisco: HarperCollins.

Foucault, Michel. 1970. *The Order of Things: An Archaeology of the Human Sciences.* New York: Random House.

————. 1980. *The History of Sexuality.* Vol. 1, *An Introduction.* Translated by Robert Hurley. New York: Vintage.

French, Marilyn. 1985. *Beyond Power: On Women, Men, and Morals.* New York: Summit.

Frentz, Thomas S., and Janice Hocker Rushing. 1990. "The Technological Shadow in *The Manchurian Candidate.*" In *Communication and the Culture of Technology,* edited by Martin J. Medhurst, Alberto Gonzales, and Tarla Rai Peterson, 239–56. Pullman: Washington State University Press.

Genovese, Eugene D. 1976. *Roll, Jordan, Roll: The World the Slaves Made.* New York: Random House.

Gioia, Dana. 1991. "Can Poetry Matter?" *Atlantic Monthly* 267/5:94–106.

Goethals, Gregor T. 1990. *The Electronic Golden Calf: Images, Religion, and the Making of Meaning.* Cambridge: Cowley.

————. 1991. "Audio-Visual Icons and Rituals." *ARTS: The Arts in Religious and Theological Studies* 3/2:9–15.

Gould, Eric. 1981. *Mythical Intentions in Modern Literature.* Princeton, N.J.: Princeton University Press.

Graves, Robert. 1966. *The White Goddess: A Historical Grammar of Poetic Myth.* Rev. ed. New York: Farrar, Straus and Giroux.

Green, Peter. 1986. "Hellenistic Technology: Eye, Hand, and Animated Tool." *Southern Humanities Review* 20/2:101–13.

Grossberg, Lawrence. 1992. *We Gotta Get Out of This Place: Popular Conservatism and Postmodern Culture*. New York: Routledge.

Grossberg, Lawrence, Cary Nelson, and Paula A. Treichler, eds. 1992. *Cultural Studies*. New York: Routledge.

Habermas, Jürgen. 1973. *Legitimation Crisis*. Boston: Beacon.

Harvey, David. 1989. *The Condition of Postmodernity: An Enquiry into the Origins of Cultural Change*. Cambridge, Mass.: Blackwell.

Hassan, Ihab. 1987. *The Postmodern Turn: Essays in Postmodern Theory and Culture*. Columbus: Ohio State University Press.

Havel, Václav. 1986a. "The Power of the Powerless." Translated by P. Wilson. In Vladislav 1986, 36–122.

———. 1986b. "Politics and Conscience." Translated by E. Kohák. In Vladislav 1986, 136–57.

———. 1986c. "Thriller." Translated by P. Wilson. In Vladislav 1986, 158–63.

———. 1990. "Words on Words." Translated by A. G. Brain. *New York Review of Books*, January 18, 5–8.

———. 1992. Interview. "Europa steht am Kreuzweg." *Der Spiegel* 48 (November):172–75.

Heidegger, Martin. 1977. *The Question Concerning Technology and Other Essays*. Translated by William Lovitt. Martin Heidegger, Works. New York: HarperCollins.

———. 1971 [1950, 1960]. "The Origin of the Work of Art." In *Poetry, Language, Thought*, translated by Albert Hofstadter, 17–87. Martin Heidegger, Works. New York: HarperCollins.

Hillman, James. 1983. *Healing Fiction*. Barrytown, N.Y.: Station Hill Press.

———. 1985. *Anima: An Anatomy of a Personified Notion*. Dallas: Spring Publications.

———. 1990. "On Mythic Certitude." *Sphinx: A Journal for Archetypal Psychology and the Arts* 3:224–43.

Homans, Peter. 1977 [1961]. "Puritanism Revisited: An Analysis of the Contemporary Screen-Image Western." In *The Popular Arts in America: A Reader*, edited by William Hammel, 83–98. New York: Harcourt.

Hynes, William J., and William G. Doty, eds. 1993. *Mythical Trickster Figures: Contours, Contexts, and Criticisms*. Tuscaloosa: University of Alabama Press.

Irigaray, Luce. 1985. *Speculum of the Other Woman*. Translated by Gillian C. Gill. Ithaca, N.Y.: Cornell University Press.

Jaffé, Aniela, ed. 1983 [1979]. *C. G. Jung: Word and Image*. 2d ed. Bollingen Series XCVII:2. Princeton, N.J.: Princeton University Press.

Janson, H. W., Dora Jane Janson, and Joseph Kerman. 1968. *A History of Art and Music*. Englewood Cliffs, N.J.: Prentice-Hall.

Jay, Nancy. 1981. "Gender and Dichotomy." *Feminist Studies* 7/1:38–56.

Jencks, Charles. 1977. *What Is Post-Modernism?* Academy Editions. New York: St. Martin's.

———. 1987. *Post-Modernism: The New Classicism in Art and Architecture.* London: Academy Editions.

Jewett, Robert, and John Shelton Lawrence. 1989 [1977]. *The American Monomyth.* 2d ed. Lanham: University Press of America.

Jordan, June. 1980. *Passion: New Poems, 1977–1980.* Boston: Beacon.

Jung, C. G. 1960/69. "The Transcendent Function." In *The Structure and Dynamics of the Psyche,* vol. 8 of *The Collected Works,* translated by R. F. C. Hull. Bollingen Series XX. Princeton, N.J.: Princeton University Press.

———. 1961. *Memories, Dreams, Reflections.* Recorded and edited by A. Jaffé, translated by R. and C. Winston. New York: Vintage.

———. 1966. *The Spirit in Man, Art, and Literature.* Translated by R. F. C. Hull. Princeton, N.J.: Princeton University Press.

———. 1972. *Mandala Symbolism.* Translated by R. F. C. Hull. Princeton, N.J.: Princeton University Press.

———. 1975. *Letters.* Selected and edited by G. Adler with A. Jaffé, translated by R. F. C. Hull. Bollingen Series XCV. Vol. 2. Princeton, N.J.: Princeton University Press.

———. 1977. *C. G. Jung Speaking.* Edited by W. McGuire and R. F. C. Hull. Bollingen Series XCVII. Princeton, N.J.: Princeton University Press.

———. 1978. *Psychology and the East.* Translated by R. F. C. Hull. Princeton, N.J.: Princeton University Press.

———. 1988. *Nietzsche's Zarathustra.* Edited by J. L. Jarrett. Bollingen Series XCIX. Vol. 2. Princeton, N.J.: Princeton University Press.

Kalaidjian, Walter. 1989. *Languages of Liberation: The Social Text in Contemporary American Poetry.* New York: Columbia University Press.

Karatheodoris, Stephen. 1993. "Male Desire in the Political Economy of Sexual Difference." Edited by William G. Doty. In *Gender, Race, and Identity,* edited by Craig Barrow, Katherine Frank, John Phillips, and Reed Sanderlin. Chattanooga: Southern Humanities Council Press.

Keen, Sam. 1986. *Faces of the Enemy.* San Francisco: HarperCollins.

Kenner, Hugh. 1971. *The Pound Era.* Berkeley and Los Angeles: University of California Press.

Kessler, Jascha. 1985. *Classical Illusions.* New Paltz, N.Y.: McPherson.

Kittay, Feder, and Diana T. Meyers, eds. 1987. *Women and Moral Theory.* Totowa, N.J.: Rowan and Littlefield.

Kochhar-Lindgren, Gray. *Narcissus Transformed: The Textual Subject in Psychoanalysis and Literature.* Philadelphia: Temple University Press.

Koyré, Alexandre. 1968. *From the Closed World to the Infinite Universe.* Baltimore: Johns Hopkins University Press.

Kramer, Heinrich, and James Sprenger. 1971. *The "Malleus Maleficarum" of Heinrich Kramer and James Sprenger.* Translated by Montague Summers. New York: Dover.

Kreiswirth, Martin, and Mark A. Cheetham, eds. 1990. *Theory Between the Disciplines: Authority/Vision/Politics.* Ann Arbor: University of Michigan Press.

Kristeva, Julia. 1982. *Powers of Horror: An Essay on Abjection.* Translated by Léon S. Roudiez. New York: Columbia University Press.

Krois, John Michael. 1987. *Cassirer: Symbolic Forms and History.* New Haven, Conn.: Yale University Press.

Kroker, Arthur, and Marilouise Kroker, eds. 1991. *The Hysterical Male: New Feminist Theory.* CultureTexts. New York: St. Martin's.

Krupat, Arnold. 1983. "The Indian Autobiography: Origins, Type, and Function." In *Smoothing the Ground: Essays on Native American Oral Literature,* edited by Brian Swann, 261–82. Berkeley and Los Angeles: University of California Press.

Lasch, Chrisopher. 1978. *The Culture of Narcissism.* New York: Norton.

Lash, Scott. 1989. *Sociology of Postmodernism.* International Library of Sociology. New York: Routledge.

Lauter, Estella. 1984. *Women as Mythmakers: Poetry and Visual Art by Twentieth-Century Women.* Bloomington: Indiana University Press.

Lazer, Hank. 1986. "Criticism and the Crisis in American Poetry." *Missouri Review* 7:201–32.

———. 1988. "Radical Collages." *The Nation* 2/9:24–26.

———. 1990a. "Poetry Readings and the Contemporary Canon." *American Poetry* 7/2:64–72.

———. 1990b. "The Politics of Form and Poetry's Other Subjects: Reading Contemporary American Poetry." *American Literary History* 2/3:503–27.

———. 1992a. *DOUBLESPACE: Poems 1971–1989.* New York: Segue.

———. 1992b. *INTER(IR)RUPTIONS: Poems.* Mentor, Ohio: Generator.

Leitch, Vincent. 1979. "The Book of Deconstructive Criticism." *Studies in the Literary Imagination* 12/1:19–39.

Leonardo da Vinci. 1949. *Paragone: A Comparison of the Arts.* Translated by Irma A. Richter. London: Oxford University Press.

Lerner, Gerda. 1986. *The Creation of Patriarchy.* New York: Oxford University Press.

Liszka, James Jakób. 1989. *The Semiotic of Myth: A Critical Study of the Symbol.* Bloomington: Indiana University Press.

Lockhart, Russell Arthur. 1987. *Psyche Speaks.* Wilmette, Ill.: Chiron.

Lyotard, Jean-François. 1984. *The Postmodern Condition: A Report on Knowledge.* Translated by Geoff Bennington and Brian Massumi. Theory and History of Literature, 10. Minneapolis: University of Minnesota Press.

MacIntyre, Alasdair. 1984. *After Virtue.* 2d ed. Notre Dame, Ind.: University of Notre Dame Press.

———. 1988. *Whose Justice? Which Rationality?* Notre Dame, Ind.: University of Notre Dame Press.

———. 1990. *Three Rival Versions of Moral Enquiry: Enyclopaedia, Genealogy, and Tradition.* Notre Dame, Ind.: University of Notre Dame Press.

Makarushka, Irena S. M. 1990. "The Good Mother, The Good Father, and Other Myths of Evil." *Union Seminary Quarterly Review* 44:121–36.

Mani, Lata. 1992. "Cultural Theory, Colonial Texts: Reading Eyewitness Accounts of Widow Burning." In Grossberg, Nelson, and Treichler 1992, 392–408.

Marcuse, Herbert. 1978. *The Aesthetic Dimension.* Boston: Beacon.

Márquez, Gabriel García. 1970 [1967]. *One Hundred Years of Solitude.* Translated by Gregory Rabassa. New York: Avon.

Merleau-Ponty, Maurice. 1968. *The Visible and the Invisible.* Translated by A. Lingis, edited by Claude Lefort. Evanston, Ill.: Northwestern University Press.

Minnich, Elizabeth. 1990. *Transforming Knowledge.* Philadelphia: Temple University Press.

Mitchell, W. J. T. 1986. *Iconology: Image, Text, Ideology.* Chicago: University of Chicago Press.

Morris, Wright. 1975. *About Fiction: Reverent Reflection on the Nature of Fiction with Irreverent Observations on Writers, Readers, and Other Abuses.* New York: Harper-Collins.

Morrison, Toni. 1987. *Beloved.* New York: Penguin.

Mulvey, Laura. 1975. "Visual Pleasure and Narrative Cinema." *Screen* 16/3:6–18.

Nelson, Cary. 1989. *Repression and Recovery: Modern American Poetry and the Politics of Cultural Memory.* Madison: University of Wisconsin Press.

Noel, Daniel C., ed. 1990. *Paths to the Power of Myth: Joseph Campbell and the Study of Religion.* New York: Crossroad.

Nussbaum, Martha. 1990. *Love's Knowledge: Essays on Philosophy and Literature.* New York: Oxford University Press.

Olsen, Tillie. 1978. *Silences.* New York: Dell.

Owens, Craig. 1992. *Beyond Recognition: Representation, Power, and Culture.* Edited by Scott Bryson, Barbara Kruger, Lynne Tillman, and Jane Weinstock. Berkeley and Los Angeles: University of California Press.

Pagels, Elaine. 1979. *The Gnostic Gospels.* New York: Vintage.

Paul, Sherman. 1986. *In Search of the Primitive: Rereading David Antin, Jerome Rothenberg, and Gary Snyder.* Baton Rouge: Louisiana State University Press.

Pavese, Cesare. 1989. *Dialogues with Leucó.* Translated by William Arrowsmith and D. S. Carne-Ross. Boston: Eridanos; orig. 1947; transl. 1965.

Perlof, Marjorie. 1984. *The Poetics of Indeterminacy.* Princeton, N.J.: Princeton University Press.

———. 1985. *The Dance of the Intellect.* New York: Cambridge University Press.

———. 1986. *The Futurist Moment.* Chicago: University of Chicago Press.

———. 1990. *Poetic License.* Evanston, Ill.: Northwestern University Press.

Pirsig, Robert M. 1992. *Lila: An Inquiry into Morals.* New York: Bantam.

Polanyi, Michael. 1964. *Personal Knowledge: Towards a Post-Critical Philosophy.* New York: HarperCollins.

Postman, Neil. 1985. *Amusing Ourselves to Death: Public Discourse in the Age of Show Business.* New York: Viking.

Quasha, George, and Jerome Rothenberg, eds. 1973. *America a Prophecy: A New Reading of American Poetry from Pre-Columbian Times to the Present.* New York: Random House.

Raboteau, Albert J. 1978. *Slave Religion.* New York: Oxford University Press.

Ragland-Sullivan, Ellie. 1986. *Jacques Lacan and the Philosophy of Psychoanalysis.* Urbana: University of Illinois Press.

Rasmussen, David. 1990. *Universalism vs. Communitarianism.* Cambridge, Mass.: MIT Press.

Reuther, Rosemary Radford. 1990. *Lift Every Voice: Constructing Christian Theologies from the Underside.* Edited by Susan Brooks Thistlethwaite and Mary Pottern Engel. San Francisco: HarperCollins.

Reynolds, Frank, and David Tracy, eds. 1990. *Myth and Philosophy.* Toward a Comparative Philosophy of Religions. Albany: SUNY Press.

Ricoeur, Paul. 1986. *Lectures on Ideology and Utopia.* Edited by George Taylor. New York: Columbia University Press.

Ronell, Avital. 1989. *The Telephone Book: Technology, Schizophrenia, Electric Speech.* Lincoln: University of Nebraska Press.

———. 1992. *Crack Wars: Literature Addiction Mania.* Lincoln: University of Nebraska Press.

Rothenberg, Jerome. 1970. *The 17 Horse Songs of Frank Mitchell X–XIII.* London: Tetrad.

———. 1972. *Shaking the Pumpkin: Traditional Poetries of the Indian North Americas.* New York: Doubleday.

———. 1974. *Poland/1931.* New York: Doubleday.

———, ed. 1978. *A Big Jewish Book: Poems & Other Visions of the Jews from Tribal Times to the Present.* New York: Doubleday.

———. 1981. *Pre-Faces & Other Writings.* New York: New Directions.

———. "A Personal Manifesto." In Rothenberg 1981.

———, ed. 1985. *Technicians of the Sacred: A Range of Poetries from Africa, America, Asia, Europe, & Oceania.* 2d ed. Berkeley and Los Angeles: University of California Press.

———. 1989. *Khurbn & Other Poems.* New York: New Directions.

———. 1991. "A Poetics of the Sacred." Manuscript.

———. 1992. "'We Explain Nothing, We Believe Nothing': American Indian Poetry and the Problematics of Translation." In *On the Translation of Native American Literatures,* edited by Brian Swann, 64–79. Washington: Smithsonian Institution Press.

————, and Diane Rothenberg, eds. 1983. *Symposium of the Whole: A Range of Discourse Toward an Ethnopoetics*. Berkeley and Los Angeles: University of California Press.

Rowe, John Carlos. 1992. "Postmodernist Studies." In *Redrawing the Boundaries: The Transformation of English and American Literary Studies*, edited by Stephen Greenblatt and Giles Gunn, 179–208. New York: Modern Language Association of America.

Rushing, Janice Hocker. 1986. "Mythic Evolution of 'The New Frontier' in Mass Mediated Rhetoric." *Critical Studies in Mass Communications* 3:265–96.

————, and Thomas S. Frentz. 1989. "The Frankenstein Myth in Contemporary Cinema." *Critical Studies in Mass Communication* 6:61–80.

Said, Edward W. 1978. *Orientalism*. New York: Random House.

Sayre, Henry. 1982. "David Antin and the Oral Poetics Movement." *Contemporary Literature* 23/4:428–50.

Schutz, Alfred. 1970. *Collected Papers*. Edited by Maurice Natanson. The Hague: Martinus Nijhoff.

Selby, Henry A. 1973. Roundtable Discussion. In *Myth and Reason: A Symposium*, edited by Walter D. Wetzels. Austin: University of Texas Press.

Sergent, Bernard. 1986. *Homosexuality in Greek Myth*. Translated by Arthur Goldhammer. Boston: Beacon.

Sexson, Lynda. 1990. "Let Talking Snakes Lie: Sacrificing Stories." In Noel 1990, 134–53.

————. 1992 [1982]. *Ordinarily Sacred*. Charlottesville: University Press of Virginia.

Shils, Edward. 1981. *Tradition*. Chicago: University of Chicago Press.

Siebers, Tobin. 1992. "Cold War Criticism." *Common Knowledge* 1/3:60–90.

Silliman, Ron. 1987. *The New Sentence*. New York: Roof.

————. 1990. "Canons and Institutions: New Hope for the Disappeared." In *The Politics of Poetic Form: Poetry and Public Policy*, edited by Charles Bernstein. New York: Roof.

Smith, Barbara Herrnstein. 1988. *Contingencies of Value: Alternative Perspectives for Critical Theory*. Cambridge, Mass.: Harvard University Press.

Steele, Thomas J., S.J. 1982. *Santos and Saints: The Religious Folk Art of Hispanic New Mexico*. Santa Fé: Ancient City Press.

Stella, Frank. 1986. *Working Space*. Cambridge, Mass.: Harvard University Press.

Stewart, Susan. 1987. *"Ceci Tuera Cela*: Graffiti as Crime and Art." In Fekete 1987, 161–80.

Suleiman, Susan, ed. 1985. *The Female Body in Western Culture*. Cambridge, Mass.: Harvard University Press.

Taylor, Mark C. 1984. *Erring: A Postmodern A/theology*. Chicago: University of Chicago Press.

————. 1992. *Disfiguring: Art, Architecture, Religion*. Religion and Postmodernism. Chicago: University of Chicago Press.

Thompson, John B. 1990. *Ideology and Modern Culture: Critical Social Theory in the Era of Mass Communication.* Cambridge, England: Polity.

Tillich, Paul. 1957. *Dynamics of Faith.* New York: HarperCollins.

Toulmin, Stephen. 1970. "Contemporary Scientific Mythology." In *Metaphysical Beliefs,* edited by Stephen Toulmin, Ronald W. Hepburn, and Alasdair MacIntyre, 3–71. New York: Schocken.

Turner, Victor. 1982. *From Ritual to Theatre: The Human Seriousness of Play.* New York: Performing Arts Journal Publications.

Underwood, Richard A. 1965. "Hermes and Hermeneutics: A Viewing from the Perspectives of the Death of God and Depth Psychology." *Hartford Quarterly* 6/1:34–53.

Vattimo, Gianni. 1992. "Optimistic Nihilism." *Common Knowledge* 1/3:37–44.

Vladislav, Jan, ed. 1986. *Václav Havel; or, Living in the Truth: Twenty-two Essays Published on the Occasion of the Award of the Erasmus Prize to Václav Havel.* London: Faber and Faber.

Weber, Max. 1984. *The Protestant Ethic and the Spirit of Capitalism.* Translated by Talcott Parsons. London: Unwin.

Wehr, Demaris. 1987. *Jung and Feminism: Liberating Archetypes.* Boston: Beacon.

Wetzels, Walter D., ed. 1973. *Myth and Reason: A Symposium.* Austin: University of Texas Press.

Whitmont, Edward C. 1982. *Return of the Goddess.* New York: Crossroad.

Winnicott, D. W. 1989. *Psycho-Analytic Explorations.* Edited by C. Winnicott, R. Shepherd, and M. Davis. Cambridge, Mass.: Harvard University Press.

Wolf, Christa. 1984. *Cassandra: A Novel and Four Essays.* Translated by Jan Van Heurck. New York: Farrar, Strauss and Giroux.

Wulff, David M. 1991. *Psychology of Religion: Classic and Contemporary Views.* New York: Wiley.

CONTRIBUTORS

Jeffery Byrd, assistant professor of art at the University of Northern Iowa, completed a BFA at the University of Alabama, and an MFA at the University of Florida. His photographs have been exhibited across the country, and his work was discussed in a review essay in *Genre* (1993).

William G. Doty is professor of humanities in the department of religious studies at the University of Alabama/Tuscaloosa. A regular reviewer for Atlanta's *Art Papers*, he also has contributed to many journals and published fifteen books in several fields.

David H. Fisher is associate professor of philosophy at North Central College in Napierville, Illinois. Recently he has published essays on the work of Julia Kristeva and Jacques Lacan, and at present he is working on a book treating elements of a postmodernist ethic. Fisher teaches courses in the history of ideas and in an MA program in liberal studies, as well as in his primary specialities of ethics and aesthetics.

MATTHEW FOX is the internationally known author of many books on Western spirituality and the Christian responsibility for global civilization, especially as "creation spirituality" is a parallel to liberation theology for First World peoples. His *Creation Spirituality: Liberating Gifts for the Peoples of the Earth* (1990) and others of his many writings have led him into confrontations with church authorities. He argues that "we must learn to ground our struggle for justice, rights, and responsibilities in the most common ground of all: our shared experience of awe" (1990, 150).

STEPHEN KARATHEODORIS (1945–90) was a brilliant sociologist at the University of Alabama whose early death from cancer deprived us of major contributions he would have seen through to publication. Following early interests in mathematics, physics, and philosophy, he worked across a number of fields, including science and rationality, medical sociology, dialectics and rhetoric, and the semiotics of gendered language.

GRAY KOCHHAR-LINDGREN lives with his family in Rabun Gap, Georgia, and teaches contemporary fiction at Emory University. He is the author of poetry and essays in several journals, and of *Narcissus Transformed: The Textual Subject in Psychoanalysis and Literature*, based on his PhD dissertation in the Graduate Institute of the Liberal Arts, Emory.

HANK LAZER, assistant dean for humanities and fine arts and professor of English at the University of Alabama, writes criticism and poetry. He has edited two books of criticism, and his essays on contemporary poetry appear in a wide range of journals. Two books of poetry were published in 1992: *DOUBLESPACE: Poems 1971–1989*, and *INTER(IR)RUPTIONS*. In May 1993 Lazer met with poets, students, critics, and scholars in China as part of a cultural exchange program that included the bilingual publication of his poetry and essays.

MARK LEDBETTER is associate professor of religion at Millsaps College in Jackson, Mississippi. He is the author of *Virtuous Intentions: The Religious Dimension of Narrative* (Scholars Press), and *Doing Violence to the Body: An Ethic of Reading and Writing* (Macmillan).

IRENA MAKARUSHKA teaches in the department of religion at Bowdoin College, Brunswick, Maine, where she has taught a variety of historical and thematic courses, and developed new courses such as The Problem of Evil; Religion, Women, and Nature; and Adam and Eve and the Moral of the Story. In addition to publishing a number of scholarly essays and film critiques, she is the author of *Religious Imagination and Language in Emerson and Nietzsche.*

DANIEL C. NOEL (PhD, Drew University) is professor of liberal studies in religion and culture at Vermont College of Norwich University. He is the author of *Approaching Earth: A Search for the Mythic Significance of the Space Age,* and editor of *Seeing Castaneda* and *Paths to the Power of Myth: Joseph Campbell and the Study of Religion* (Doty, Noel, and Sexson, among the contributors to this volume, also contribute to that volume). He publishes in Jungian as well as scholarly journals, and lectures widely.

JEROME ROTHENBERG is the author of over forty-five books of poetry and translation, and the editor of such ground-breaking anthologies as *Technicians of the Sacred: A Range of Poetries from Africa, America, Asia, Europe, & Oceania; Shaking the Pumpkin: Traditional Poetry of the Indian North Americas; America a Prophecy;* and *Symposium of the Whole: A Range of Discourse Toward an Ethnopoetics.* He is professor of visual arts and literature at the University of California at San Diego.

LYNDA SEXSON is professor of humanities at Montana State University in Missoula and coeditor of *Corona,* anticipating a special issue for that journal on the Nature of the Book. She is the author of *Ordinarily Sacred* and a book of extraordinary fictions, *Margaret of the Imperfections.* Her current research focuses upon metaphor and iconoclasm.

INDEX